A Beast the Color of Winter

Douglas H. Chadwick

A Beast the Color of Winter

THE MOUNTAIN GOAT OBSERVED

Sierra Club Books
SAN FRANCISCO

The Sierra Club, founded in 1892 by John Muir, has devoted itself to the study and protection of the earth's scenic and ecological resources—mountains, wetlands, woodlands, wild shores and rivers, deserts and plains. The publishing program of the Sierra Club offers books to the public as a nonprofit educational service in the hope that they may enlarge the public's understanding of the Club's basic concerns. The point of view expressed in each book, however, does not necessarily represent that of the Club. The Sierra Club has some fifty chapters coast to coast, in Canada, Hawaii, and Alaska. For information about how you may participate in its programs to preserve wilderness and the quality of life, please address inquiries to Sierra Club, 530 Bush Street, San Francisco, CA 94108.

Library of Congress Cataloging in Publication Data

Chadwick, Douglas H.
A beast the color of winter.

Bibliography: p. 195
Includes index.
1. Mountain goat.   I. Title.
QL737.U53C44   1983   599.73'58   83-4737
ISBN 0-87156-805-5

38,202

Jacket design by Bonnie Smetts
Book design by Marianne Ackerman
Illustrations by Carla Simmons
Printed in the United States of America
10 9 8 7 6 5 4 3 2 1

*For my father, who loves books and always
took me with him outdoors*

Contents

Acknowledgments

I'VE GIVEN MOST of these in the introduction, because I wanted to relate a bit more about the people who helped me in the mountains and the organizations that supported my work than just their names. Many of the researchers whose findings I refer to in various chapters made a special effort at one time or another to provide me with detailed data, new theories, and other valuable assistance. This is no more or less than the way science works. I think, however, that it works better than usual among the relatively small group of men and women who spend their time following bearded white beasts on steep cliffs.

The only people I really need to thank here are, to begin with, Dr. Bart O'Gara, leader of the Montana Cooperative Wildlife Research Unit, and Dr. Victoria Stevens, whose thesis on the mountain goats of Olympic National Park will be published by the time this book is. Both of them reviewed drafts of my manuscript, and I am fortunate to have had their helpful comments on it. Carl D. Brandt, my agent, and Diana Landau, my editor, knew how to make those drafts into a finished book, and I want to thank them very much. Lastly, I should mention my debt to Joe Judge and Mary G. Smith, both of *National Geographic*, who encouraged me to keep writing and taking pictures.

The High, Free Places

IT IS ONLY a statement of physical fact to say: Mountains are as close as the surface of our planet reaches toward the heavens. The purest air, the purest water, and the purest light on earth are found amidst these great uplifted forms. They are the source of awesome natural power, shaping winds and weather and the rivers that flow across the land. And they are the home of very special communities of living creatures.

In North America there is one large animal that belongs almost entirely to the realm of towering rock and unmelting snow. Pressing hard against the upper limit of life's possibilities, it exists higher and steeper throughout the year than any other big beast on the continent. It is possibly the best and most complete mountaineer that ever existed on any continent. *Oreamnos americanus* is its scientific name. Its common name is the mountain goat.

> It ain't a buffler, proper, nor a white antelope, neither, though you hear that name put to it and a sight of others. They keep to the high peaks, they do, the tip top of mountains, in the clouds and snow. . . . Not many's seen a live one. A man has to climb some for that. He does now.

The dialogue, from A.B. Guthrie Jr.'s splendid novel of mountain men in early Montana, *The Big Sky,* is fictional but historically accurate. The first white men to travel through the American West were far from sure just what sort of animal it was that lived up on the tip top of those colossal alps they were "discovering." Buffalo and antelope were common guesses. "A variety of polar bear," suggested Captain James Cook after finding mountain goat pelts among Pacific Coast Indians. These tribes knew the beast as *mazama*. From its horns they carved ceremonial spoons, and from its fur—which was sometimes woven together with cedar strips —produced durable blankets and rugs. Some coastal Indians still practice the weaving, and I used to collect goat hair shed on spring and summer ranges to send them.

Seeing their first mountain goat hides in Shoshone Indian tipis near the base of the Rockies, Lewis and Clark took them as evidence of a new species of bighorn sheep, thus initiating a persistent tradition of confusing these two high-country creatures. One of the more freewheeling contributions along this line came from an early observer who noticed mountain goat tracks in freshly dug earth around alpine marmot burrows and announced the discovery of a bighorn sheep that lived underground. If the strange, shaggy peak-dweller falls from a precipice, claimed another report, it will land on its horns and bounce back onto all fours— this being its particular method of avoiding injury. Again, it sounds as if someone had mountain sheep in mind, particularly the rams with their coiled horns.

A few reasonably accurate descriptions of mountain goats did make their way back East. One of the better early taxonomic descriptions of *Oreamnos americanus* was ventured in 1817 by Samuel Constantine Rafinesque, a naturalist whose other work included the formulation of evolutionary theories which considerably predate those of Charles Darwin. Precisely where among the hooved animals *Oreamnos* ought to be classified remained a subject of debate for some time, and well into the second half of the century there were those who still had doubts that it existed at all.

Even the truth about the beast sounded improbable. It was said to be draped in a long coat of pure white, like the everlasting snow of glaciers. A bushy goatee was observed growing from its chin, and its muscle-humped forequarters tapered to a narrow rump, giving it an overall shape akin to a bison. Yet the thin, rapier-sharp horns rising from the top of its head were unlike those of any bison, goat, or sheep.

Consider where it was reported to live throughout the year: in a realm where adventurers found unsurpassed beauty but also some of the harshest environments yet known. Winter there, they said, was as long as or longer than the other three seasons combined. What food and shelter this land above the trees offered became buried by snow, often whipped by gale-force winds into drifts over 50 feet deep, while temperatures sank to 50 degrees (F) below zero and shivered there for days on end. Moreover, to stay on the sheer sides of those forbidding peaks meant that the creature confronted avalanches, rockfalls, and—always—the possibility of a fatal slip as well. All it would take is one misstep, one foot failing to hold on an icy glaze or wet moss or crumbling rock, in a lifetime of climbing.

If anything was clear to the skeptics, it was that another shaggy myth had shambled in from the wilderness. Lord knows, they probably thought, mountain men out there make an art of exaggeration. "Naked savages" climb summits in search of visions while explorers, snowbound and starving, have visions despite themselves. And what of those other men always drawn to frontiers, the sort who seem forever in search of legends and hopeful of monsters? Any one of them could have been responsible for this mixture of frost, altitude, and imagination.

Nevertheless, enough specimens inevitably were shot and shipped to museums and laboratories to settle the issue. The biologists opened the crates. They took fur, horns, and bones between their fingers, and there it was: a bearded, climbing beast the color of winter.

The first time I went in search of the mountain goat I hiked into the Selway–Bitterroot Wilderness of western Montana. I had been told I might find the beast there. But the month was December, and the huge country around me was itself covered by a thick white coat. My telescope swung in futile arcs between snow mounds, gleaming crusts, chalk-colored rocks, weather-bleached snags, and icicles standing in dimly lit caves.

I made temporary camps away from the paths of snowslides to eat and rest. Otherwise my time was spent snowshoeing and scanning new sets of frozen cliffs and pinnacles, without success. After a good deal of searching I ended up with no more evidence than the early explorers to prove the creature a real one. No evidence, save perhaps distantly seen tracks which the wind and snow quickly covered.

Then one afternoon as I looked upward from a dark valley bottom to where sunlight and clouds of fine ice crystals flared across a promontory, my binoculars caught the four-legged images I was after. They seemed, in a way, to be just that: images. Horned wraiths dissolving and reforming in swirls of drifting snow like figments of the imagination—mine, or maybe the mountains'.

I started up for a closer look ("A man has to climb some for that. He does now."), and it was slow, tense going. When I finally heaved up onto the ledge where I had seen the apparitions standing, they were gone. Tracks led to an ice-rimmed escarpment. My own hands and feet dug into the snow as I lay on my stomach and stretched forward to look where the prints of their feet disappeared into the airy gulf beyond.

I hugged my way around a corner to get out of the wind. Pausing to rub my nose and cheeks to chase the frost out of them, I became aware of two black horns and two liquid black eyes turning toward me. They hovered disembodied against the snow-filled sky and slopes. Behind the eyes a mound of snow began to shift, then erupted as the creature stood up from its bed and shook the last of the freshly fallen flakes from its back. Time passed—I don't recall how long—before the eyes and horns moved again and floated across a fissure. Suddenly, like a clot of tumbling snow, the beast bounded down a series of narrow ledges on a winter-slick wall of stone and was gone.

Where it had lain bedded, its body heat had melted a small impression. Wisps of fur were frozen to the ice in the bottom of it. I worked some strands loose and, somewhat like those scientists of an earlier day, rolled them between my fingers to assure myself that this was, after all, a flesh-and-blood animal.

The mountain goat is a real enough beast; to remind me of that I have a faint scar on my knee where a huge male once gored me. Precisely what sort of beast it is in terms of behavior and ecology was still not very thoroughly understood when I began my research early in 1971. It had remained the least studied of the hooved "big game" species in North America. For a long time it had also remained the one large mammal on the continent whose range and numbers were not seriously affected by human development.

The first place I lived with mountain goats was among the Swan Mountains of northwestern Montana, in a remote and lovely valley named Bunker Creek, just beyond the boundary of the Bob Marshall Wilderness. "The Bob," set aside by Congress back in the 1940s, is today adjoined on its northern end by the Great Bear Wilderness and on its southern end by the Scapegoat Wilderness, both established during the 1970s. Together, the three areas comprise the largest unbroken stretch of pure backcountry in the lower 48 states—1,535,707 acres rippling along the Continental Divide. Skipping across the asphalt of U.S. Highway 2 on the Great Bear's northern border (as many spectacular wildlife populations do), the one million acres of Glacier National Park can be added to this officially protected mountain ecosystem.

Virtually every species that has belonged to this part of the Rockies since the last immense Ice Age glaciers retreated 10,000 to 12,000 years ago is present here in vital, interacting populations. The exception—and it is unfortunately a major ecological one—is *Canis lupus irremotus,* the northern Rocky Mountain timber wolf. Following decades of truly devout persecution on our part, wolves are only rarely seen in the region now and mostly as solitary silver or gray shadows, loners on a circuit

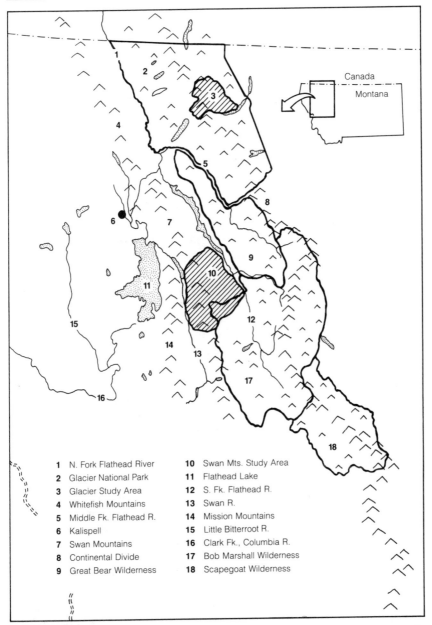

Canada
Montana

1	N. Fork Flathead River
2	Glacier National Park
3	Glacier Study Area
4	Whitefish Mountains
5	Middle Fk. Flathead R.
6	Kalispell
7	Swan Mountains
8	Continental Divide
9	Great Bear Wilderness
10	Swan Mts. Study Area
11	Flathead Lake
12	S. Fk. Flathead R.
13	Swan R.
14	Mission Mountains
15	Little Bitterroot R.
16	Clark Fk., Columbia R.
17	Bob Marshall Wilderness
18	Scapegoat Wilderness

1. Map of the Rocky Mountains in western Montana, showing areas where the author studied mountain goats.

down from Canada, though there is hope that they might be able to re-establish a viable population here.

At the beginning of the 1970s, Bunker Creek was as rugged and woolly as any place in the Bob and its allied wildernesses, supporting the same rich diversity of mountain fauna. Conservationists had argued for years that the wilderness boundaries should be expanded to take in this neighboring drainage. Instead, while I was there, a road was blasted and bulldozed to the head of the valley, and its steep sides were heavily logged. I had known an end was at hand for Bunker Creek's long isolation and had come specifically to try to find out what effects this might have on the resident herd of mountain goats.

Such investigations were overdue at that point. Set in motion by accelerating rates of consumption in the rest of the United States and Canada, logging, mining, and petroleum-drilling operations had been penetrating farther and faster into the high country of the continent than ever before. Increasing numbers of men with guns followed closely behind on the new roads. Because goat population surveys were generally so sketchy and sporadic, it took some time for game managers to realize what was happening: the white climbers, so long aloof from man and his multiplying needs, were now declining over wide sections of their range —in many cases drastically—leaving one empty cliff after another.

Greater access, more disturbance, intensified hunting: fewer mountain goats. The correlation seemed obvious, but it was not necessarily a straightforward one. Other hooved game species had withstood worse pressures without succumbing. Some, such as the white-tailed deer, seem to thrive next to man; there are at least three times as many deer in the highly developed state of Pennsylvania alone as there are mountain goats in all of North America. Further, why were many herds of the crag-dwellers faring poorly even where game managers had set quotas to limit hunting pressure?

It was a good bet that the goat's high-altitude, cliffside lifestyle incorporated unique movement patterns, elements of social organization, or population dynamics—some factor or combination of factors which made herds especially vulnerable to disruption or overharvest. But this was by no means a sure bet. Disease epidemics, increased predation, competition from other ungulates, climatic change, and any number of other liabilities had yet to be ruled out.

The problem of dwindling mountain goat populations prompted a number of studies, including my own, at roughly the same time, and the thin stack of existing reports on the animal's biology began to thicken. Among the earlier investigators whose findings all of us new goatwatchers relied upon, I think it is fair to single out Stewart Brandborg. His

Life History and Management of the Mountain Goat in Idaho, published in 1955, still stood as the most complete description of the bearded beast available. Brandborg eventually left the goat rocks to become director of the Wilderness Society in Washington, D.C., a post he held for many years.

During the three years we spent in the Swan Mountains my wife, Beth Ferris, and I expanded the study from Bunker Creek to include other valleys and other goat herds nearby. Some of the herds were within the Bob Marshall. A few remained near areas that had been roaded and logged, enabling us to make additional comparisons between disturbed and undisturbed groups. All, however, had been subject to fairly heavy hunting pressure—the harvest of game animals being permitted within wilderness areas as well as without—and so were never easy to get very close to. The sight of a nearby human figure typically would send goat bands stampeding up and away across the rocks for at least a quarter of a mile.

All the same, we managed to place acrylic collars containing a miniature radio transmitter on five animals, braided nylon collars with colored flagging on five more, and small patches of temporary dye on several others. We were also able to keep track of individual goats that had natural markings—bent or broken horns, scars, other deformities, and, for short periods each spring and summer, distinctive patterns of shed and unshed fur. Distant though we usually had to remain to avoid unsettling the climbers' daily routines, we even came to be able to identify a few herd members by their personalities.

Our own daily routines had more to do with patience and bushcraft than with any sophisticated scientific methods: keep track of as many animals as you can locate on the mountainside for as long as there is enough light to squint through the telescope, and try to write down (in the shorthand code we soon developed out of desperation) everything they do. We hiked and searched. Sat and watched. Day after day—and sometimes night after night—we used binoculars to follow the white beasts when the moon waxed full, then turned to an image-intensifying sniper scope during darker periods. And we did it month after month. You might call it a life of useful obsession, a slightly manic distension of normal curiosity.

We stayed with the mountain goats through one complete mountain winter and portions of others. No one else had tried to keep tightly focused on individual mountain goats and their activities from the beginning of this most crucial of seasons to the end. We quickly came to appreciate why. Our efforts at minute-by-minute observation blew away in blizzards, and we were sometimes too busy trying to keep from freezing or getting caught out in avalanche conditions to give any thought at all to what our white neighbors were doing. Plans ended at impasses on iced ledges, and numb fingers refused to write. But the notes we did obtain were valuable ones, and sooner or later they led into spring.

All in all, Beth and I divided the project's chores about equally, from keeping up spirits and momentum in sieges of storm weather to setting off alone to survey distant drainages. Yet we also had help and good company from time to time in the form of friends and volunteers, among them: Karen Cox, whose observations fill many pages in my notebook; Steve Shanewise, now managing waterfowl habitat for a private hunting club; Rod Flynn, who has since studied endangered rhinoceros in Indonesia and bobcats in the American Southwest; Bob Ream, an assistant professor at the University of Montana and my advisor when I was a graduate student there during the first years of the goat study; and Jack Nixon, fresh out of the Special Forces and Vietnam when I met him in the Swan Mountains backcountry. He said, "If you've got work to do so that I can stay up here, I'm your man. All you have to do is feed me some grub once in a while." Jack had vowed once, in a Vietnamese jungle, that if he got back he would never again pass a cold, clear mountain stream without drinking, and I don't think he ever did during the months he was with us.

Finally, I would like to record for posterity the contribution of one Parker R. Waite, who sallied forth across the Swan Divide bearing seven steaks and a case of beer for us, plus three bottles of salad dressing because he knew we often filled out our meals with wild herbs. He arrived, my buddy Parker, with no steaks and barely enough beer to dampen my tongue, having consumed everything but the salad dressing en route.

The Montana Department of Fish, Wildlife, and Parks initiated the idea of a goat-logging study in Bunker Creek and supported me for the first two years there with a graduate research stipend. The third year, I received a fellowship from the National Wildlife Federation, then a grant from Defenders of Wildlife. These enabled me to make surveys of other big mountain mammals—my special interest was the grizzly bear—in an attempt to compare their densities in roaded and unroaded drainages while continuing my long-term studies of the goats.

We left the Swans in mid-1974 and moved some 70 miles north, to the center of Glacier National Park and new mountain goat herds. That separation was followed by another, for Beth and I grew apart and were divorced. She is a filmmaker today. Her movies, which have won international awards and appeared on television, often deal with wilderness and wildlife. One has the mountain goat as its subject, so we still share some of the affections that once bound us. Be that as it may, I did the rest of

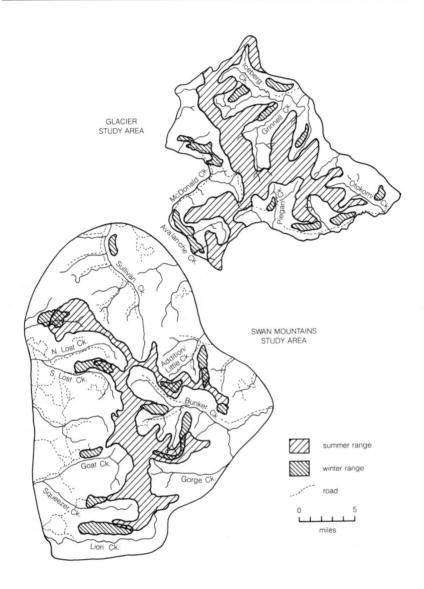

GLACIER
STUDY AREA

Iceberg Ck.

Grinnell Ck.

McDonald Ck.

Otokomi Ck.

Piegan Ck.

Avalanche Ck.

Sullivan Ck.

SWAN MOUNTAINS
STUDY AREA

N. Lost Ck.

Addition/
Little Ck.

S. Lost Ck.

Bunker Ck.

Goat Ck.

Gorge Ck.

Squeezer Ck.

Lion Ck.

summer range

winter range

road

0   5

miles

2.   *The Swan Mountains and Glacier National Park study areas, showing major drainages and winter and summer goat ranges.*

my work mostly alone, though for one summer in Glacier I was assisted by Dan Brandborg, Stewart Brandborg's son, on his way to a career in forestry and wildlife.

I was to stay in Glacier through 1977. Through 1976 I was seasonally employed by the park as a biologist, my only duties being to continue my research on mountain goats. The arrangement worked out nicely. I got steady and sound advice from chief biologist Cliff Martinka, who had invited me to work there, and only occasional complaints from the safety-conscious rangers, who figured me for an accident waiting to happen. For the last year and a half I was in the park the National Geographic Society gave me generous photographic assistance.

In Glacier I found myself among higher peaks and deeper snowfields than before. The park is named for the more than 50 glaciers within its domain, still actively sculpting the 9,000 to 11,000-foot-high massifs. Among the Blackfeet Indians this portion of the Continental Divide was known as "the backbone of the world." My study area spanned it, and I felt as though that was truly where I lived.

I was also among a much denser population of mountain goats, which had not been hunted or disturbed by development for many generations. With its continuous exposures of rock strata stacked up like blocks— tilted, twisted, and planing out above the forests—Glacier is optimum goat country. There may be none better. The park chose the bearded climber on a crag as its symbol based on the estimate that between 600 and 900 goats live within its 1,500-plus square miles. The park naturalists were being too modest. After taking representative counts here and there throughout Glacier, I told them they could justifiably claim closer to 1,500 of the creatures. My 120-square-mile main study area alone was inhabited by 300 to 350 goats.

By contrast, I had never found more than 80 to 90 goats in the 190 square miles of the Swans that I surveyed. There, sticking tight to one herd or another I had been able to fill plenty of notebooks in chronicling the life and times of goats I knew by name. But I was also stuck with the fact that a sample of 80 to 90 goats was just not big enough to allow me to draw very far-reaching conclusions about birth rates, survival in the different age and sex classes, or other aspects of population dynamics in this species. Glacier was exactly what I needed. No matter where I hiked I was rarely out of sight of a goat for long.

My goal became to try to locate and classify by age and sex every one of the 300-some goats in the Glacier study area once every month from early May, when lingering snows still confined the white climbers to winter ranges, through the end of September, when they were drifting back down toward the wintering sites just ahead of the first heavy snowstorms. Covering each valley, side valley, hidden valley, cirque, and plateau kept me moving pretty steadily. I averaged about nine miles a day, on trails and off. Come October I was ready to take off my climbing boots and sit down to analyze data, write reports, and put on winter fat, though I would put on ski boots and head out to make winter observations every so often. After keeping up this routine for three years in order to build a fairly precise population model, I turned again to following individual goats, but much more closely than I ever could have in the Swans.

Because the white climbers in Glacier had no overwhelming reason to fear man, I no longer needed to spend half a day crawling and slinking around the rocks like a hungry cougar to get a close-up glimpse of their life. A few of the herds I became acquainted with were used to having backpackers pass through their range and tolerated me within 200 feet, and one actually accepted me within their midst. I had waited a long time for such a herd.

At last I could travel with these creatures, rest alongside them on the slopes, turn with them to watch an eagle floating past. I could hear each sound they uttered and the rumbling of their four-chambered ruminant stomachs, see every flower or blade of grass they snipped, scrutinize the most subtle details of their social interactions. When I assumed certain postures and behaved in accordance with certain goatish rules, they even interacted directly with me. To be treated like a peculiar but passable mountain goat might not appeal to many people. I took it as a compliment of sorts. More importantly, I felt that by seeing the world through the animals' eyes, if only for an instant or two at a time, I understood both them and myself much better than before.

Seven years is a long time to go goatwatching, I suppose, and it leaves you unfit for a lot of other occupations. I have nonetheless turned to different projects since then. No longer do whole months go by when it seems I could count on one hand the number of times I strolled on level ground. Yet I've traveled to look over a lot of goat country in Canada and Alaska, and I still spend a good many days each year on pilgrimages to familiar Montana cliffs, where I take notes and photographs and occasionally recognize companions by a notched ear or busted horn. I doubt I'll break the pattern soon. I hope not.

There are so many things to be learned on the mountainside. Begin with new data, new insights into the living order and the process of natural selection which creates it. In the quest for scientific facts in the high country, you quickly confront some hard-edged facts of survival yourself and develop a powerful habit of self-sufficiency.

Then there are those relationships that can not quite be grasped as facts, but prove equally rewarding to know. What kind of weather a faint smell in the air forecasts. Where, given the lay of the rocks, a band of bighorn sheep will go next. What slight contour to follow across crusted snow to keep from breaking through. How much farther you can push your legs before they start to fail. How much further you can push your courage up a cliff face before it begins to falter. How to walk at night in the forest without a moon. When you are in the sort of spot where elk will be watching you from their midday beds. Call it developing some of the skills of the tracker or pioneer. Call it coming to feel at home in the country and in yourself.

We tend to forget that we are designed for knowing these things, for we too are the consequence of millions of years of evolution among wild animals in wild landscapes. We tend to forget that we too are animals, at once new and ancient, endlessly different and endlessly the same. There is perhaps no better way to appreciate that fact than to spend time near the crest of a mountain range with every gift that makes up your human heritage—each muscle, gland, nerve and instinct, as well as each faculty of reason—being called upon to express itself. I suppose this is the real reminiscence I'm after when I return to the goat cliffs.

Science, which is essentially an organized form of wonder, has its special rewards, just as it has its special techniques. But for me the excitement of discovering new dimensions of a little understood animal's life was only part of the pleasure of being so alive myself in the high, free places.

It will be helpful to preface the early chapters with a quick look at a few definitions and a synopsis of some key mountain goat characteristics. Following a gestation period of almost exactly six months, mountain goat kids are born in late May or early June, usually singly, occasionally as twins. Females are commonly called *nannies*, males *billies*. With very rare exceptions, they do not become sexually *mature* and take part in the late October to early December *rut*, or breeding season, until at least 29 to 30 months of age; that is, when they are about two-and-a-half years old. Thus females usually are first capable of giving birth at the time they turn three years of age.

I use the term *juvenile* to refer to both kids and yearlings, and *subadults* to encompass kids, yearlings, and two-year-olds. While *adult* therefore should be taken to mean goats three years of age and older, the white climbers do not really attain full size until at least four. An exceptionally

TABLE I. *Physical characteristics of mountain goats by age and sex classes.*

	Age (months)	Weight (pounds)	Horn length (inches)
Kid	0–11	7–50	0–3.5
Yearling	12–23	45–70	3.0–6.5
Two-year-old	24–35	65–110	5.5–8.5
Adult	36+	150–225 (avg. male) 120–160 (avg. female)	8–11

big billy may weigh in the neighborhood of 300 pounds, and a rare billy or nanny will carry horns reaching 12 inches in length. A mountain goat older than 10 years is nearing the end of its natural lifespan in the wild; the oldest one I've encountered among the peaks was 13. Goats in captivity or transplanted to a benign nonnative range may live somewhat longer. The wearing down of adult teeth to the gumline is an important built-in limit to longevity.

I remember periods early in the study when it seemed I was spending an awful chunk of my own lifespan just trying to pin down the age and sex of bearded white beasts. The problem is that yearlings and two-year-olds are tough to tell apart from one another or, at a distance, from adult goats. Nannies and billies also look alike as subadults and, seen from far off, even as adults. In the past, many researchers settled for classifying

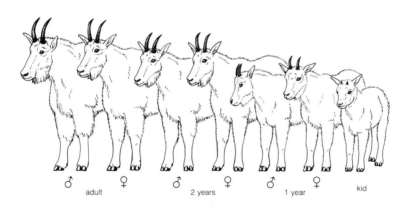

3. *Mountain goat age and sex classes.*

4. *Variation in horn shape between male and female mountain goats.*

all goats as either kids or adults. Others picked out yearlings and separated adult males from adult females. But two-year-olds were invariably
lumped with adults in inventories, and they still are, in most studies.

With steady practice I found it possible to train my eye to consistently
identify kids, yearlings, two-year-old males and females, and adult males
and females with the aid of an ordinary 15-to-45 power telescope. I occasionally had to be willing to wait an extra hour for an animal to get up
from bed so I could get a better view of its horns, and be willing to follow
a particularly generic-looking goat until it moved close enough to some
others for me to compare relative sizes, and so forth. But I could cut
corners once I learned certain behavioral clues. An obvious example is
that nannies squat to urinate while billies remain standing and stretch
out their legs. A more complex example would involve certain postures
two-year-old billies begin to use in social encounters, which distinguish
them from both two-year-old nannies and yearling billies. And this is the
point of making an extra effort to sort out the various sex and age classes.
Each behaves differently and is subject to different pressures from both
mountain goat society and the mountain environment—more so than was
appreciated until recently. Some major criteria for distinguishing age and
sex classes are summarized in Appendix I.

Nannies tend to remain faithful to a traditional home range year after
year. Billies typically move out to take up peripheral or wholly separate

ranges, usually at about the time they turn three, though sometimes considerably earlier. Thereafter, most billies seldom associate with mature females and subadults outside the rutting season. Neither males nor females defend any kind of fixed territory. Instead, goat society is organized as a dominance hierarchy, in which an individual's ability to defend or assert a mobile personal space reflects its relative rank. Aggressive behavior of this type is an almost constant feature of everyday life within groups, though much of it is fairly subtle.

Local herds are made up of solitary individuals and bands. The bands usually contain between two and five or maybe six goats, but at times up to 15 or 20. Kids remain close to their mother's side for nearly a full year, as a rule. Older subadults tend to continue following adult nannies, especially adult nannies with a kid at heel, but they do not necessarily choose their own mother to follow. In other words, a typical goat band consisting of a nanny, her kid, a two-year-old, and perhaps a yearling or two may look like a family unit—and that is how such groups have often been described—but the evidence from marked goats suggests otherwise. Bands turn out to be fairly loose associations whose composition changes frequently. Adult billies spend much more time alone than adult females or subadults, but commonly join in small bachelor bands during part of the year, notably in summer.

Finally, though I will refer to the snow-colored creatures as mountain goats and—for the sake of convenience—as just plain goats, they are not really true goats at all, as we will see in Chapter 2. At the least, we ought to steer away from the tradition of calling them Rocky Mountain goats, because they are spread throughout North America's northern Pacific Coast mountain chains as well as through the northern Rockies.

I have called the mountain goat a beast, a beast the color of winter. It is a beast. And in the same sense that we are more than just human it is more than just a beast. Indian tribes believed each creature that dwells among these mountains—Goat, Eagle, Wolverine, Salmon, Otter, Raven, Marten, Wolf, and all the others—possesses a spirit. Insofar as by "spirit" they meant some glimmer in an already bright eye, some shared quality of consciousness, I believe they were right, particularly for the large mammals. Here are beings with languages and elaborate societies of their own, possibly a sense of self and the ability to make judgements, and certainly—if you will only watch them long and closely enough to see—a large capacity for curiosity, frustration, misery, companionship, and joy.

CHAPTER ONE

Early Days of the Sundance Kid

THE NANNY ON the northernmost cliff had gradually stopped keeping company with the rest of the herd in the upper valley. For the past several days her movements had been confined to ledges about halfway down the outcropping of tile-red argillite rock. It was one of the cliff's steepest sections. Several of the ledges, though, were wider than those around them, and were overhung by stone shelves that offered some shelter in case the weather turned foul. These were the ones she frequented. A few Douglas fir had driven roots into the widest ledges. The older trees were squat and ragged, their tops shattered by past windstorms and avalanches.

The last week of May had just arrived. Across the terraced rock and lower meadows the last flattened brown husks of long-frozen vegetation were quickly disappearing beneath a swelling green. Meltwater poured over cliff faces everywhere in glistening waterfalls as deep snowpacks toward the summit softened. Engelmann spruce and silvery-barked subalpine fir, their densely packed, flexible branches and spire shape designed to withstand the winter load of snow, emerged taller each day against the white background of mountainside. Farther down the valley the new needles of western larch shone like green fire.

Though chill and sometimes frosted, the mornings were no longer silent. Varied thrush, olive-sided flycatcher, pine siskin, mountain bluebird, Townsend's solitaire—all were singing before the first flares shot through the passes from the east to announce the sun's arrival.

The nanny fed indifferently, then stood sleepily in the first channeled light to chew her cud. I was observing her closely, sitting on a block of firewood outside my tent in the Swan Mountains. It was an ideal location, one I had found the year before after weeks of snowshoeing, sliding up and down skyscraping terrain each day, and crawling into my down-filled bag early each night for the dreamless sleep of the exhausted. No one, not the game managers who set hunting seasons for the animals or the foresters who planned to cut more high-elevation timber in the area, knew quite where the resident mountain goats roamed during the various seasons or even how many lived in the area to begin with. But here were close to thirty of them, by far the largest concentration I had yet located and, as it turned out, the largest I would ever find in this part of the Swans.

Many of the valleys in this mountain range are miles across from rim to rim, having been widened by Pleistocene glaciers. This one, drained by a fast, talkative stream named Little Creek, was more canyon-shaped. Camped on the opposite side of the valley from the blocks and bands of cliffs but at about the same altitude, Beth and I were between a half-mile and three-quarters of a mile from the mountain goats. We were close, but not so close that they were distracted by our presence.

The solitary female was young; I judged her age to be three years. She had conceived during the rutting season of the previous fall. Now as she stood in the sun she made sudden hunching motions from time to time. I knew then that she had been able to find enough food over winter to nourish both herself and the embryo growing within her, and that it had become a baby kicking within her womb. If my estimate of her age was correct, this would be her first pregnancy. What, I wondered, did she make of this heavy thing moving inside her?

The following day she fed little and slept in the shade of one of the Douglas firs. About six o'clock the next morning I found her standing near the same tree. Beside her, also standing—but quaking as it did—was a tiny goat, perhaps seven pounds in weight. Its coat was pale and wet, its eyes big and round, as though it were astounded by the size of the place —and the possibilities.

The mother licked her baby carefully. When she licked along its spine the infant straightened its legs and stood taller than before. Then it tottered beneath its mother, found one of her teats, and butted up against it to make the milk flow faster. Stimulation of the newborn animal in order to get it moving, standing, and finally nursing is one of the specific functions of licking. We mimic this pleasant stimulation when we pet a domestic animal like the family cat or dog. This behavior pattern in mammalian mothers also serves to clean the coat of birth fluids and fluff it up to dry before evaporative cooling chills the infant. At the same time, the mother becomes imprinted with the smell of her offspring.

The kid's tail stood erect like a pennant as it suckled. The upraised tail was, in fact, a signal. Seeing it, the mother bent around and thoroughly licked the exposed anus of her infant, cleaning it to prevent irritation and infection, and further imprinting herself with the youngster's odors. (After the two of them later rejoined the herd, I often saw her trying to tell her baby apart from the kids it was playing with. As a last resort she would sniff the anus of each of the identical-looking youngsters, then chase the imposters away.) When it finished suckling, about three minutes after it started, the kid knelt—collapsed would be more accurate—and rested at its mother's feet.

I had tried the year before to find nannies during their time of seclusion, but the newest kids I had observed were already days old. Now I had one that, taking into account the wetness of its fur and its struggle to remain standing, was only minutes old. Beth and I agreed to take turns at the telescope to record the infant's development second by second as long as the light lasted each day—some 17 hours from dawn to dusk.

Backaches and throbbing neck muscles beset us before twilight gathered on our first day. Though I had trained myself to focus for long intervals through the telescope with one eye while using the other to guide what I was writing in the notebook on my lap, this marathon vigil soon left my writing fingers stiff and my eyes bleary, red, and feeling as if they were permanently cocked at different angles.

All the same, the view through the tube was spellbinding. As we sat spooning cold meals past the tripod and into our mouths, the image unfolded and grew in miraculous patterns and with a speed that reminded me of movies in which time-lapse photography makes plants germinate, stretch upward, and flower in the space of one long breath. Over half a century ago naturalist Ernest Thompson Seton reported seeing a mountain goat kid hopping into the air within ten minutes of its birth in captivity. A Montana old-timer I know tells a story of following a pregnant nanny for two days, intending to capture her kid and raise it himself. He swears he saw her give birth and reached the birthsite within fifteen minutes to half an hour, only to have the kid outhop him on the jumbled rocks. True or not, the tale is within the realm of possibility for this species. The kid I watched waited only slightly longer to begin hopping about. And within five hours of being dropped onto the mountainside, it was ardently trying to climb it.

Unable to walk very far without occasionally sprawling, the kid would skitter and wobble away from its mother and promptly place both forefeet up against whatever was higher than it was—ledges, boulders, tree trunks—and try to see what sort of progress it could make in a vertical direction. Then, returning home, it might try to climb the mound that was its bedded nanny. Early that first day this prodigy gained the top of a medium-sized boulder. Without hesitation, as if its muscles had plans of their own, the baby sprang from there high into the air—only to land more on its nose than its feet. Then it went back up the boulder and repeated its performance, including the crash landing.

In between nursing, resting, and attempting to go upward the hours-old kid whirled in circles, made spasmodic hops, mewed and bleated in a voice that echoed through the valley, danced on its hind legs, and butted still nonexistent horns at the sunbright sky. Its rubbery legs could not yet match all its inborn aspirations. Yet it could scamper very quickly from place to place, if never very stably.

In quieter moments the baby explored its mother, mostly by sniffing. It appeared to favor her moist mouth and nose; the intriguing triangles of her ears, which flapped to keep away insects; her long, thin horns; and of course the area around her udder.

For her part, the nanny's attention to the tiny one was nearly absolute. Although she seemed restless and paced back and forth in the shade while her baby slept, the mother never went more than 20 feet from the infant. She ate only a few plants, and then halfheartedly. However, during the day this vegetarian bent her head to the ground and consumed the remains of her afterbirth, then licked the soil where birth fluids had spilled out of her. Whether or not she recouped some essential nutrients in the process, her actions were ensuring that no ripe smells would waft from the birthsite to the nose of a predator prowling the mountainside. Among hooved species in which the mother and newborn abandon the birthsite very soon after partuition (as many antelope and wild horses do), the female is less likely to eat the placenta.

The kid preferred to be uphill from its mother, but was often more concerned with whatever it happened to be doing at the moment than with its position relative to her. The nanny, though, kept track of such things. When the leaping baby lost its balance she was there below, so that it fell against her legs rather than toward the mountain's edge—and possibly on down through the sky. With her neck and head she gently nudged the baby uphill while it explored, and she made certain that during its many naps the youngster slept tucked against the summit side rather than the valley side of her thick coat. Even so, she was likely to awaken with the kid clambering atop her as it prepared to vault into space once again. (Young goats, it seems, take the term "offspring" literally.) Rising, stretching, and yawning, she would prepare to continue following its every move. I could hear her literally cry out when the baby took a hard spill, and she would rush over to lick and nuzzle it, and then encourage it to nurse.

The second day also was warm and clear. As I sat by the telescope with my shirt off, the sun began to redden one pale shoulder that had not felt much of its heat for many snowbound months. Young mountain goats are not always blessed with fair skies. In later years, I watched them huddle against their mother in bed while three or four inches of fresh snow drifted over their backs and gales blew the May blossoms off their stalks. But for all this particular kid knew, the peaks were endlessly sharp against a blue sky and gaily-colored flower petals left their stalks only in the form of butterflies that floated past its nose.

Markedly faster on its feet after the first 24 hours, the baby was venturing farther, climbing more—especially over the white slopes of its bedded nanny—and leaping higher. It was also falling harder, though not as often. Still, when it lifted a rear leg to scratch behind its ear, there was a fair amount of doubt as to whether the result would be a successfully scratched itch or yet another collision with the ground. No setback deterred the kid for long, though. In its hurry to live, the infant rarely walked anywhere. Instead, it pronked, bucked, scampered, and slid, then pawed at its mother's side if she was bedded, until she stood to let it refuel by nursing. This diminutive, milk-fed, milk-white sprite's upward pushes at the teat were already strong enough to joggle the nanny's 100 to 125-pound body, and even threw her off balance at times.

If the kid seemed utterly entranced by motion for motion's sake, there was at least a pattern to it. In the way this two-day-old baby spun in circles and butted imaginary opponents, I could discern many of the basic elements of fighting as performed by older mountain goats with much more serious intentions. Similarly, I noticed elements of male courtship in the mounting stance the kid sometimes assumed when climbing upon its nanny, and in the way it rubbed its chin over her back and neck as she lay bedded. This did not imply that the kid was a billy. Female kids exhibit generalized versions of several of the sexual postures used by mature males, mounting being the most prevalent, as do female yearlings (as well as both male and female juveniles in many other ungulate species). As anyone who has paid attention to our own species is aware, every individual appears to have the potential for performing the behavior patterns of either sex. Roles usually become more fixed as the individual matures and produces more sex-specific hormones.

We saw the kid nurse 17 times for a total of 58 minutes the first day; 10 times, totaling 31 minutes the second day; and only six times, for 20 minutes altogether, the third day. As it took less milk the kid spent more time sniffing vegetation in the area where its mother was grazing, occasionally mouthing the stalk of the same plant its mother had just snipped. By day four the kid was biting off the stalks.

It was also, by the fourth day, able to keep up with its parent over broken terrain. Accordingly, the nanny began to feed farther afield, though she avoided leading her offspring onto the steeper ledges. The total distances traveled by the pair during the first four days were 35, 85, 135, and 200 feet, respectively. This was all back-and-forth movement within 100 feet of the bedsite, but it was a bit more experience for the youngster each day and a bit less confinement for the nanny. We envied them, for though we were as restless as the nanny we remained tied to the telescope just as tightly as on the first day.

In regard to early movements of the mother goat and infant, Brandborg describes:

> . . . a Salmon River (*Idaho*) kid that was unable to leave the ledge where it had apparently been born. When first observed, the kid was attempting to climb a 10 foot face of rock above the narrow ledge (approximately 20 feet in length and 5 feet wide) upon which it was confined. The mother stood above her offspring on the top of this barrier, waiting expectantly as the kid tried time after time to scale it. Finally, after several minutes of these efforts, the kid bedded and the mother began to feed on the slope above the ledge. She returned an hour later to allow the kid to nurse and again the kid attempted to scale the rock face. The mother goat descended and, after nosing the kid for a few seconds, would climb the rock again as though to demonstrate the ease with which this could be done. In the succeeding five days it was necessary for the mother to leave the kid for periods of more than an hour while she fed on slopes above the ledge. The kid sometimes grew restless and would walk back and forth on the narrow rock shelf or repeat its attempts to scale the wall. The mother, upon her return, was always received enthusiastically by the young animal which was quick to receive the food she provided. On the fifth day the nanny happened onto the one place on the ledge where the cliff was broken, making descent to a lower slope possible. She followed this and was able to lead the kid onto the adjacent hillside. This was the only observed instance of a kid being separated from the female because of its inability to traverse the goat range. Occasionally, a young animal was forced to find another route in order to keep up, but this never resulted in the separation of the mother and the offspring.

On day five, the kid Beth and I were watching began to forage alongside its mother wherever she went, though when she concentrated her grazing in one spot the baby might kneel and lie down to catch a quick nap. Along with their spring staples of new bunchgrass and sedge, the pair snipped many of the same things we had been harvesting for our dinner salads: wild onion shoots, wild strawberry leaves, and the fiddle-heads of ferns growing in shady rock crannies. The white climbers liked the blossoms of avalanche lilies, yellow bells, and spring beauties. We and the bears preferred the leaves of these three early green-up species and, most of all, the bulbs, which have a crisp, delicately nutty flavor. Toward evening the kid bedded down again, crossed its forelegs casually like a scaled-down replica of a grown-up mountain goat, and began to chew its cud for what I believe was the first time and with what looked to me like tremendous satisfaction.

Three weeks after the kid's birth the nanny would begin stepping over it to end nursing sessions. These sessions by then have grown fairly short and perfunctory anyway, more a bonding interaction between the two than a source of critical nutrition for the youngster. The kid would be effectively weaned four weeks after coming into the world, though it would still attempt to nurse from time to time for many weeks longer.

It was evident by the fifth day that the nanny was ready to rejoin the herd, a new member at her heels. The time of isolation had allowed the infant to build strength and coordination in an environment where it was concealed from—and largely inaccessible to—predators and where there was little to distract the nanny's attention from its welfare. Their seclusion also gave the two animals an important opportunity to become more familiar with one another's distinctive scents, voice, and physical features. Mothers and infants are, after all, strangers in a sense. How many human mothers would be able to immediately pick out their own infant from the others in a large maternity ward without an identification bracelet?

Once reunited with the herd, the nanny needs to be able to do more than select her kid from a group of playing infants. I once watched a large band of goats crossing a talus slope, when a grizzly launched itself toward them from behind a boulder. Panicked kids are wont to flee at the heels of the nearest large goat at the moment of crisis. Separated during their escape, a mother and kid I had observed were later able to cover their huge vertical world independently, each calling and listening and searching out the other's unique odors amidst a landscape saturated with the smells of other goats, to become reunited.

Lastly, the seclusion period gave the three-year-old nanny and her kid a setting in which to forge strong links of affection, as each repeatedly fulfilled the other's strong needs and was the sole animal to do so. Hormones had aroused potent maternal urges in the nanny; there to requite them was the kid, which in turn received constant nourishment and support.

The young of most hooved species stay with their mother the first year.

The typical mountain goat kid, however, not only stays with its mother for 10 to 11 months, but sticks exceptionally close to her side practically the entire time. Mike Hutchins, who studied mountain goats in Olympic National Park, Washington, came up with a revealing statistic: just about half the kids he observed would be within one meter of their mother at any given moment throughout the summer. This is about as close as the youngster can get without being stepped on. My notes show the average distance between mother and young decreasing only slightly thereafter. A kid might wander up to 30 feet from its parent for a short time, but to see one linger much farther away was uncommon. As for the nanny, she remains perhaps the most attentive and protective of ungulate mothers, following her offspring's actions almost as devotedly as it follows her footsteps until at least late winter.

Although I am very fond of mountain goats I am not trying to prove here that they have some remarkable quality of fondness themselves. Quite the opposite: apart from mother–kid ties, the sharp-horned species is distinctly aggressive toward members of its own kind. As we will see in Chapter 6, the white climber's social environment can be every bit as rigorous as its unforgiving physical surroundings. Each developing youngster requires an extra measure of protection from both; by keeping within its mother's personal space the kid can avoid harassment by goats of lower rank in the social hierarchy than its mother. An unusually tight and prolonged mother–infant bond is simply one more necessary adaptation for survival in the mountain goat's world of extremes.

Although it had been this nanny's wish to be completely alone with her offspring for several days, things did not work out exactly that way. To begin with, two kinds of ground squirrels frequent mountain goat cliffs in this part of the Rockies. (Or, from the rodents' standpoint, mountain goats frequent the ground squirrel cliffs.) Golden-mantled ground squirrels favor the high, stony, exposed locations, while Columbian ground squirrels are more common on dry, sunny slopes with plenty of loose digging soil.

On the second day of the kid's life one of these rodents—I was too distant to tell which kind—scurried up a rock above the two goats. There it proceeded to eat a bouquet of what looked like penstemon, then hurried right past the kid en route to another flower cluster. The kid saw it and popped straight up into the air, bleating.

Upon having this white explosion go off next to it, the ground squirrel jerked to a stop, whistled its piercing cry, turned, and scrambled away on a different tack. Unfortunately, it failed to notice that it was escaping in the direction of a much larger detonation until it had climbed partway across the bedded nanny's rump. The nanny, alerted by the bleat of her babe, was just beginning to get up, and when she felt the unknown invader on her rump she bucked with the kind of sidewinding twist that rodeo hands call "sunfishing." Which transformed the hapless ground squirrel into a flying squirrel for a long moment before it became, emphatically, a ground squirrel again. As the rodent staggered to its feet, the first thing it focused on must have been a gigantic, enraged mass of flying fur propelling two black rapiers capable of gutting a lynx in its direction.

At about the same time that the dizzy squirrel might have realized it was going to have to climb a stone wall as fast as any squirrel had ever climbed one, the nanny appeared to become aware that (a) the enemy was not especially large or well-fanged and (b) it was a living definition of full retreat. She stopped, and the frightened kid took shelter underneath her, looking out from behind the stockade of four shaggy legs to see what was next. Nothing very exciting was next. The nanny stamped her foot once or twice in annoyance, and the squirrel completed its retreat. So the kid began nursing, and its mother, responding as always to the signal of the upraised tail, licked its rear end thoroughly.

Later the same day the kid ran to huddle beneath its mother twice more: once when a jay-like Clark's nutcracker flew close overhead (good practice in case the swooping bird turned out to be an eagle), and again when a passing band of mountain goats appeared over the top of the ledge.

These last intruders temporarily forgot to maintain the personal space they usually insist on through low-key intimidation or, that failing, through outright battles and chases. They clustered shoulder-to-shoulder and haunch-to-haunch to peer down over the rock shelf at the tiny creature peering back up at them from between leg pillars. The last goat band I had seen so closely packed together was being harassed by coyotes, and I could not recall the last time I had seen a group so intrigued. Then it dawned upon me: not only was this the first infant I had seen on the slopes this year, it was the first the other white climbers had yet seen in this birth season.

Mutual astonishment, in which wide-eyed heads craned up and down and sideways, lasted for quite some time. The kid alternated between a front-leg view and one from the side, while the crowd shoved a little and edged forward to get a better look. My attention was concentrated upon a particular intruder. She was a three-year-old female, like the kid's nanny, and was herself to give birth about ten days later. Fitted loosely around her neck was a radio collar. She was the first mountain goat Beth and I had trapped, and though I gave her a number rather than a name in my notes, I will call her Pandora.

Pandora appeared wonderstruck by the baby. Upon first coming into sight of it she had stared without twitching a muscle for over 40 seconds. I recalled the way she and I had stared at one another when we first met on the slopes of that valley which was to be roaded and logged: Bunker Creek, just over two miles along a connecting ridge from our present site at Little Creek.

Pandora was unblinking then, a 70 to 80-pound two-year-old who watched as Beth and I approached in the gathering dusk. She stood by a mossy seep of mineral water that issued from the lower part of a blue-grey scarp of limestone. It was a place she was probably used to visiting each spring and summer to lick the salty deposits at the edge of the seep. But in the summer of 1971 she found wooden slats set around the salt lick, and when her hoof struck an all-but-invisible trip wire of nylon filament, a weighted net had suddenly fallen, linking the open ends of the cage and trapping her within it. The cage was likely the first thing in her life she had never been able to climb away from. And then we were staring at each other; two kinds of beings, each with illusions about the nature of the other, and what it would do next.

It is hard to guess what feelings lie behind an animal's eyes. What you see in those orbs may be the animal's true emotions or a reflection of your own state of mind. In the large brown-black eyes of Pandora I thought I saw frustration and, naturally, fear—but also an unexpected amount of resolve.

Beth and I were inexperienced and hesitant, which only made us more awkward in the failing light as we tried to throw one noose over her head and another around her hind foot. Time after time Pandora kicked away the foot snare and butted away the descending head loop in mid-air, then whirled to face us again with those unflinching eyes and horn daggers, breathing heavily. Through the wooden slats Beth tried a quick strike with a hypodermic syringe containing tranquilizer. But the needle snapped on the goat's thick hide, and Pandora bloodied her nose against the trap while turning to defend herself.

Feeling that I was accomplishing little besides sadism, I walked a short distance away to begin another of the conversations I periodically hold with myself. Since a crucial function of my study was to discover why mountain goat populations were declining in the Swans, I had to know more about the animals' movements: daily travels; seasonal migrations; the overall size and extent of an individual's home range; differences in the way males, females, adults, and juveniles use an area; and how widely the repercussions of large-scale human disturbance at one site would be felt. Brightly colored collars would help me identify individuals a long distance away and under conditions of poor visibility—which were more the rule than the exception in many months. By adding a radio transmitter to a collar, I could eventually relocate an individual even after it had disappeared from view and journeyed ten miles to a completely unsuspected destination—as later happened with a young collared billy.

Before me now was a terrified young mountain goat that I wanted very much to let go with my best wishes. The possibilities of a collar hampering her in some dicey climbing situation, either by snagging on a rock or by throwing her off balance with its extra weight, bothered me to begin with. And here I was bloodying her, trying to get one around her neck. But if I were to turn her loose unmarked, what good would such a gesture be if the herd as a whole continued to dwindle? In some valleys where, two decades earlier, old-timers and hikers had seen 30 and 40 mountain goats, I now searched for days to find three or four.

I returned and managed to get a wide loop over her head, as a decent cowboy would have done ten minutes earlier. She hooked at me, leaping wildly, and crashed into another wooden slat, loosening a horn and cutting her mouth. Beth made a foot catch and stretched the goat's leg out. Frantic now, Pandora reared and banged into the slats again. Equally frantic, I threw the rope away and tackled her, and she hit the ground with a strange whimper. As I struggled to blindfold her eyes and then administer a tranquilizer, she suddenly went limp. The long and clumsy harassment had taken a great toll. The mind had sealed itself off from the pain and fear and shut down the body's systems as well. The first mountain goat I had ever touched was now in shock.

What now? The tranquilizer had not yet taken effect. When it did, would it bring her around or slow her to a complete stop? We could try injecting a strong stimulant, but it might cause her to go into worse shock after reviving. What about smelling salts? It was Beth who suggested it —of all things. They just might work, but they were back at camp in our personal first aid kit. Beth raced down the mountainside in the darkness.

I found myself walking back and forth on a ledge, holding an unfamiliar and unconscious creature in my arms and telling it not to die. It was too late now to wish I had never tried to get information in this way, and I felt too hollow to try and rationalize the circumstances. It was useless to do anything but carry this young female, try to support her loose body and make it walk and begin functioning again—and try to drive from my mind the persistent knowledge that other goats had died from shock on other mountainsides during trapping and transplanting operations. Pandora's legs made weak, reflexive attempts to go forward, but the rest of the animal only inflated and deflated with shallow breaths so irregular I could never be sure another would follow.

I heard Beth calling from below and guided her with my voice up the black cliffs. We cracked an ammonia capsule beneath Pandora's nose.

Then another. And then we saw her try to raise her head. After long moments the eyes opened. Her breathing grew stronger. Soon I had to hold tightly to keep her from breaking free as she began to walk under her own power. She would make it.

The blindfold (which I replaced), combined with the tranquilizer, which was now beginning to work, kept her calm while we fastened the collar around her neck. The collar carried radio circuitry, its antenna, and battery power sources, all sealed in hard acrylic. We fitted it to leave plenty of room for Pandora's neck to grow. Working as fast as we could by flashlight, we wrapped a ring of brightly colored plastic tape around each horn. This way we could identify her in case the collar somehow came off. Next we took several body measurements. Finally, we removed the blindfold, backed away, and shut the cage door behind us.

Afraid she might slip groggily off a ledge or become easy meat for a predator in her current condition, we wanted to keep her confined until the tranquilizer wore off. We walked out of sight, built a small fire, and waited. And waited. In the pre-dawn light, just before the peaks started to turn rose and salmon pink, we restored her to freedom.

A year later Beth and I were a far more efficient and painless goat-roping team (though I still think the glamor of capturing wild animals is perhaps best experienced via television—after editing). The important thing is that Pandora also was there a year later, a healthy, pregnant, and findable mountain goat, her trap-loosened horn as rigid and sharp as before we first met. And now, on the Little Creek cliffs, she continued to stare at the newborn baby as though she beheld the future of the species in it. Pandora stayed back while the other goats, including two typically rambunctious and helplessly curious yearlings, edged forward.

The baby's mother was in a troublesome position. Normally, if she wished to be left alone, she would have run off the intruders and perhaps prodded them on their way, catching tufts of rear end fur on her horn tips to remind them to respect her privacy. But the infant would not have been able to keep up during a fast chase, and she was reluctant to leave it even a short distance behind. So she made false starts and threatened the others with tosses of her horns. The yearlings would retreat a few feet, then—realizing she was bluffing—approach once more toward the miniature goat that so held their interest. It was not until another quarter of an hour had passed that the older onlookers took their leave and the yearlings reluctantly followed, after fleeing a final, short rush by the annoyed mother.

Soon after the nanny and kid departed the ledges around the birthsite to begin visiting other portions of the cliff, they were resting on a rimrock when yet another goat intruded upon them. It was a very large adult female. She had noticed the pair from a distance and approached, as goats will, to mingle for a spell and, while she was at it, to determine who was the more dominant animal.

The mother rose from bed but did not rise to meet the challenge, again, I think, for fear of creating an unstable situation around her youngster. Instead of circling and arching her back as she might be expected to do, she faced the incoming female head-on with the kid at her heels and refused to budge. The other mountain goat, seemingly perplexed by this noncommital behavior, circled warily. When that drew no standard response either, she returned to stand rigidly before the mother and flourish her horns. At this point the tension in the air apparently infected the kid. It raced out in front of its startled parent and performed a spectacularly inspired series of leaps in which it spun this way and that, and thoroughly punctured the air around the other female's ankles with its imaginary horns. Now, I thought, I know why they call tough guys The Kid.

Its final display was so enormous that the young berserker hurled its own feet out from under itself in several directions at once and came down in a pile in front of the strange nanny. The big female let down her guard for a moment and sniffed the fallen warrior. Then she looked up from it to its mother with the blankest expression I had ever seen on a mountain goat's face, and departed.

CHAPTER TWO

A Long, Uphill Climb

HAVING SEEN HOW one mountain goat comes into its high, cliffside world, it may be a good time to look at how the species itself came into existence. How did any large hooved animal end up living on terrain so steep that a mother must keep constantly below her offspring to minimize its chances of tumbling away downhill? And why did it settle so far up the slopes, more closely tied to the wintry crest of mountains than to the sheltered habitats occupied by most of its hooved neighbors?

Nature is the consummate improviser, creating probabilities where none existed before. The evolution of the mountain goat is a case in point, and the more we know about the origins and long history of the white climber, the more fully we will be able to appreciate how it manages to survive in its extraordinary niche. We begin with the basic questions the nineteenth-century scientists had to ask when they first handled specimens of the beast that turned out to be improbable only by human standards: exactly what is this animal, and where in the world did it come from?

The common name of mountain goat implies that we are dealing with —what else?—a species of goat that lives in the mountains. But the mountain goat is not a true goat, despite a superficial resemblance to whitish, short-horned breeds of the domestic goat, *Capra hircus.* Moreover, several wild species of true goats such as the ibex *(Capra ibex)* and markhor *(Capra falconeri)* of Eurasia dwell in high, rugged country and are also referred to—with more justification—as mountain goats.

When we turn to our mountain goat's scientific name for clarification a third problem arises: *Oreamnos* literally means mountain *(ore)* lamb *(amnos),* suggesting that the creature might be some sort of sheep after all. It is not, though mountain sheep do inhabit many of the same chains of peaks in North America, and two races in northern Canada and Alaska known as Dall's sheep wear a coat of the same snow-white color.

Now what? We start thumbing through wildlife biology texts, and find that most authors have tried to resolve the matter by describing the mountain goat as a "goat-antelope" or "mountain antelope." As if the mountain goat's own identity crisis were not bad enough, antelope is the common name for animals in at least two quite separate families and half a dozen different tribes. Worse, the mountain goat has no overwhelmingly close ties to any of them, least of all to the pronghorn, the only Northern American version of an antelope.

The situation is intriguing, not to say confusing. The best way to resolve it is to describe the mountain goat by another of its taxonomic names: rupicaprid.

The Rupicaprini tribe is a subdivision of the large and diverse Bovidae family, to which the tribes of true goats and sheep; true antelope; and bison, cattle, and their relatives also belong. Just five species are generally classified as rupicaprids (*Rupes* = rock, *capra* = goat). They are: the goral (*Nemorhaedus goral*), serow (*Capricornis sumatraensis*), and Japanese serow (*C. crispus*) all of Asia; the chamois (*Rupicapra rupicapra*) of Europe and the Caucasus; and our mountain goat of North America. (Some authorities recognize six rupicaprids, distinguishing the red goral, *N. cranbrooki*, of northern Burma from the common goral.) Thus, from the entire spectrum of hooved and horned animals, the nearest kin of *Oreamnos americanus* turn out to be a handful of creatures that live a continent away and are unfamiliar to most Americans.

One thing about the winter-colored beast's closest relatives is not surprising: each is an expert climber in its own right. However, the characteristics that chiefly serve to separate the Rupicaprini from other bovid family members have to do with horn and skull anatomy.

Bovid horns are usually permanent*—as opposed to being periodically shed and regrown like antlers—and all have the same basic structure. They are hollow, formed by a sheath of keratin (the same fibrous, sulfur-containing protein that builds mammalian hair and nails) growing around a shorter bony core, and are always unbranched. Beyond that formula they have evolved into a marvelous array of designs. Five-foot-long spirals adorn the greater kudu antelope. Musk oxen wear broad, tight-fitting helmets. Male Marco Polo sheep carry up to 40 pounds of

---

*Until recently, they were thought to be permanent in every case, but some bovids, including the chamois, have been found to shed their horns once or twice during their lifetime.

5. *The mountain goat and its closest relatives.*

massively curling headgear. And so it grows, each species performing its variation on the tribal theme.

For the rupicaprid tribe the theme is distinctively daggerlike. The horns of all five members are short, thin, and sharply pointed. This, and the fact that the horns of both sexes are highly similar in size and shape, amount to a diagnostic trait. The skulls of the Rupicaprini are also readily identifiable, being quite thin-boned and light—mere eggshells compared to the massive cranium of, say, water buffalo, wildebeest, or mountain sheep.

Anatomy translates into behavior patterns, behavior patterns into survival strategies. This is the fundamental reason I have emphasized the need to avoid mixing up mountain goats with true goats, sheep, or antelope. The mountain goat's horns are of a more primitive, lethal design; its skull more fragile; its males and females more alike in appearance, as a rule. Every rupicaprid quality that makes the mountain goat physically different from species belonging to other branches of the Bovidae family tree generates important differences in fighting techniques, courtship, the way its society is organized, and, ultimately, the way its populations interact with the environment.

While nothing else looks or acts quite like the mountain goat and its closest kin, the Rupicaprini are considered to be related to four other tribes in particular. These include the single tribe that contains both true goats and sheep, the Caprini; a smaller tribe consisting of two rather odd Asian antelopes, the Saigini; and, interestingly, the equally small musk-oxen tribe, the Ovibovini. In fact, two Asian species, the tahr and takin are occasionally found wandering back and forth between tribes in a sort of taxonomic limbo. The present consensus is that the shaggy tahr is a true goat with a number of rupicaprid traits and the takin more of a musk-ox than a rupicaprid, though not all that much more.

A closer look at the taxonomy of the Rupicaprini and adjacent tribes is available in Appendix II. The classification of animals is a subject that can quickly grow tedious, but we have enough names now to go on to the evolutionary history in this province of the animal kingdom. Such intermediate species as the tahr and takin are living evidence of the course it took. The Rupicaprini probably developed from primitive antelope stock; a beast called Pachygazella, whose fossil remains have been found in China, is a possible progenitor. It appears that the early rupicaprids gave rise in turn not only to more advanced rupicaprids but, through offshoot branches, to the tribes of both musk-oxen and true goats. Then from a divergent line of true goats came the animals we know as sheep. In a sense, then, the mountain goat's ancestors are also the forefathers

6. Heads and horns of various members of the subfamily Caprinae.

(and mothers) of the domestic goats and sheep so closely linked to many human cultures.

Rupicaprids are thought to have been around since the Miocene, 25 million years ago, and the musk-oxen and true goat lines began to diverge from them sometime during the same epoch or at least by the early Pliocene, 12 to 13 million years ago. The focus of all this species shaping was the Himalayan Mountains, rising ever since the Indian subcontinent collided with the land mass of Asia some 60 million years ago, isolating old species and building environments for new ones.

Primitive rupicaprids may not have looked too different from the present-day goral, which still inhabits the central Himalayan region, its populations extending southward into Burma and eastward through China into Manchuria, Korea, and southeastern Siberia. The goral is small and grayish or reddish, coarse-haired, short-horned, and short-legged. It occurs typically in small groups on terrain that is steep, rocky, and high, but often fairly heavily forested as well. Because it is adapted to both cliff dwelling and forest dwelling, it is not highly specialized for either. In all, the goral seems the very sort of generalized, unembellished creature you expect as an evolutionary prototype.

The next geologic epoch, the Pleistocene (beginning perhaps two million years ago), saw those *himals*—meaning "snow peaks" in Nepalese— thrust farther upward to become the highest on earth. Meanwhile the rupicaprids developed various new forms of their own and spread throughout Eurasia and possibly into northern Africa. But, geologically speaking, their time in the sun was brief. Most of them disappeared before the Ice Ages were over.

While such European rupicaprids as the Balearic cave goat, a buck-toothed contemporary of Neanderthal man, and the large *Gallogoral* ran their course toward extinction, the chamois went on to claim the Alps, Apennines, Pyrenees, and the Caucasus and Carpathian mountains as its modern range. During most of the year this brown and white species is a committed crag-dweller, favoring some of the tallest, most precipitous territory those European mountain ranges have to offer. With the onset of winter it generally descends into the higher forests and uses somewhat gentler terrain.

An adult chamois usually weighs 100 pounds or less, carrying its weight on a frame that is longer-legged and slimmer than those of its stocky rupicaprid brethren. Easily the fleetest of its tribe, the chamois is a remarkable leaper by any tribe's standards. It is more gregarious than the goral; groups of over 20 can be found when typical family-sized bands join together.

Because of a long proximity to European civilization, the chamois is the rupicaprid best known to science. While an American may not be quick to recognize chamois as the name of a mountaineering beast—it is also called the gems—he is likely acquainted with the pliant but durable cloth known as "shammy" or "shamoy". Now made synthetically for the most part, this material originally was a leather product: the hide of Europe's representative of the Rupicaprini.

Serow remain in the opposite end of Eurasia. Their range extends from the central Himalayas southeastward into Malaya and Sumatra and northeastward as far as Japan. Isolated when the Japanese archipelago became detached from the mainland, the island population of the serow evolved into a distinct species, the Japanese serow.

Reddish brown to gray-brown in color, serow resemble a robust version of the goral, often weighing 200 pounds or more in contrast to the goral's 50 to 75. They are even less social than goral. Serow have seldom been seen in groups larger than three or four. For that matter they have rarely been seen at all except by local hunters, for they lead secretive lives on steep hillsides covered by dense vegetation. In contrast to the chamois, both the goral and serow are among the least studied of the world's large animals, though the Japanese serow has begun to receive some attention recently. Yet, like the chamois, their historical range and numbers have been radically reduced by human activities. That some subspecies of goral and mainland serow are endangered is one of the very few things known about them.

Each time the ice sheets of the Pleistocene spread outward from the polar regions much of the world's water became locked up in those land-engulfing glaciers. Sea level fell as much as 300 or 400 feet. The Bering Straits between what are now Alaska and Siberia dried up, leaving a wide isthmus that connected the Old World with the New. Given the modern distribution of goral and serow in northeastern Asia, it is not hard to imagine some ancestral rupicaprid continuing a bit farther in that direction and eventually crossing the Bering land bridge.

The upheaval of mountain ranges and repeated scouring of the northern regions by great glaciers did much to establish a new order in the animal world. Yet these forces also obliterated much of the fossil record of their own handiwork. Normal erosional processes, which occur at an accelerated pace in high, steep terrain, have further obscured it. Reconstructing the history of the proto–mountain goat is a matter of fitting together a few widely scattered skeletal fragments, with a lot of guesswork for glue.

We can assume that the emigrant was already adapted to cold, or it would not have been able to withstand the arctic conditions of the Beringian region. We may assume, too, that it was already something of a climber by dint of its rupicaprid heritage. But was it still sufficiently unspecialized that its population simply extended across the mostly flat tundra and taiga of the land bridge? Or did some adventurous and lucky band of true mountaineers spurt across from the highlands of Siberia's Chukchi Peninsula to a cluster of rugged terrain almost 2,000 feet above sea level near the center of the bridge—now the Diomede Islands—and then on to the other side? Whatever the case, the rupicaprid soon took to the cold hills of its adopted continent.

It by no means had the hills to itself. Other hardy hooved Eurasians were making the transcontinental trek to take up residence there, among them the forerunners of modern moose, elk, musk-oxen, bison, and mountain sheep. And the hills had long been occupied by native American ungulates, including members of the camel and horse families. Also present was a gauntlet of predators, again of both native and recent Eurasian origins. Their ranks included such formidable Pleistocene hunters as the huge dire wolf and saber-toothed cats; the predecessor of the grizzly; other wolves, big cats, and bears; and the precursors of current-model coyotes and wolverines.

Pressure from its fellow grazers and from increasingly sophisticated predators, some of which were developing extremely efficient social hunting techniques, pushed the sole American rupicaprid ever deeper into the mountains and ever higher and steeper on their slopes.

Whereas the major glacial phases used to be numbered at four, it is now believed that the ice sheets came and went at least seven times during the Pleistocene. When they came they buried nearly half of North America beneath ice up to 10,000 feet thick. Yet each time they withdrew the climate was as warm as today, perhaps warmer. Millenia-long spells of mild weather called interstadials occurred even during periods of glacial advance.

Encroaching ice compressed populations of hill and mountain-dwellers and, as it did, predation and competition for living space grew intense. Then, whenever the ice retreated and temperatures rose, another substantial shift in the balance between species occured. The most cold-proof and mobile among them led the way in recolonizing habitats relinquished by the glaciers while tall forests grew back over barren-looking landscapes of tundra and stunted trees.

It was a time of flux, a time of testing and opportunity, and every animal's response was strictly judged in the court of natural selection. It was, therefore, a time of rapid evolution. We can guess that the rupicaprid experienced particularly keen competition for newly available mountainside niches from evolving mountain sheep. The sheep were doing well at establishing themselves on moderately precipitous rocky terrain throughout the Cordillera (a collective term for the mountain chains of western North America).* As a result the rupicaprid was under pressure to specialize in exploiting still more sheer-sided, rockbound habitats.

Onward and upward. No one knows just when in its climbing career the proto–mountain goat underwent the final stages of metamorphosis into what we recognize as *Oreamnos*. The earliest *Oreamnos* fossil yet unearthed cannot be dated with any certainty back further than the last major interglacial period—about 100,000 years. It is known that during cold phases the mountain goat extended its range southward along the Cordillera. Fossils of *Oreamnos harringtoni*, a smallish species two-thirds the size of *O. americanus*, have been located at mountainous sites in California, Nevada, Arizona, and north-central Mexico. All of them were preserved in caves and are from the Wisconsinan glaciation, the last major advance of the continental ice sheets.

O. harringtoni was probably a contemporary of *O. americanus* rather than its predecessor. The reasoning behind this view is that the climate warmed at some point and part of the *Oreamnos* population returned northward leaving the other part isolated on the highest and coolest of the southwestern mountains to evolve along a separate course.

When the Wisconsinan finally ended, just 10,000 to 12,000 years ago, so did *O. harringtoni*, apparently unable to adapt to considerably warmer temperatures. It may have been overwhelmed by the intensified predation and competition that followed rising timberlines as well as by its inability to cope with heat stress.

---

*There are either six or seven species of true sheep (*Ovis*) in the world, depending upon which expert you prefer to go by. North America has two distinct species, which probably diverged from a common ancestor after advancing Pleistocene glaciers confined part of the population to an ice-free northern refugium while the rest was pushed southward:

1. *Ovis dalli*, known as thinhorn sheep, are found north of Canada's Peace River Valley, a gap in the north-south trending Cordillera. Three living subspecies are recognized. Two, called Dall's sheep, are snow white. The third, called Stone's sheep, is grey, dark brown, or black above with a white underbelly; "like a Dall's sheep in evening dress," as researcher Valerius Geist put it.
2. *Ovis canadensis*, known as bighorn sheep, are found from the Peace River south to the desert mountains of northern Mexico. Eight subspecies are recognized. Seven are living; the eighth, the Audubon's or badlands race of the Dakotas, succumbed to livestock grazing and unregulated shooting a century ago.

O. americanus withdrew still farther northward in the wake of the glaciers. Today native mountain goat populations are found only in Washington, Idaho, Montana, British Columbia, Alberta, the Yukon Territory, and southern Alaska, with a minor group in the extreme western edge of Canada's Northwest Territories.

It would be difficult to point to such a thing as a perfect representative of the modern mountain goat. Alaskan goats tend to have larger bodies and somewhat thicker horns than mountain goats toward the southern limit of the species' distribution. If you take calipers to the skulls of goats in museum collections you would also pick up some variation between, say, Pacific Coast and Rocky Mountain populations. For that matter, some white climbers in the Selkirk Range of British Columbia are actually brown-and-white climbers. The Selkirk population as a whole is noted for producing individuals with brownish hairs among the white, especially along the dorsal ridge—the line of mane-like fur following the center of the back. (Brown fur appears on mountain goats in other areas but does not seem to occur as frequently. The best explanation for this dark pigmentation seems to be that it is a throwback to the original color of this rupicaprid line. It is most prevalent among young animals, as is usually the case for vestiges of ancestral appearance and behavior. I have seen three Montana mountain goat kids with brownish back stripes.)

Taxonomists once focused on the minor physical differences that exist among mountain goat populations as a basis for dividing North America's rupicaprid into several modern species. But the taxonomists themselves have evolved over the years, in their case from avid "splitters" to "lumpers." At one stage it was generally agreed to recognize just one species but keep four separate subspecies. Reference to mountain goat subspecies persists in some texts. At the moment, however, the taxonomist tribe regards existing differences as too blurry to justify even that. A definitive 1970 paper by Ian McTaggart Cowan and Wayne McCrory, who analyzed 167 mountain goat skulls from all parts of the climber's continental range, concluded that there is just *Oreamnos americanus,* period. No other living species and no subspecies. Goat biologists today speak only of clines (variations due to gradual change in a common trait over geographic distance) and ecotypes (populations distinguished by particular adaptations to a local or regional environment).

Ecotypes at opposite ends of a cline, subject to dissimilar environments, may be easy to tell apart from one another but not from the populations in between. Before they can develop into true subspecies, and perhaps eventually different species, something must act as a barrier to gene flow along the cline. A tongue of glacial ice or the formation of a desert has served that function for other creatures. Just as an interstate highway fringed by housing and business developments can do a pretty good job of segregating, say, salamander populations.

With this concept of potential speciation in mind, let's briefly turn to the subject of transplanted mountain goat herds. Since the turn of the century mountain goats have been introduced to something like three dozen nonnative ranges, mostly by wildlife managers seeking to establish a greater variety of game for local hunters. Some of these ranges are within the northern Cordillera; for example, Kodiak Island in Alaska, the Crazy Mountains of Montana, the Olympic Peninsula of Washington, and the Wallowa Mountains of Oregon, where a small and unproductive herd clings to existence on the barren mountaintop that serves as its new home.

Other introductions have been made in states which the mountain goat has probably not occupied since the demise of *Oreamnos harringtoni*. Bearded beasts can now be found measuring rocky pitches in Wyoming, Colorado, Utah, and Nevada. Then there is unlikely South Dakota; six white climbers from Alberta were delivered there in 1924. The idea was to keep them in an enclosure at Custer State Park for display to the public. Two, an adult nanny and a yearling billy, escaped the first night and took up residence in the nearby Black Hills around Mount Rushmore. I like to envision one perched on George Washington's monumental nose, but no one has ever reported it. Five years later the escapees were joined by the other four after a tree fell across Custer State Park's improved enclosure fence. Those six have since become a stable population of 300 to 400. Custer could have used their kind of luck.

Six animals do not constitute a very large initial gene pool. Most of the other introductions also involved less than a dozen mountain goats. Given this fact, in addition to the atypical nature of the ranges, the elimination by man of many big predators from most of those ranges, and the isolation of all the transplanted herds, the stage has clearly been set for more than a little inbreeding and divergent evolution. It may be that before too many centuries have passed, future taxonomists are going to have to revert to the old splitting tradition insofar as the mountain goat is concerned.

Counting native and non-native herds, there are probably more than 40,000—and less than 100,000—of the white climbers in North America at the present time. Obviously population sizes have been very difficult for regional biologists to estimate; the largest groups of goats are spread throughout some of the most rugged and remote country left on the continent. British Columbia and southern Alaska contain at least three-quarters of the current total, which, whatever it may be, is still less than the number of human beings in a single modest city such as Billings,

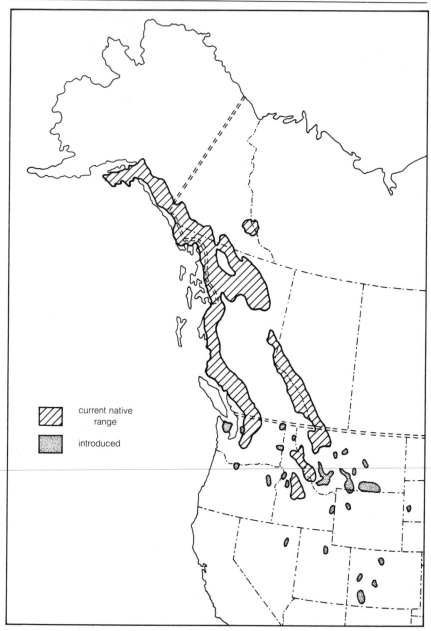

7.   Distribution of mountain goats in North America, showing locations of native and transplanted populations.

Montana. Whether the continental mountain goat population prior to the declines of recent decades was a quarter again as large or up to twice as large is anybody's guess. As for the introduced populations, they account for fewer than 5,000 goats altogether.

Putting transplanted herds aside for the moment, the argument might be made that the species is still living under Ice Age conditions, or as near to Ice Age conditions as it can get. Native herds are intimately bound to alpine and subalpine topography that was powerfully glaciated in the past and is for the most part still capped by remnant glaciers or permanent snowfields. In Glacier Bay National Monument and adjacent sections of Alaska's coastal mountains, the white goats can be found working their way across cliffs whose sides are even now being ground away by glaciers larger than an average county—larger than the state of Rhode Island in a couple of instances. The periglacial conditions that directly shaped *Oreamnos americanus* are what the species remains best adapted to today.

Juvenile mountain goats bear a noteworthy resemblance to the most primitive member of their tribe, the small, short-horned, short-muzzled goral. By the time they mature, however, all the long history of transformation from Old World hill and forest dweller to master of the New World's loftiest ice-honed domain is revealed in their form.

In adults the rather undistinguished basic profile of the rupicaprid group becomes fully bearded and crowned by the longest of the tribe's stilletolike horns. Behind the base of each horn is a crescent of black spongy tissue, the supraoccipital gland (also called the postcornual gland). Chamois are the only other hooved animal that possesses this type of gland. The chamois use it for scent-marking during the rutting season and in association with aggressive social encounters outside the rut, by rubbing the horn gland against vegetation. Mountain goats scent-mark in this way, but less frequently, and the overall effect of such behavior as a means of proclaiming personal space and social status appears to be less significant for them. The gland probably evolved in a forest-living ancestor which used the secretions to mark the boundaries of a fixed territory.

Behind the whiskers and horns a thick neck swells toward a deep chest and tremendously developed shoulder musculature, which lends strength for climbing and also for pawing snow. The beast seems all forequarters when contrasted with its kin.

Over the craggy build of the climber, first making a high dorsal ridge and then rippling down to flare about the legs in wide pantaloons, is the thickest and longest coat of the rupicaprid tribe. In fact, of all the wild members of the bovid family only the musk ox—that walking carpet of the North Slope tundra—and the Tibetan yak, now probably extinct, are dressed in shaggier coats for low temperatures. The mountain goat's outer fur consists of coarse guard hairs, up to eight inches in length. They are hollow—that is, air-filled—and dead air spaces make excellent insulators. Beneath the outer fur are two to three inches of densely interwoven wool as fine as cashmere (some say finer). This wool creates a foamlike quilt of trapped air, and little cold can penetrate this second line of defense. As it is, the mountain goat spends much of the summer simply trying to stay cool by lying on snowbanks and keeping to shaded slopes most of the day—and this at a time when most of its winter wool has been shed. Here may be a partial explanation of why *Oreamnos americanus* is naturally found only as far south along the Cordillera as Idaho and Washington.

Finally, the fur itself of this rupicaprid is as white as . . . Of course. The color that is not a color is the perfect camouflage. Fresh snow can be expected in the high country anytime from September through May, and it may fall any time at all. I have celebrated two Fourth of Julys huddled in a tent with a thick layer of fresh, white flakes on it. In the height of sunny summer weather the climber remains usually just one more patch of white in the landscape, for it follows the receding snowline upward in much the same way that populations of its ancestors followed the receding glaciers. (Given the beast's susceptibility to high temperatures, the white coat may also be helpful in reflecting the rays of the summer sun.)

There, from the rising Himalayas to the top of the Cordillera half the planet away, is a summary of how a bearded, climbing beast the color of winter was formed. Now we can move our attention to the way it lives from day to day, making good its claim to the New World peaks. The first subject we will take up is, naturally enough, the mountain goat's climbing abilities.

Before leaving this chapter, though, I want to offer one thought for consideration. Knowing what we do today about geologic processes and the factors that cause climatic change, it looks as though the main justification for believing the Ice Ages ended for good a few thousand years ago, and that we are now in a brand new epoch called the Holocene, is that it makes us feel better. There is precious little rational evidence against the alternative prospect, that we are merely in yet another interglacial period. As I said earlier there have been other such periods every bit as warm or warmer, and there have certainly been others every bit as long or longer.

Another prevalent idea is that the onset of a phase of global cooling and

glacial advance is so gradual a business that, even if we *are* in an interglacial, it's nothing we need concern ourselves about for countless generations. This too appears to be based primarily upon wishful thinking. The
cold, hard data coming out of drill holes down through the history of the
Antarctic icefield suggests that the change from interglacial to glacial
may happen rather abruptly: within a century's time, maybe within one
or two decades.

The scenario begins with a series of severe winters followed by cool
summers, which leave snow covering more of the earth's surface than
usual. This causes more of the sunlight striking the planet to be reflected
back into space than usual. Hence, less heat is absorbed, which leads to
a slight drop in global temperature. This in turn causes more snow to fall
in winter, and less of it to melt in summer. Again (envision a satellite
photograph of North America in winter) the albedo, or reflective quality
of the continents, rises, bouncing more sunlight away. Warm air masses
continue to rise from the oceans, the heat-storage areas of the planet. But
these cool more rapidly now as they cross land surfaces, precipitating
more snow than ever, which reflects more sunlight, which leads to further deterioration of global temperatures. Vast stretches of the polar seas
begin to stay permanently covered by icepacks—white, sun-reflecting
icepacks . . . .

This is a self-propelling feedback system. Once kicked into motion it
could conceivably start the glaciers grinding from the poles toward the
equator within a couple of generations of mountain goats. At least that's
what a number of climatologists believe has happened before, and could
happen again. The scenario I have outlined is riddled with "ifs." Meanwhile, some experts predict that man's current doings on the planet—
chemical emissions, agricultural practices, and so on—will heat the place
up through a greenhouse effect until it resembles the tropical age of the
dinosaurs. Others, however, hold that we are indeed ensuring the early
arrival of the next Ice Age. Still others believe that volcanoes will be the
trigger for the next glacial phase.

Nevertheless, I want to point out that learning about the Pleistocene
and about the evolution and survival of man and his fellow mammals
during that time may not be an entirely academic enterprise. What many
might conceive of as the past, a relict dry and dead and done with, could
become our future. Rather suddenly.

The point which follows is that we in an interglacial period could be
doing ourselves a grave disservice if we fail to preserve large, vital populations of northern mammals. Appeals to aesthetics and altruistic emotions
aside, we or our descendants may *need* these beasts nearly as much as
Neanderthal and Cro-Magnon people did before us. Mountain goats,

thinhorn sheep, musk oxen, caribou—they and their wild neighbors have much to teach us about adapting to periglacial conditions. In their genes are coded eons of physiological and behavioral expertise. I don't believe it is at all farfetched to imagine us drawing upon that knowledge for utilitarian purposes. In a cooler climate than we now enjoy we might find it easier to raise them than the livestock we have been relying upon for fur, milk, meat, and hides these past few millenia. The Laplanders with their domesticated caribou, the reindeer, present an existing model of such a periglacial situation, as do the Himalayan peoples with their domesticated yaks. Or, we could take the best of both wild and traditional domestic stock by hybridizing them through breeding programs, or perhaps directly through gene splicing, embryo transplants, and other advanced techniques now being explored. Yaks and cattle have long been successfully crossbred, and some North American ranchers believe cattle will soon be replaced on northern ranges by beefalo, a blend of cow and the winter-hardy bison, or buffalo, that we came so close to exterminating.

The reader will have to sort out how much of all this is a goatwatcher trying to justify his odd occupation a little more by saying: Look, every obscure bit of knowledge about this beast could one day be of intensely practical value, or if it is the argument of a conservationist grasping for compelling commonsense arguments as to why we must continue to share our environment with a rich diversity of wild species. Or a matter undeniably worth some serious thought and planning. I'm not absolutely sure myself.

CHAPTER THREE

The Sudden Edge of Earth and Sky

THE DANGER INHERENT in climbing a given pitch is largely a matter of perception. Like so many things in life, believing—believing deep down—that you can do it makes your chances of carrying it off that much better. The Kid of Chapter 1 had that kind of confidence on the edge of things. It and the other mountain goat youngsters I watched were clearly born with it. That all of them went out of their way to challenge vertical terrain—under their mother's watchful eye—before they had mastered walking on level ground is not surprising. The genes young mountain goats carry were not passed on by the uncertain, the unwilling, or the uncoordinated.

I am not a climber. A happy scrambler, maybe, but not really a rock-climber, and to put my study of mountain goats in perspective it is time for me to admit it. Of all the ice-white beasts I kept track of, the one I was best able to relate to was a young adult female I called Nanny Not-Me. Where other mountain goats pranced and played, Nanny Not-Me was sometimes reluctant to set foot. Long after her companions of the day had traversed a wildcat route Nanny Not-Me would still be at the beginning of it, making false starts; I once counted 50 aborted leaps on her part at the base of a small arête. Then she would paw, feed with a vengeance, scratch repeatedly, or perform some other activity that I recognized as a symptom of stress. After giving vent to the worst of her frustration she might lie down on the threshold of the pitch, paw a bit in her bed, get up, shake, and make a few more halfhearted steps. Finally she would just stare after the others or off into space as though contemplating the unfairness of her lot. Why, oh why did she have to have been born a mountain goat instead of an antelope out on some endlessly flat plain?

I can think of no simple explanation for Nanny Not-Me's acrophobia. The climbing she did attempt was not obviously clumsy. She may have been afflicted with something like poor vision, though her senses appeared to be normal enough in other situations. (One of the most astonishing descents of a palisade I ever saw, by the way, was performed by a one-eyed billy.) Perhaps she had taken a bad spill at some point in her career and never quite recovered her poise. Yet she was timid in social situations too. In a reversal of the usual mountain goat hierarchy of who butts whom, she was easily dominated at times by two-year-olds and even by yearlings when I first met her.

Contrary to what I just said about passing on genes Nanny Not-Me not only survived but produced a kid (who turned out to be a normal, self-assured climber) the following year. She had improved a little by that time, though, and continued to become a more aggressive climber thereafter. Nonetheless, there is—or appeared to be for a while—such a thing as a mountain goat that is afraid of heights. I never laughed at Nanny Not-Me's trials. I knew only too well how she might have felt.

The steepest pitch on which loose rock material will remain without sliding is called the angle of repose. It is a delicate point of balance between the inertia of objects at rest and the tireless pull of gravity. Once, clambering up a pile of truck-size boulders that seemed securely anchored by their own weight, I stepped on precisely the wrong spot. The pile creaked ever so slightly, then shifted again, and in another instant I was astride an earthquake. Four or five fortunate leaps across monstrous turning stones, followed by a headlong plunge, brought me to the solid safety of a ledge. Meanwhile several thousand tons of rock whose repose a single footfall had disturbed roared on to take up new positions closer to the valley floor.

Naturally the farther you go below the angle of repose on a mountainside the more stable rock debris becomes. Soils build to greater depths, and plant succession proceeds toward climax communities such as forests.

Very little talus stays put much above 40 degrees (90 degrees being vertical). The mountain goats I recorded spent 70 percent of their time on slopes whose overall angle was steeper than 40 degrees. Since bedrock —the intact mass of the mountain—is chiefly what remains above 40 degrees, this is only a slightly different way of saying that about three-quarters of all the mountain goats I saw were on cliff faces. Almost without exception the remainder were on meadows or fellfields—slopes of talus rubble or boulders—a short dash away. Only a fraction of one percent were located within a canopied forest.

We know *Oreamnos* to be associated with cliffs, and now we have some quantitative measure of how extensive that association may be. Putting it in terms of time spent above the angle of repose is a reminder (which Nanny Not-Me seldom forgot) that gravity can tell the difference between the right step and the wrong one with no trouble at all.

My records go on to show the mountain goats spending ten percent of their time on slopes steeper than 60 degrees. I find this impressive. At such angles ledges consolidate into immense, skyrocketing ramparts, and the rock on your uphill side begins to press against you as though actively resisting further ascent. Still more impressive is the fact that the species' use of steep slopes generally tends to *increase* during winter, the season of slanted snow and slick ice. In the Pahsimeroi Mountains of Idaho, for example, biologist Lonn Kuck found 60 percent of the mountain goats wintering on slopes of at least 50 degrees. As we will see in greater detail in Chapter 5, the main reason behind this increase is perfectly logical; the more perpendicular the cliff, the better it sheds the snow that inundates virtually all the rest of the high country.

If you are not a mountaineer but want to form an idea of what Kuck's and my herds were contending with from October through May you might try this: Take a typical staircase in your home (30 to 35 degrees), tilt it to match the angle of the sides of Egypt's Great Pyramids at Giza (52 degrees), remove some of the steps, and shovel ice and a couple of feet of snow over the whole affair. Then, as long as this is only mental exercise, try moving the concocted cliff atop an apartment building. Place it right on the edge so that the next step below the bottom is at least a couple of stories down, because even moderately sloping sections of a mountain goat cliff may have forbidding dropoffs at their base.

There are doubtless more practical ways to envision the beast's life, but this one will do to reemphasize the two major themes of this chapter. First, a very great deal of what the mountain goat does, from courtship to play, takes place on cliffs and therefore depends upon climbing skills. Second, the question constantly asked by natural selection—whether an animal is fit or unfit to survive—must be answered foothold by foothold throughout much of each mountain goat's life.

Figure 8 is a vertical profile of goat range in relation to typical mountain topography, soil succession, and basic types of vegetation. Understandably, since the scheme is so simplified, it is not very hard to think of minor exceptions to it. However, I can also think of a major exception

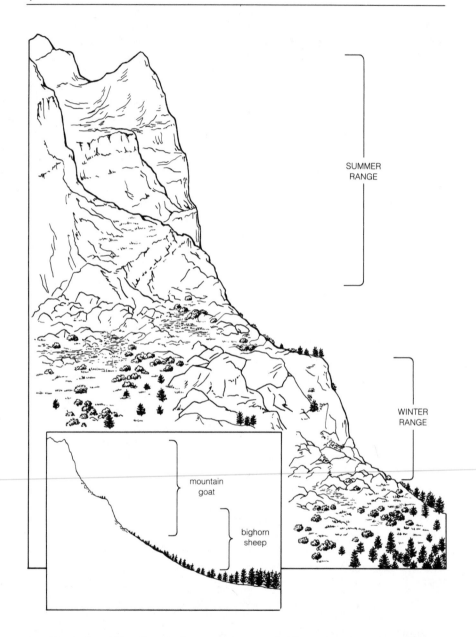

SUMMER RANGE

WINTER RANGE

mountain goat

bighorn sheep

8. *Vertical profile of typical mountain goat habitat, showing parts of range generally used by goats in winter and summer, and a comparison of mountain goat and bighorn sheep ranges.*

—one we need to become acquainted with before going on. It involves the goats that belong to what British Columbia biologist Daryl Hebert first defined as the coastal ecotype.

This ecotype comprises populations that, for the most part, inhabit mountain ranges right along the edge of the ocean and its inlets; in some cases, the animals descend practically to the beaches in winter. Such maritime populations can be found all the way from northern Washington through southern Alaska. They are characterized by smaller average group sizes and lower overall densities than are generally found for goats farther east in the Pacific region or for those in the Rockies.

In addition, according to recent studies by Hebert, Joseph Fox, John Schoen, Christian Smith, and others, they use densely timbered habitats more than was previously realized, and to a far greater extent than goats do elsewhere. While goats in noncoastal environments may move down into the forest zone during the snow months, they usually remain high enough that the mountainside offers extensive open cliff faces between stands of trees. This is the main reason that so few goats I watched were in actual forest habitats. Goats belonging to the coastal ecotype spend more time at lower altitudes. Some reside in relatively low mountains to begin with. Others are forced down when Pacific storms swamp the upper elevations with snow too wet and heavy for winds to sweep away. In both instances, the goats often find themselves limited to bluffs or other small but very steep outcroppings, and to the steep, broken slopes immediately adjacent to these rocky patches. More often than not, this places them directly within the timber, beneath an overarching green canopy of limbs.

I wouldn't go quite as far as to claim that the coastal goat's niche, at least in winter, resembles that of the goral or serow, but the bearded beast certainly seems to be putting its forest-dwelling background to use here. Yet note the words I borrowed from coast area researchers to describe the terrain that these goats consistently pick out among the trees: broken, rocky, steep, and very steep. For example, Smith reported that the largest percentage of goats wintering near Ketchikan, Alaska were on slopes of between 50 and 65 degrees, and the next largest percentage were on slopes of *over* 65 degrees.

Consequently, although I'll sometimes have to modify a statement in order to account for variations between the coastal ecotype and populations farther toward the interior, I don't feel a need to hedge very much of what I've already said about the mountain goat's pervasive connection with precipitous ground. The beast remains first and foremost a climber, wherever it lives.

To see how this species literally clings to existence, a good place to begin looking is where mountain goat meets rock: at the two-toed hooves. These are not anything like suction cups, though that popular misconception clings tenaciously to an existence of its own. But neither are they simple clublike appendages. They are rather plain-looking but ingenious rock-gripping devices.

The sides of a mountain goat's toes consist of the same hard keratin found on the hoof of a horse or deer. Each of the two wraparound toenails can be used to catch and hold to a crack or tiny knob of rock. The front edge of the hoof tapers to a point which, though not quite as sharp as that of many artiodactyls (ungulates with an even number of toes), is useful for digging into dirt or packed snow when the goat is going uphill. So far, nothing special. But a horse or deer or a typical bovid has a concave hoof; that is, the hoof cups upward, and the animal is essentially walking on the rim of its toenail(s). By contrast, the mountain goat is shod with a special traction pad which protrudes slightly past the nail. This pad has a rough-textured surface that provides a considerable amount of extra friction on smooth rock and ice. Yet it is pliant enough for any irregularities in a stone substrate to become impressed in it and thereby add to the skidproofing effect. Four hooves. Two toes per hoof. Eight different specially adapted soles. Now we are getting somewhere.

Next, the two toes of each hoof naturally spread fairly far apart from one another, giving the white climber a distinctively squarish footprint. In fact the two toes can easily spread farther apart than the hoof is long.

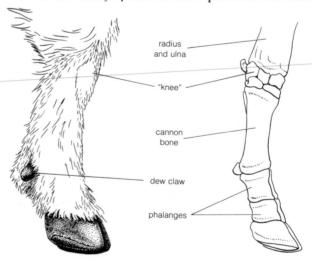

radius
and ulna

"knee"

cannon
bone

dew claw

phalanges

9. *External and internal anatomy of the lower foreleg.*

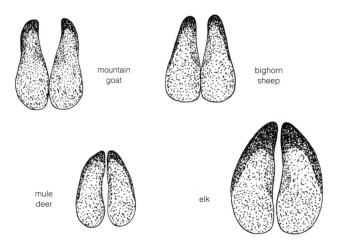

10.   Comparison of mountain goat and other ungulate tracks.

This acts to distribute the animal's grip onto a wider segment of ground, so that if part of the hoof is on crumbly footing the other might still catch on something firm. Or, if part of the hoof is on a slick surface the other can extend to grab something rough.

In addition, the simple mechanical procedure of toe-spreading adds several more subtle dimensions of skid-proofing. These are most noticeable when the animal is descending a slope or leaning forward downhill, perhaps to feed or to have a better look at something below—for that is when the toes spread most widely apart. These dimensions can be visualized as follows:

Make a wide V with your index and middle fingers and try pressing down against something with their tips. Since walking on an artiodactyl hoof is anatomically similar to walking on the tips of two fingers, the mountain goat feels muscles and tendons working against each other somewhat the same way you do. It adjusts the tensions accordingly in order to fine-tune its grip on uneven surfaces. That is the first dimension.

Now you will find that the more weight you put on your fingertips, the more they want to diverge sideways. In like fashion the mountain goat's toes divide the downward force of the weight on a hoof. When your fingers, or the toes of the hoof, are placed on an inclined surface, part of the total weight continues to be directed sideways—a horizontal vector of force as distinct from a vertical vector. There is thus less net force being exerted in a single downward line; hence there is less likelihood of overcoming the force of friction along that line and beginning to slide.

This is not a fancy way of restating the effect of distributing and balancing the grip I just described. What is going on here is a fanning out of forces. If *all* the downward force could be converted into opposing sideways forces, it would in effect be cancelled out. If you stand in a narrow hallway, place your hands on the opposite walls, and push as hard as you can against them you can very nearly hold your weight off the ground. With the mountain goat's foot, we are only talking about one two-toed hoof and only a partial sideways component of force, but the result is the same to a degree. Bring your two fingers together and press them down against the same inclined surface, and you'll find they will slide more readily than they did when held in a V.

The third and final dimension is simpler to explain. Solid rock, talus, dirt, or snow can become wedged in the crotch of the V and act as an additional brake.

In addition to their many functions when widely spread, the same two toes of the hoof can close pincerlike around a knob or crease of rock to grasp it.

During the course of ungulate evolution, as the basic five-toed vertebrate foot was being specialized for rapid toe-tip locomotion, the Bovidae completely lost their equivalent of our big toe (and thumb). The second and fifth digits were greatly reduced, but they are still around. Partway up the ankle of a mountain goat project two "dewclaws", which are actually small, crescent-shaped versions of the two main toes. They give the goat extra footing when it is descending rocky slopes and a lot of valuable drag when it is headed down dirt, ice, or snow. For that matter the animal's conformation is such that its entire lower rear leg and also its rump can be pressed against the slope for added stability and traction during descents.

Friction and more friction: after hearing hunters talk about how hard it is to drag shaggy goat carcasses across ice and snow I examined some of the long outer guard hairs with a microscope. The surface of each strand consists of overlapping scales that give it a slightly fringed or frayed outline under magnification. It is a rougher surface than is found on the hairs of such neighbors as deer or sheep, and the hairs are much longer. I suppose this does add a resistance that is occasionally valuable to live goats—if an animal slips onto its side when crossing a steep, snow-filled couloir, for instance; or when the rump is purposely used as a brake going down crusted snowfields. I was told that some Montana Indians wore moccasins with goat hair soles for climbing steep snowy slopes, but I haven't yet been able to track this claim down for a fact. (In his book *Grizzly Country*, naturalist Andy Russell does mention that the Stoney Indians, an Assiniboin tribe whose territory was mainly mountain country on the eastern flanks of the Rockies in Alberta and Montana,

11. Conformation during descent of a steep slope.

used the goat's hide for moccasin soles. They removed the fur first, as the thick spongey skin itself offered superior traction on rocky ground.)

As ungulates go, *Oreamnos americanus* is comparatively short-legged. A tourist in Glacier Park said to me that he supposed the animals just wore their legs down with all the climbing they did. I've also heard one tourist tell another that the legs on one side of a mountain goat are shorter than on the other. This, she allowed, was how they coped with such tilted slopes. (Of course, they had to always keep circling round the mountain in the same direction.)

Among the Bovidae the two main metapodial bones (for us, located in our palms and the fleshy part of our foot) have become fused and elongated into a single structure called the cannon bone. Like toe-tip walking and elongation of other leg bones, this gives an animal more leverage for propulsion when running and leaping. Over eight inches long in modern deer and a foot long in modern horses, the cannon bone seems to have remained comparatively short in the rupicaprid line. In the mountain goat it is a squat four inches long.

What the beast loses in fleetness it makes up for in maneuverability. The bones of the foot below the front "knee" and rear "hock" (equivalent to our wrist and ankle, respectively), being much closer together, allow the muscles that are attached to them to rotate and flex the foot in tightly synchronized patterns. And the winter-colored beast's center of gravity is that much closer to the ground—right where a climber wants it to be. Compared to a mountain goat, an elk or antelope is walking on stilts.

The distance between the front and rear legs is also relatively short in mountain goats; that is, both the heavy neck and low rump appear to extend beyond the feet somewhat farther than in typical bovids. Having a stance in which all four feet naturally come rather close together is an important advantage when maneuvering in a cubbyhole on the cliffs or picking a path over boulders—wherever standing room is at a premium. It is the stance that produces the classic mountain goat pose—the perch on a pinnacle, the white beast on the tip top of the continent, the sentinel left by the Ice Ages to keep watch over their old domain until the time comes for the glaciers to claim it once again.

That quintessential pose of a mountain goat hunched on a crag illustrates very well how disproportionately massive its forequarters are in relation to its compact rear end. The creature may not be able to spring from rock to rock with the grace of a high-rumped mountain sheep, but with its thick chest and bulging shoulder hump it is an unparalleled puller. I have seen mountain goats perform what amounted to one-handed chin-ups. Having only a scrap of momentum behind them they reached out, hooked one hoof on an overhead shelf, and hauled themselves up by it alone. With its center of gravity not only low but far forward, all *Oreamnos* really needs is good footing for the front legs. It can lift and wheel its hindquarters about so effortlessly that it can worry about where to set them down later.

One mountain goat I happened to be observing continued along a thin and steadily tapering ledge for some time after I was certain it could go no farther. It stopped, reconnoitered, and then went farther still. At last it decided to call a halt and head back. But at that point its footing had dwindled so seriously that the animal was no longer able to simply turn around. It did not even seem to be able to lean out far enough to see over its shoulder in order to back up.

I had watched mountain goats in similar predicaments work their uphill front hoof along the rock until they found a hold. With that they were able to draw themselves up to a sort of standing position, and then it was only a matter of carefully dropping back down to face the opposite direction. But for this mountain goat, either there were no suitable crevices to catch a hoof on, or the strip of ledge where it had finally become

12. The Great Northern Railroad logo: the classic billy on a crag.

stuck was too narrow for even that kind of last-ditch strategy. After some tentative foot shuffling the mountaineer braced its front hooves on the ledge and slowly raised the rear of its body off the ground. Clenching my hands tighter and tighter on the binoculars, I watched the beast lift its hindquarters higher and higher and begin to roll them straight over its head. The rear hooves touched the wall here and there for an instant, yet what the creature had effectively carried off by the time it was finished was a complete slow-motion cartwheel, or, technically, what gymnasts call a rollover. I put down my binoculars and remembered to breathe, and this mountain goat, an average-sized billy, strolled off in the direction from which it had come.

Rapid Rosie was like that: a gymnast of a climber, who made up the rules as she went along. The first time Beth and I visited her cliffs in a distant part of the Swan Mountains study area, this two-year-old nanny was bounding head-on and heedless up a slate grey tower. Airborne as often as not she soon reached the base of a sheer, twelve-foot-high rock facet. It looked to us like an uncompromising barrier, and we were sure she would at last have to go some way other than straight up. There seemed to be good alternative routes to either side. But Rapid Rosie hurled herself—where else but vertically again.

Seven times Rapid Rosie jumped, and her front legs struck invisible seams from which she propelled herself upward in search of another hold. Seven times she had to turn in mid-air and skid selectively down-ward to land on the slim ledge she had started from. Had she overshot that—and it would not have been hard to do—she would have plunged 25 or 30 feet on down to the next one, and probably would not have been able to stop there either. Well, I thought, maybe she had been spooked by something on the order of a grizzly.

The next time I visited those outcroppings, there was Rapid Rosie (who, by the way, had somehow made it on the eighth try) going at the same pace, only downhill. She descended one 20-foot-tall limestone band in three diagonal hops, then shot down a smooth-walled chute by bouncing from side to side in a sort of free-form ricochet. I wish she had possessed some equally distinctive physical characteristics, because I lost track of her after a long interval between visits and so will never know what became of this particular goat and her hot-rod ways.

All mountain goats are capable of Rapid Rosie's brand of razzle-dazzle. But to tell too many stories of daring traverses and fancy hoofwork would obscure the more important point that the species' approach to mountaineering is fundamentally conservative. Not hesitant, like Nanny Not-Me, but methodical. A pace based upon three-point suspension—lifting only one limb at a time, just as human climbers are trained to do—is standard goat mountaineering technique. Also standard is the practice of punctuating the climb with frequent pauses to assess the situation, test footing and, often, to turn back and select a safer course.

An extra measure of safety comes from knowing a passage before attempting to negotiate it, and mountain goats do much of their traveling on familiar trails, as opposed to pioneering routes as they go. A well-populated goat range is webbed with clearly visible paths, most of them along an obvious course of least resistance for a given section of cliff. The main arteries are paved with accumulated dung pellets, while a lusty, fertilized plant growth marks their edges. I have even come across trails worn into solid rock by centuries of constant use.

It only makes sense: slow and sure and consistent is the policy that keeps generation after generation above the angle of repose while the very cliffs around them are being gradually torn down by erosion. The slow and sure part of the policy has become built right into each animal. Short-legged and musclebound as it is, the beast is left panting for breath by a galloping 100-yard sprint. Yet it is able to plod steadily from the cuff to the crest of a cloud-busting palisade without resting or visibly tiring. "They can gain 1,500 feet in altitude . . . in about 20 minutes with little apparent effort," noted John Holroyd in a paper describing mountain goats in Kootenay National Park, British Columbia. "The same climb made by a good [human variety] mountain walker would likely take an hour to an hour and a half."

As for the part of the policy concerning consistency, this has become built into each herd's behavior. Keeping to the same seasonal ranges from one year to the next, each animal comes to use them in predictable, and therefore safer, patterns. And the social system ensures that the oldest goats' knowledge of the area is largely passed on to the younger goats that follow them.

There is plenty of call for inspired acrobatics by the most cautious of goats anyway. Drifted, ice-glazed snow will transform even a gentle defile into a test of every quality of strength and balance the animal owns. Although I always tried to find the least risky path from ledge to turret; although I shied away from the least risky path itself in many places; I somehow ended up risking everything time and again. Similarly, an electrifying burst of twisting leaps or a fly-like crawl across an almost chinkless escarpment is often the only option left for a mountain goat that began by merely extending a lazy promenade in a new direction.

In the long run I found that it was immature goats which provided most of the truly spectacular examples of go-for-broke climbing. Lacking the home range experience of their elders, they are the most likely to wander into a tight spot to begin with. And lacking the strength and skill of adults, they are the most likely to try to get themselves out of it by an all-or-nothing gamble.

The disadvantages of very young kids are partially offset by their mother's presence, as we saw in Chapter 1. If the youngster hesitates too long at the brink of a pitch the mother usually clambers back to lead it over a less demanding corridor before it can decide to undertake one of its headlong rushes. But watch a gang of three yearlings who have gone off to play and explore and generally knock about the rocks by themselves for a while. First they spy a fat marmot sunning itself on a boulder splotched with orange lichen. Being yearlings, they are almost sure to move over that way and egg each other on to see who will sniff at it from the closest distance. Soon they are on a detour but too busy bumping and chasing each other to really notice how steep this bypath is growing. And before much longer there is the gang, milling in a knot above some yawning chasm and looking at each other as if to say, "No, I've never come this way before. I thought you had." I made a special category in which to list occasional observations of leaderless subadults like these. I could have entitled it: Headed for Trouble.

Although some may be perhaps more foolhardy than others, each mountain goat does appear to have a keen awareness of when it has reached the limit. Watch again, this time as a climber struggles to find room for its outer hooves on a slender cliffside crease, or as it suddenly feels the talus underfoot start to slide toward a drop-off. All the signs of fear are now plain. The ears are flattened. The tail is raised straight up.

(The tail flag, hoisted by kids in need of their mother's milk and attention, has become an indicator of anxiety level when lifted by older individuals. A partially erect tail means, "I'm worried." A completely erect tail means, "I'm good and scared," or maybe it is the same old cry: "Help, Momma!" Although Momma will no longer come for the older animal, the behavior still functions as a signal of danger for others to read.) The mountain goat crouches and nervously flicks its tongue past its lips (the tongue-flicking may also derive from infantile behavior related to nursing).

Every so often as I was traversing the base of a cliff I would come across the broken body of a mountain goat. And every so often I would notice another individual with a bent or busted horn, or a leg that it either limped upon or dragged uselessly along. But going from this to an accurate estimate of the frequency of injury and death from climbing accidents is difficult.

Existing reports don't have much to say on the subject except to note the rare incident of a serious slip or fall or the finding of a fallen body. Possibly the very scarcity of such observations tells us the goats stay pretty safely glued to the cliffs. Possibly it only tells us we've overlooked a lot. Underlooked may be a better word for it. Severely injured or ill mountain goats tend to take refuge in caves and on inaccessible ledges where their bones turn to dust out of sight of any man. Others tumble, and their corpses lodge where no one is likely to find them. There have been sporadic discoveries of dead or weakened, oddly behaving goats miles from the nearest suitable cliff. These hint that at least a few animals which have become sick—from disease, or maybe originally as a result of an injury—begin wandering downhill, some aimlessly, others perhaps in search of mineral salts or something we aren't yet aware of. Whatever the case, most probably die in places no one would think of looking for them and so add little to our overall picture of goat mortality.

During his years of research in Idaho and Montana Brandborg located 25 goat carcasses. Half of them were at the bottom of cliffs, but he, probably wisely, declined to do more than speculate as to the actual cause of death. For one thing avalanches as well as errors snap bones and deposit mountain goats at the bottom of cliffs. Two decades later, in an intensive study of some of the same Bitterroot Mountains goat herds Brandborg had observed, Bruce Smith found 12 carcasses, three of them at sites where either falls or snowslides could have done them in. I have thus far found only 30 carcasses and could positively attribute death to falling in just five cases (17 percent).

Turning to injuries, I can say that I saw 22 different white climbers with bent or broken horns and 17 with impaired legs. I can say that the affected animals comprised two to five percent of my study population at any given time. But I cannot say for sure that some of these injuries did not result from fighting among the goats. Nor, again, do I have any way of telling how many injuries were the consequence of what human mountaineers term "objective dangers": rockfalls, icefalls, and avalanches —the things that get you simply because you are on the mountainside, regardless of how well or how poorly you are climbing.

The Bitterroot herd that Bruce Smith kept particularly close track of contained an average of 30 goats. Three of them (ten percent) had broken or deformed horns according to Smith, and there were "several others with chipped horn tips." He goes on to report, "I saw a nanny and kid fall 15 feet from a narrow ledge while attempting to turn around. The kid landed upright, unharmed, but the nanny crashed back first onto a juniper bush inflicting a wound on her foreleg."

We still need some more precise estimate of the risk associated with the kind of climbing done by *Oreamnos*. Let's try a different tack. I put in 4,400 goat-hours observing nonbedded animals in the Swans. (Goat-hours derive from the number of goats I was focused on multiplied by the number of hours I observed those goats; for example, 2 goats watched continuously for 3 hours = 6 goat-hours.) During that time I saw hundreds of missteps. Most were so slight the beasts paid no particular attention to them. Only 29 caused the climbers to lose their balance, and only five of these occurred in terrain I judged to be dangerously steep. By these observations, we might expect an individual goat to experience, on the average, one unbalancing misstep every 13 to 15 days, but one in dangerously steep terrain only about once every 75 to 90 days, or about four to five times a year.

Here is a nice, clearcut statistic. And like many nice, clearcut statistics it has a lot of suppositions underlying it, some of them a little messy. I think we can use it, but first let me point out some of these assumptions, if only to illustrate what can go into the making of a scientific "fact."

First, to translate from slips per goat-hour of observation to slips per day I assumed that goats are active (nonbedded) between ten and 12 hours out of every 24, with nocturnal activity accounting for an average of three of those hours. I believe this is reasonably accurate, though the amount of time goats spend feeding, traveling and—in spring and summer— licking salt at night varies widely, depending upon how much moonlight is available. I also assumed that climbing accidents are no more frequent at night than during daylight hours. This may not be reasonable at all, but I usually couldn't see well enough to pick out nighttime slips, so it will have to do.

Beyond that, I did not include the climbing of very young kids in my count of missteps, since they were scrambling, tossing themselves about, and generally experimenting so much of the time. Nor did I count any wild, hastily improvised climbing flurries on the part of older mountain goats unless the animal looked totally out of control. The matter of control was itself awfully tricky to judge; I ended up giving the benefit of the doubt to the climber in nearly every instance, reasoning that by its own amazing standards the beast still had the situation in hand—in hoof, that is. Still further, 17 (59 percent) of the unbalancing missteps I witnessed were related to wet or icy conditions. Yet when the cliffs were wettest, storm clouds often prevented me from seeing anything; and avalanches, snowstorms, and extreme cold all kept me from making nearly as many observations in winter as I did under less icy conditions. As it was, I surely missed some slips during those goat-hours I claim to have put in, for I did plenty of turning away from the telescope to rub my eyes, swat mosquitoes, shake the snow from my neck, and so forth.

All of these qualifications argue that the statistic of four to five potentially serious missteps per year for a mountain goat is an underestimate, not to mention slightly arbitrary. Nevertheless, to my mind it would still bespeak an astonishing surefootedness even if doubled; the more so because a misstep is really only as serious as the final result, and the animals I saw salvaged the situation in every instance.

Several observers have commented on the mountain goat's unsettling predilection for walking along the edges of overhanging cornices, which seems to stem from the creature's general habit of keeping an alert eye on the world below. Here again the risk may be significant in the context of the observer's values but minimal in the context of the beast's skills and mountaineering judgement, including its ability to recover if the cornice should collapse beneath its weight. To rephrase that, the beast may not only be a better climber than we suppose but a better climber than we lowlanders *can* suppose. Just when you imagine that the goat you are watching must be clinging for dear life to a shred of ledge, it calmly lifts a rear foot and begins scratching an ear with it.

This is quite a bit of analysis to go through to confirm an ecological truism—that the species is every bit as good at climbing as it has to be to maintain its numbers under natural conditions. However, I was specifically trying to gauge the importance of various sources of natural mortality, hoping this would in turn help explain why many mountain goat populations have declined so abruptly when confronted by various sources of human-caused mortality and disturbance. My hunch was that for a creature that spends something like three-quarters of its time above the angle of repose, at least half of that under winter conditions, a very substantial part of normal mortality might come from accidents suffered in the course of just getting from place to place; i.e., climbing. The evidence for that hypothesis does not seem to be there: not enough of the right kind of corpses, not enough walking wounded in populations, not a high enough frequency of dangerous missteps—unless all of these represent very serious underestimates indeed.

The best conclusion is, I believe, that climbing accidents do take a constant toll of a magnitude which few other species have to deal with, and it is a factor to consider in the equation of population stability, but the major sources of natural mortality must be searched for elsewhere. We will consider the role of parasites, other disease organisms, and predators in the next chapter, which is a long, wide-ranging sort of hike through the animal communities of goat country. Right after one brief story.

The rock strata of Glacier Park and the Swan Mountains consist primarily of upthrust and overthrust limestones, shales, and argillites—all compacted ooze from the bottom of ancient seas. Very ancient seas. Some of the limestone formations here have been dated at 1.6 billion years of age, meaning they were formed in the latter half of the earliest geologic era, the Precambrian. Some of the first cell types on earth are in these stones—not chiefly as fossils, for we are talking about microscopic beings with soft cell walls, but as chemical traces of complex sugars and proteins. The true fossils show up in bands of rock near the top of Glacier's escarpments. They are peculiar ones called stromatolites, which look like petrified cabbage heads and are thought to have been formed from clumps of bacteria and possibly very primitive algae. Standing on these rocks with some of our planet's primal organisms interred within them always gives me a pleasant awareness of the continuity of living plasm.

Because they come in layers, sedimentary rocks such as these erode on certain exposures to make plentiful steplike ledges and terraces—platforms where a little soil can pause on its downhill journey and nourish plant growth. So in one sense they provide good footing for the mountain goat—as long as the strata are not tilted too much on end—and good foraging habitat as well. But from another standpoint the same strata create pretty shaky climbing conditions. Sedimentary formations, especially the softer shales and argillites, tend to weather quickly. Water leaches limey minerals along fracture cracks and in the seams between layers, and the exposed rocks turn as crumbly as masonry that has lost its cement. There is a saying that you have to hold the rocks together to climb them in this particular part of the Rockies, and it is true.

I was working my way along an outcropping near the stromatolite layer in Glacier when I ignored my general rule of keeping to the easiest route and decided to short-cut up a cream-colored belt of limestone. Once past that barrier it would be an easy scramble to the top and then a fast slide down some snowfields into the next big valley.

Halfway up the pitch I was back to the old, familiar realization that everything I had done, owned, thought about, cared for, or needed was getting compressed into that infinitely small space between fingertips and stone. In other words, things had once again arrived at the stage where what I hoped to do in my life depended upon what I did next with one hand. What I did next with it was grip a squarish lip of rock. I tried wriggling it to be sure it was firmly set in place. There was no give. So I transferred my weight to that hand and started to pull myself up, and the rock came out of the mountain like a drawer out of a chest. All the way out. I still had it tightly gripped in my hand as I toppled straight backward and then began falling head first.

All very simple and very clean, I remember thinking. Pluck. Damn. And you are gone. Yet my body was working with an optimism of its own, twisting to turn me around and aim my feet downward. When I hit I had already free-fallen 30 or 35 feet, but I did not slam into the mountain. The rock where I happened to land was steeply angled and smooth enough that I glanced off it, struck again, glanced off that, and then came to a sliding stop. My momentum had been slowed in stages. When I got around to checking my bones they were all straight and attached the way they are supposed to be. Everything else felt sprained and bruised, and I had some bloody scrapes, but I was able to hobble back to camp before I stiffened up.

I have been presenting a fair amount of condensed data in the past couple of chapters. And I guess the reason for my tale is that amidst all the biological determinism, amidst all the sorting of the fit from the unfit and the grinding out by immense forces of species and their unique characteristics, there is one special factor I may have passed over. It is an inexplicable factor, yet it is part of every equation. For want of a better word we sometimes call it luck.

CHAPTER FOUR

Neighbors

I SAW MY first wolverine tracks near Bunker Creek. They were everywhere in the snow, their circuitous design telling of an animal that makes its living by keeping constantly on the move and investigating every possibility in its path.

While I was goatwatching in the Swans, biologists Maurice Hornocker and Howard Hash undertook the first intensive study of wolverine ecology in North America, working in essentially the same area I was—the South Fork of the Flathead River drainage. In some cases their radio-collared wolverines covered 75 to 100 miles every few days wandering back and forth through this rugged countryside. En route these 20 to 50-pound members of the mustelid, or weasel, family were making meals of anything from frogs and birds' eggs to carrion and whatever warm-blooded prey they could bring down.

Although they don't make a habit of it, wolverines can on occasion bring down some fair-sized animals, and the fact that they have been seen attacking adult deer and even elk and caribou has given them an unmatched reputation for ferocity. Which goes along with historical descriptions of them as greedy, malicious, loathsome, and downright evil.

So many moral failings attributed to a single animal—the wolverine was commonly known as "the glutton"—are usually a good measure of the extent to which it competes for something people would rather have exclusively for themselves. In this case the same far-roaming habits and highly developed sense of smell that make the wolverine a virtuoso opportunist among the predator–scavengers make it a talented pilferer of cabins, food caches, and traplines as well.

As Ernest Thompson Seton notes in his book *Arctic Prairies,* "Its habit of following and raiding all traps for the sake of the bait is the prime cause of man's hatred, and its cleverness in eluding efforts at retaliation give it still more importance."

To fight such odious crimes, that sweet-tempered embodiment of self-less virtue who has named himself *Homo sapiens* shot, trapped, and poisoned the wolverine completely out of existence in the lower 48 states. As late as the mid-1930s even Glacier Park was still engaged in killing "bad" animals—i.e., predators—to save the "good" animals. Rangers shot wolverines and cougars on sight, and poisoned bait was scattered indiscriminately across the mountainsides of this region by airplane to eliminate any and all carnivores vile enough to be eating meat in a national park or forest. Not surprisingly, a couple of decades later Glacier, like other parks that had pursued the same policy, was contending with disease epidemics and overgrazing among the good animals, and had to reduce the numbers of some—namely elk—by shooting.

Only within the last two or three decades, following a decline in the use of poisons, has the wolverine been able to return to Montana and parts of Idaho from Canada. It ventured back mainly via the Glacier Park–Great Bear–Bob Marshall–Scapegoat ecosystem of protected wilderness habitat. This is still the epicenter of the wolverine population in the lower 48, a stronghold from which the species may continue to expand and re-establish itself in other intact portions of its former territory.

When a wolverine tore into our tent in the Swans and shredded a sleeping bag to see if any meat went along with all those feathers, we cursed and bought another tent. A black bear took care of that one. We lost still more food and equipment to woodrats, coyotes, strong-beaked ravens, and grizzlies. While we were off on a goat search one grizzly busted open a cabin we had been using. By the time we returned home, the place had been picked over by a black bear, deer (they ate the spilled salt and grain), porcupines, and jays, along with the usual armies of mice, and a wolverine.

Over the years porcupines alone, with their craving for salty minerals, gnawed sweat-tinged axe handles, boots, packs, pants, aluminum cooking gear, styrofoam pads, and the plastic casing on my binoculars. Worse, they chiseled through the rubber brake lines of my truck parked at a trailhead—twice, forcing me to begin wrapping the entire vehicle in chicken wire.

Beth and I told ourselves from the outset that if any unwarranted intrusions were being made here in the backcountry, they were ours. We believed it too. But I realize now how deeply ingrained in us was the habit of assuming human dominion over space and food. Having always lived outside the wilderness, we were just not used to being pressed to consider the presence and needs of so many other kinds of beings. It took all those lessons, those wolverines and porcupines, and more before we caught on intuitively to the competition over finite resources that occurs at all levels of life in a rich, native ecosystem.

With experience we learned to take better care in what we did with food scraps, avoided leaving a tent standing for days at a time while we were off ridgerunning, and secured our gear by hanging it from tree branches by a rope. One night when we hadn't bothered to string the stuff up, we awoke to the sound of a woodrat and mice chewing our equipment close to the sleeping bags. We dutifully bundled it together and hauled it into the spruce. An hour later we were awakened again, this time by the squealing of a porcupine that had somehow claimed both the bundle and rope and was trying to drive off a flying squirrel.

As if to prove the point that the only things that are truly yours and yours alone in the wild are your thoughts, a bushy-tailed woodrat once ran straight up to my best boots while I was lying by a late-night fire and began chiseling away at the salty leather. The really bushy-tailed part of this woodrat was that I hadn't taken the boots off yet.

The best home I ever had was a small scraped circle of pine needles and dirt around a stone fire ring. Over it, a clear piece of plastic was strung between tall spruce, and above that, the sky. On three sides stood the forest. The fourth side was an avalanche meadow growing up in high grasses and flowering brush. At the top of the meadow began the goat cliffs, and there were two natural salt licks near their base where the white climbers came daily. Bunker Creek pooled behind beaver dams at the bottom of the meadow, reflecting the mountains, the forest, and the summer sky.

In the cool mornings I would walk barefoot through dewy grasses spangled with spiderwebs to a spot where I had an open view of the cliffs. Some of the goats would be feeding and others contesting the best licking sites, the young ones playing while they awaited an opening. By late morning the last goats were bedding down to chew their cuds. The sun, nearing its zenith, shone directly onto the creek's clear bed, and I would turn to watching westslope cutthroat trout in the pools.

Westslope cutthroat are a rare race. The upper reaches of the Flathead River system, most of which was added to our National Wild and Scenic River System in 1977, form one of the principal breeding areas that remain to it, and also to the Dolly Varden trout, a big salmonid fish related to arctic char.

The cutthroat in Bunker Creek are small, for the waters are cold and summer brief. In the pool I kept the closest eye on—usually while lying naked on an overhanging log—the largest trout was 11 inches long. This fish occupied the head of the pool, positioning itself in the apron of the gentle current that flowed through a break in the beaver dam above. It therefore had first chance at the insects that fell off overhanging plants upstream and were borne along on the surface.

Behind the first fish was the next largest one, about 10 1/4 inches from mouth to tail tip. Behind it was a 9 1/2-inch trout, and so on, the fish becoming progressively smaller on down the pool until, at the downstream end, those left were no longer than my little finger. Fry smaller than that tended to stay under the bank in the shadows.

From time to time each fish would leave its place and check for floating insects near the edges or hunt larvae among bottom debris. In its travels it often brushed against another's temporary territory. As when the goats I had just been observing argued over licking sites and feeding areas, there followed either a threat, a short chase, or a battle.

When fighting, the fish aligned themselves the same way mountain goats did: side by side and head-to-tail (antiparallel). Whereas the goats arched their backs and erected the ridge of hairs along it, the trout flared their fins to increase their apparent size, and the subtle dappling on their sides became neon warning signs of scarlet and purple. Then, again like the goats, they began rigidly circling one another. If neither lowered its fins, turned off its colors, and fled, the circling escalated into biting.

All day beneath the placid quicksilver surface of this pool fish flared and fought, maintaining an elaborate social definition of living space and access to protein.

At the top of the hierarchy the 11-inch fish claimed the most desirable space. It had to battle the most frequently to defend that area, but it obtained the most to eat by remaining there—an average of eight to 12 floating bugs hourly, compared to three to five for the second and third-ranking fish, and one or none for the fingerlings at the far end. Nevertheless, a fingerling could always hope to beat the consequences of the rigid social order by leaping up to snap an insect on the wing: a stonefly, or a gossamer mayfly, some day, maybe even one of those enormous green dragonflies hunting midges and mosquitoes close to the surface. I noticed that the dragonflies meanwhile defended territories of their own, as did the olive-sided flycatchers and tree swallows that nested in snags along open sections of the creek and also hunted dragonflies.

Things came together in this home shared by so many. I had all the possessions I could have wanted but few personal belongings, and those few seemed more trouble than they were worth. The more I learned to look, the more there was waiting to be seen and absorbed. The world was generous to the eye and made eloquent sense, more than I could have imagined, had I always lived where most of my neighbors were people.

Griz

Even if we had wanted to ignore the patterns of life around us and carry a full pack of human conceits about being the rightful owners of all we surveyed, we could not have. Not as long as Griz lived there too.

Nature has few creations like the great bear to enforce respect for the order she has wrought; few remaining works whose very spoor, once seen, can make the mountains suddenly higher, the valleys wider, the wind louder as it bends around a rise. And fewer all the time. Two hundred years ago, 100,000 grizzlies—possibly many more—inhabited the lower 48 states. At present 800, probably fewer, dwell there. Like the wolverine, their major stronghold in the U.S. outside Alaska is the section of the Rockies included in the Glacier–Great Bear–Bob Marshall–Scapegoat wilderness ecosystem.

Having no more real acquaintance with Griz than most folks, Beth and I looked around for something to render us bearproof before first going into the Swans in early spring. An acquaintance recommended that Beth and I carry a magnesium emergency flare to be ignited in the presence of a troublesome bear and held resolutely between the prospective biter and bitee. Had this worked for him in actual practice, we asked? Kind of, he replied. The one black bear he had subjected to the flare had only walked curiously up and bitten it instead of him.

We finally settled on a pressurized foghorn from a boat supply house. It was the world's loudest can. Upon a press of the plunger it emitted a bellow capable of stopping anything but an avalanche in its tracks. We hoped.

So we each carried one slung from a shoulder—next to the camera, lenses, binoculars, telescope, tripod, drinking cup, and pack already hanging from us. Spring snow is a practical joke to walk on, and when you are rigged out like a traveling pawnshop it is bound to have the last laugh. The crust carries you along just until you start to relax, then gives way all at once where a buried log or brush has weakened its structure. And you plunge onto your side, pack frame banging your head, binoculars filling with snow, and—in our case—your foghorn accidentally pressed on and blasting warnings to any ships that happen to be near your ear.

We persisted in carrying these wonderful bleeping beepers until the middle of one night in May. I opened a sleepy eye and saw a porcupine eating my boots (the first of several pairs that were to be reduced to near sandals by the efforts of the local rodents). It was time to give the bear-beeper its first real field test on wildlife. With demented glee I turned the foghorn on the pricklybear and jammed the plunger down. As on most spring nights the temperature had fallen below freezing; out of the can came a wee shivering "feeeep."

It seemed that everything to do with Griz that first year was haphazard. Our initial encounter was with a sow and cubs not long out of hibernation. They appeared on a ridge well above us as we were climbing upward. I wanted to turn back. Beth, who was not nearly as spooked, held out for going closer. The bears got our scent soon afterward and began to run as if frightened, but they fled more toward us than away, and we took to the nearest trees.

It is early summer that same year. I am sliding on my boot soles down leftover snow on a ridgeline, humming to myself, making wide turns, picking up speed. A mother grizzly and cub stand up from where they have been bedded in a shady cleft between a boulder and the snow directly below me. Ho! No time to brake. Believing herself and her youngster attacked, she runs away a dozen feet. Stops. Spins back toward me.

I angle right as sharply as I dare; if I slip I'll tumble right past her legs. Schussss, and I'm past claw's reach and tucking all out for the bottom. She is sliding after me but keeps spinning around rump first, from what I can see over my shoulder, and gives it up after a couple of hundred yards.

Now it is midsummer. I am angling up a different ridgeline, carrying my radio receiver and antenna to fix the location of a collared goat. This time I am also carrying the least imaginative of all antibear gimmicks: a gun—a .44 magnum, to be specific. And because I am carrying a gun I do not stop when I come to a Griz signpost on the trail, where the bear has freshly clawed the bark eight feet high on a fir. Farther on I find a pungent mess of dung clearly too large to be from a black bear. In it is the intact paw of a ground squirrel, disconcertingly like a miniature human hand, the rest of the animal's flesh now becoming grizzly flesh. My gun and I ignore that too and go on to the crest.

Cottony patches of goat fur are snagged on bushes along the ridgeline. I had not known the climbers were traveling this route. Which way? Down the ridge is a late-melting snowbank and the imprint of goat tracks on the moist ground beside it, headed west. I turn on the receiver, but the radio signal is bouncing around a lot, deflected by side ridges. The next knoll should be a good receiving spot. More goat tracks appear, maybe two days old. . . .

There is a grunt, and by the time I look up all three—the sow Griz and both big two-year-old cubs—are heaving toward me, whuffing with each bound. I can see spittle flying from open mouths. I hurl my antenna at them and realize I am screaming. By the time my gun is unholstered they are nearly on top of me but beginning to veer aside. The sow halts a short distance off. The two cubs, though, decide to return for some more bluff charges, while she roars and swings her huge head, urging them, I think, to come away.

To its credit, the gun helps me stand my ground and call their bluffs. But then, without this weapon I would probably have gone back before I stumbled onto the bears; I would at least have paid closer attention to the wind and stayed near climbable trees. In any case, the end of this episode is that the cubs call it quits and leave with their mother.

I race away in the opposite direction, slow to a walk, then sit, then jump up, pace, and decide that to celebrate what feels like a rebirth I am going to head up the ridge to a shallow melt lake on the shoulder of Thunderbolt Mountain and go swimming. I drop my pack and radio gear. This leaves me with: sneakers; baggy, slightly grey underpants (they are cool to hike in, and I never see anybody up here); a belt and a holster containing my .44 magnum. In this garb, charged with adrenaline, I am fairly leaping uphill toward the lake and singing as loudly as I can to warn the bears of where I am in case they have circled around this way while leaving. I sing nursery rhymes, sea shanties, whatever circulates in my overheated brain.

Sure enough, as I top the rim of the lake there are two people watching me, the only two people I will meet in that part of the high country all summer. They are watching me very carefully and standing very close together. Their eyes travel from my cannon to my seedy undershorts and up to my face, and I perceive that they are having trouble coming up with an opening conversational gambit. I undertake to explain—at about a thousand words a minute—nursery rhymes, Griz with foaming mouths, rebirth, goats. But they just smile in a pained sort of way and keep edging closer together. Finally they walk abruptly away down the other side of Thunderbolt, looking back over their shoulders, still grinning furiously. Damn, I think, these guys are pretty strange.

It is another late spring season. I see a good-sized blond grizzly swing out of an alpine gully and into a flower-lit meadow, and I feel the threat of it 150 yards away like a blow. My thoughts draw together. I know the wind favors me. I crouch in stages to remove my silhouette. The trees here won't help; they are shorter than I am. But I have kept as close to the cliffs as any goat and have my eye on a likely rock escape route.

The grizzly is rooting around at the base of a boulder. It flicks the massive fallen rock effortlessly aside—gorgeous strength!—and begins licking up what must be an ant colony. All at once two long-legged cubs come chasing each other out of the gully, wrestling and cuffing. She grunts to them, and they tumble her way. The sow plonks down on her rump and scratches an itch. I check behind me, and when I turn back she has one cub under each arm. The three of them are resting in the grass: just bears. Just bears wanting to live like bears. I have forgotten that I am supposed to be terrified of them.

I came to admire them without reservation. In Glacier, where I couldn't have carried a firearm even if I had still wanted to, the grizzlies were dense enough that I would count on seeing at least one in a week of scanning for goats. And now I try to spend time watching them there each spring and fall when they concentrate in special areas I know of, the challenge being to keep the bears from becoming aware of my presence so that they suffer no disturbance. I have become addicted to Griz.

These days my memories are of a dark bear floating in a lake on a hot afternoon, blowing bubbles through its submerged snout and then pricking them with its four-inch-long claws. Of two grizzlies wrestling over a log and one of them lying on its back and wheeling the big tree section in the air like a juggler while its roars of satisfaction carried through the basin. Of bears spending an afternoon sliding down a snowbank in play —as I was doing that time I all but collided with the sow and cub. And of a sleepy sow in huckleberry time with three nearly grown, sleepy cubs all jostling for position with their heads on one another's side in a great, grizzled, softly growling pile.

Man has had a long relationship with the grizzly and its Eurasian relative (which may have been its ancestor) *Ursus spelaeus,* the cave bear. It has been a connection, probably mutual, of wonder and fear. The Cult of the Bear is considered one of the earliest religions man devised in his dealings with the unknown and may prove to be the most durable, for there is evidence that it lasted some 20,000 years during Paleolithic times.

But if man has worshipped the great bear, he is also its most persistent and deadliest predator—its only one, really. Soon after Griz crossed to the New World it was followed by bands of Paleo-Indians. The myths continued and so did the hunting. Then came the next New World colonists—the Europeans with rifles, who reduced the numbers of Indians and bears through actions barely short of genocide. Is it surprising that the grizzly, a highly intelligent creature capable of rapid learning, should, after the systematic destruction of its race, flee from a man almost every time it meets one?

Bears have troubled my dreams more than once, causing me to lay awake thereafter, listening to faint sounds. Yet because of Griz the whole night was awake, ancient and wild. For me they are a pitch of awareness, and Griz-less backcountry sometimes seems anesthetized. For others, though, they are sheer monsters—shaggy, dark-roaming objects of fear, destroyers of our deep psychic wish to deny those things we can neither tame nor predict.

As for dreams, dogs seem to have them too. You can watch them growl and run in their sleep, anyway. If bears, close relatives of dogs, dream as well, I would imagine that we are its nightmare. Researcher John Craighead, who with his brother Frank has probably spent more time than anyone else among grizzlies, once told me that if we cannot learn to co-exist with what few of these extraordinary beings are left, it is doubtful that we will ever be able to get along with our fellow men on this planet.

Seasonal Strategies

It is just possible that some groggy bear or marmot will provide us with a key to the stars. Sometime in the fall the marmots and ground squirrels of the north country enter a state of true dormancy, a semi-vegetative condition in which their temperature falls to only a few degrees above freezing while their heartbeat, respiration, and related body functions are reduced to barely perceptible levels.

The hibernation of such animals as black bears, grizzlies, and chipmunks is less profound, more like merely a long period of drowsiness. Griz, for example, may get up and move about in their winter dens or even wander outside on warm days. In fact during the mild, almost snowless winter of 1980–81 I was crossing fresh grizzly tracks in Glacier all through January, and grizzlies have been seen running down elk in Yellowstone National Park in midwinter.

True dormancy is common among cold-blooded vertebrates of northern latitudes, but it requires much more complex and not fully understood physiological changes in a warm-blooded mammal. Once we have a better idea of how, say, a marmot's kidneys and liver handle the buildup of metabolic waste products over the months of dormancy, we can apply the information toward developing a life-support system for human astronauts placed in a state of suspended animation in order to survive an extended journey through space. Or perhaps the black bear's version of hibernation, or the grizzly's, will turn out to be more applicable to the human system.

Each of the mountain goat's neighbors has its strategy for coping with winter, the bleak season of the minimum; prolonged sleep is simply the strategy of avoiding the issue altogether. The bears disappear for almost half the year, from October or November until April or May. Ground squirrels and marmots go underground in the high country as early as the end of August to remain more or less unconscious for the next three-quarters of the year, emerging again only in May or June—and even then they often have to tunnel up through a thick snowpack to reach the light of day.

A more common strategy is to escape the worst of winter by migrating, either to an entirely different region, as many mountain-breeding birds and some fish species do, or at least to a far lower elevation, like most of the hooved animals* and predators. Only a few neighbors—notably pocket gophers, whose raised earth tunnels crisscross mountain meadows; white-footed deer mice; various voles; the lemmings of alpine tundra; weasels; and ptarmigan—remain active year round in the uppermost landscapes alongside the bearded climbers. And they are largely invisible company, as they go about most of their work burrowed into or under the deep, insulating snowpack.

The white-tailed ptarmigan of western mountain tundra is nearly invisible to begin with, being a perfect white in winter (except for its black eyes and bill), and a mottled brown in summer. Its behavior enhances its camouflage. Ptarmigan walk with an uncannily slow, measured step and hold motionless when disturbed. Many times a snowfield or meadow in goat country has grown wings and taken flight just as I was about to set my foot down on it. Molted ptarmigan feathers, like shed mountain goat hairs, have warmed quite a few of the baby birds and mammals of the land above the trees, after being gathered and worked into the lining of nests. The ptarmigan even grows feathers on its feet; they act as snowshoes until the spring molt.

The blue grouse is somewhat unique in that it may actually move upward in altitude during late fall, from valley woodlands toward treeline. There this largest-bodied of the American forest grouse spends the snow months feeding primarily on fir buds and needles. Spring overtakes blue grouse high on the mountainside, beginning their mating season. The cock inflates himself, exposing two bold red throat patches that amplify his courting call—a loud cross between a gulp and a hoot—then stretches a fan of tail feathers upward like a peacock and struts about in

---

*Investigating white-tailed deer in New England, Helenette Silver and her colleagues discovered that these artiodactyls gear down into what she terms a fasting metabolism, which might be viewed as a very mild form of hibernation. The principle behind it is the same. By lowering their metabolic rate the deer, though still active, become somewhat more sluggish than usual. Consequently they require less food energy than normal to keep them going and so improve their chances of fending off starvation in the season of scarce forage.

There is some evidence that some other members of the deer family—namely elk and moose—also dampen their metabolism slightly in winter, and there are some indications that sheep may do the same. On the other hand, measurements made of the metabolism of a captive Alaskan goat exposed to winter conditions showed it to be normal.

open areas such as the broad ledges of goat cliffs, where he can be admired by the hens.

As is true for the courtship of so many species, male blue grouse tend to become exceedingly single-minded. I've had them march directly in front of me, refusing to yield their parade ground despite my outweighing them 185 pounds to three. One I watched stood fast in the path of a two-year-old billy. The closer the billy approached, the further the cock puffed himself up and the more noisily he boomed his call. Though the billy began to toss his horns and stamp, the bird kept on strutting his stuff. Nor would the cock give up more than an inch or two at a time of his turf when the billy made short leaps at him.

The billy soon worked himself up to war-dancing and slashing vegetation, and at one point drove his horns against a fallen snag. The dead tree happened to have been precariously balanced between rocks, and the billy's thrust sent it tumbling down the cliffs with a resounding crash. As if someone had pricked him with a pin, the grouse suddenly deflated to normal size and scuttled away into nearby brush.

Seed-eating birds associated with the upper elevations in this part of the Rockies include pine siskins, pine grosbeaks, crossbills, and grey-crowned rosy finches. They travel in flocks and concentrate their feeding on the upright purplish cones of subalpine fir when passing near treeline in winter. The rosy finches summer higher than the others, and you may see them bursting like handfuls of hurled stones through the tallest passes, propelled by funneling winds.

For years the down parka I used was a red one, and every so often on a late spring hillside a calliope or a black-chinned hummingbird would appear, dazzling around me like an electron as it checked out the incredible possibility that I might be some sort of giant blossom. I didn't like to disappoint them. Blossoms were scarce enough at that time of year, and wet-flaked blizzards still likely. How—given the demands of their spectacularly high, nectar-fueled metabolism—could these bee-like birds endure being grounded any length of time by a snowstorm? And how, later in the season, could the female go without feeding during a long spell of foul, cold rain which required her to stay continuously on the nest to keep the eggs warm?

Recently it was discovered that hummingbirds have their own capacity for "hibernating." They are able to reduce their energy requirements by lowering their metabolism and entering a semi-torpid state for one or two days at a time—long enough to outlast the core of a storm without food.

I once noticed a nanny who seemed to be enthralled by something in a brushfield, which I soon saw was the courtship flight of a male black-chinned hummingbird. He would hum up nearly out of sight, then power dive straight down and at the last minute level out to sweep by a female perched on a branch. As he shot past he sparked green and lavender and—by flaring his outer tail feathers—left a VROOOOM noise in his wake along with his chattering squeal of a cry. Although this production could hardly have been set in a more pristine wildspan, it reminded me overwhelmingly of a young dude gunning his candy-colored, fuel-injected, chrome-hubbed hunk of hot pistons up and down the main drag on Saturday night, past females perched and parked on the curb.

Black-and-white Clark's nutcrackers share some ranges where goats winter on cliffs surrounded by subalpine forest. Constant association between the two species over the snow months leads to the kind of familiarity in which the nutcrackers begin riding around on the goats' rumps. The sharp-eyed birds serve at times as a type of early warning system for the goats, shrieking and flying overhead to announce the location of an intruder. They may also pick ticks off the goats' fur as their close relative the magpie is known to do in southerly portions of the mountain goat's distribution.

Ravens, Steller's jays, and gray jays, all in the same family as well, inhabit northern mountain forests throughout the year, and the wide-ranging, scavenging ravens commonly ride the winds up to see what the alpine terrain has to offer. Until the eagles return in early spring, a concentration of ravens is one of the best clues for locating the remains of winter-killed goats.

A small, chirruping song came to me one day in May from the edge of a meltwater lake gleaming between the upper and lower levels of some goat cliffs in Glacier. I couldn't remember ever hearing those notes before and searched every dwarf tree and willow thicket for the singer. The mystery continued until I saw the source staring up at me from shallow water with gold-flecked eyes, a vibrating bubble at its throat. It was a western toad *(Bufo borealis)*, performing its part of a chorus in the snow-filled amphitheater, calling for a mate. More male toads hopped across snow at the water's edge, 7,000 feet above sea level, in pursuit of a female.

Near goat rocks at the same elevation in parts of Montana and Idaho and along the Cascade Mountains in Washington and southernmost British Columbia, you might also come across the odd, voiceless tailed frog. Another noteworthy mountain amphibian found in the same regions is the Pacific giant salamander. It is the grizzly bear of North America's damp-skinned land dwellers, nearly nine inches long snout-to-tail as an adult (up to a foot long in its aquatic larval form), and given to growling at things that disturb its peace.

Micro-Predators

Some of the smallest residents of the goat's neighborhood have an out-sized effect on the white climber's life. Bees are uncommon in the cold and windy subalpine and alpine zones. Here it is the flies, being hardier and stronger fliers, that do much of the work of pollination, helping to perpetuate the goat's food supply. What some high-country hikers know as the "sweat bee" is a hover fly, belonging to the family Syrphidae, which mimics a bee's coloration, presumably to discourage predators. The sweat part of its name is accurate enough. These yellow-and-black-striped flies rode along on a lot of traverses with me, sopping up perspiration with their proboscis—the insect version of a tongue.

In other members of the order Diptera, such as horseflies, deerflies, black flies, no-see-um gnats, and mosquitoes, the proboscis and associated mouth parts are designed for piercing and sucking. Their larvae are aquatic and the bloodthirsty adults therefore especially abundant in moist habitats—around lakes and boggy tundra, and in dense vegetation on north-facing slopes and shady valleys.

On humid, windless days I watched elk and goats in high basins escalate from ear-flapping, tail-switching, stamping, and shaking to frenzied rushes and leaps away from the swarming hordes. While the goats might go on to war-dance and thrash vegetation with their horns, as they tend to when highly stimulated (or exasperated), the elk sometimes took refuge in alpine lakes, submerging like moose.

Biting flies and mosquitoes appear to be one of the main reasons why, in late June and July, mountain goats keep close to the very highest ridgetops and peaks, where there is usually enough of a breeze to disperse the bugs. I know the little—ah, let's call them proof that nature has a broader sense of aesthetics than we do—kept me as far upslope as I could get during those months.

Ticks also plague mountain mammals. Larvae of the winter tick (*Dermacentor albipictus*) emerge in late fall and become attached to the hooved residents of an area. Once its head is burrowed into a goat, the larva becomes engorged with its host's blood—a drain upon the bearded beast in the critical winter period—and begins molting through a nymphal stage. By late winter or early spring the nymph has metamorphosed into an adult, which may become engorged once more on its goat host.

At the same time—late winter or early spring, generally whenever the first warm weather arrives—another species, the wood tick (*D. andersoni*) shows up on the ledges. Having parasitized rodents such as voles and ground squirrels during its larval and nymphal stages, the adult wood tick now crawls up to the tip of a twig or grass stalk and waits with its hooked legs outstretched for a larger host to brush against it. I might remove 100 from my hair and clothing during an April day on goat range. Heavy infestations of both winter and wood ticks coming right at the end of a difficult winter can conceivably be a lethal combination to a goat already in particularly poor condition.

The wood tick is notorious as a carrier of Rocky Mountain spotted fever, which can be fatal to man if not treated in time. If mountain goats are susceptible to this or any of the other diseases ticks transmit to man and domestic animals, it has not yet been reported. The parasites do cause at least local abscesses and inflammations on the goat's skin, and these occasionally cause patches of bare, black, scaly epidermis to develop on the animal.

Kids and yearlings seem to suffer the worst irritations. Every spring I noticed pinkish stains on the fur of a few in the neck and shoulder area, where the juveniles were just beginning to shed their fur. This was not blood but blood-derived tick excrement. Later, though, an infection might develop at the site and, after continued scratching and rubbing by a youngster, become an open, bleeding sore.

I was intrigued by the care shown by the mothers of many affected kids. One nanny spent two uninterrupted hours licking a wound on her offspring's shoulder and nibbling fur (along with tick bodies, surely) away from the trouble spot. She then went on to lick the kid's back, neck, and head more thoroughly than she had probably done at any time since the youngster's birth, providing a tonic sort of stimulation and perhaps reassurance.

A third tick species known to parasitize mountain goats is the spinose ear tick (*Otobius megnini*). Its larvae find their way inside the ear canal of wild and domestic livestock and develop there to adult form, sometimes becoming numerous enough to block an animal's hearing.

A normally vigorous goat sheds or scratches off most of its tick load along with its fur in late spring and early summer. However, the list of parasites and other diseases thus far associated with goats goes on to include lice and approximately two dozen helminths variously known as roundworms (lungworms, stomachworms) and flatworms (tapeworms, flukes); harmful fungi and bacteria; viruses such as contagious ecthyma (soremouth); and a degenerative condition due to a specific nutritional deficiency (white-muscle disease). The list looks fearsome enough, and it will doubtless lengthen as goats are more intensively studied throughout their continental range. But, at least at the moment, it remains notably short compared to that for many big game species. And consider the pages it would take to tally the more obvious ailments human flesh is heir to.

The parasitic worms appear to be quite widespread among mountain goats. (Very few humans are entirely free of them either.) It is one thing to host, say, a stomachworm, but quite another to succumb to its ill effects. Harmful organisms carried by big animals do not necessarily wreak serious illness or death unless the host's defenses and vitality are first worn down by poor nutrition or other prolonged stress. This undoubtedly happens to individual goats, but the kind of epidemics and subsequent die-offs found among other ungulates (and humans), particularly in overcrowded ranges (and nations), are conspicuously absent from reports concerning the white climbers.

The best indications are that the overall health of mountain goat populations is good and that the overall role of parasite and disease organisms in regulating, or limiting, those populations is minimal. The subject will come up again in later chapters. For now we can turn our attention back to the goat's vertebrate neighbors and gradually narrow our attention to the influence of competition and predation.

Competitors Small and Large

The mammal whose natural distribution in North America is most similar to the mountain goat's in terms of geography and elevation is the hoary marmot, also called the whistling marmot. It is a more sociable creature than the lowland species most people know as woodchucks or groundhogs. Hoary marmot clan members often are seen together on the rocks, grooming one another, resting in the sun, or interacting in a ritual form of aggression that looks to the observer like a hand-pushing game of pat-a-cake. Their piercing call of warning connects every marmot for acres around on the mountainside. A hunting golden eagle spotted by just one hoary marmot is likely to be an eagle avoided by all.

By sleeping away most of the year underground they not only avoid the cold, and food shortages, but most of their predators as well. Grizzlies and wolverines, however, take advantage of this trait, excavating deep into the soil to uncover the sleeping rodents in autumn and again in late spring. The wolverines, Hornocker learned, even dig them out in winter.

Because they are almost as inquisitive as goat kids, marmots make convenient—if not always enthusiastic—playmates for them. The kids and marmots, having made a nose-to-nose acquaintance, may follow one another for a short time through the meadows and fellfields and occasionally bed side by side. At salt licks visited by both species the marmots behave much like subordinate goats, racing in to lick while the larger animal is occupied with something else, then racing away to avoid a horn prod when the big goat comes too close.

The pika is another high-altitude specialist living in stable rockslides at or above treeline. It is known as the cony, and also as the rock rabbit since it is a small relative of the snowshoe hare. The pika is no harelike leaper, though. It is a chipmunk-sized skeedaddler with fur-soled footpads to give it traction on slick stone. From its habit of stacking its daily harvest of grasses, sedges, herbs and leafy twigs in mounds beneath sheltering rock slabs comes yet another name: the haymaker. On a bright winter day you may find the haymaker out and about, spreading the food cache from its den to dry in the sunshine.

Compared to the voices of ground squirrels and marmots its call is a peep, yet it carries for long distances across the upper slopes. When stalking goats with a camera or dye-loaded gun, with marmots, ground squirrels, pikas, and Clark's nutcrackers all hollering warnings as I passed, I felt as though an enormous finger pointed out my every move.

Golden-mantled ground squirrels are better rockclimbers than the Columbian ground squirrels also found in the high country, and bushy-tailed woodrats are better still. Found on alpine ledges as well as around rocky outcroppings within the forest, woodrats will build mounds of litter to serve as nests in crevices on very steep cliff faces. Because they are active mainly at night not many people see them on the mountain goat range they inhabit. Instead they are more often encountered in cabins, and called packrats (plus a lot of unprintable names) for their habit of making off with food and belongings. But, unlike others in the brotherhood of thieves, they often leave something in return.

This trader's motives are not very mysterious. Woodrats like to decorate their nests with shiny or otherwise conspicuous items. Since the creature is likely to be carrying some food, nest material, or natural decoration in its mouth when it comes upon a more attractive object, it drops what it has and picks up the worthier load. Hence, my pen would disappear, replaced by a twig, or my compass would be swapped for an interesting bone fragment.

Discussing elk ecology in Yellowstone National Park, former chief biologist Glen Cole once pointed out that insects probably constitute ten times the total live weight, or biomass, of elk on a given range. It is an interesting perspective on wildlife biology, in that we generally think of big game animals competing only with other big game for food and living space. The perspective becomes still more interesting if you contemplate the biomass of all the small mammals from mice to marmots on a range and the amount of forage they remove in a year. Try and find a plant in late summer that has not been gnawed and chiselled or at least ventilated with bug-eaten holes. That much less remains for the big herbivores to contest in winter.

Among animals closer to its own size, the mountain goat's potential direct competitors are mule deer, elk, and mountain sheep. Most mountain goat herds rarely, if ever, see an elk or mule deer through the winter. Those that do are herds that winter well below treeline. Even there the bearded climber's insistence upon remaining on or very close to steep cliffs, combined with the reluctance of the long-legged deer and elk to use truly precipitous ice- and snowbound terrain, prevents much actual range conflict. Lonn Kuck's documentation of substantial competition between mountain goats and mule deer toward the margins of prime goat range in Idaho's Pahsimeroi Mountains is an intriguing exception. Since the Pahsimeroi Mountains are about as far south as *Oreamnos* naturally goes in North America, Kuck's finding could confirm that it is not hotter temperatures alone that have confined the goats to northern latitudes, but also the presence of competitors whose disadvantages relative to the goat on high, steep slopes diminish in less wintry climes.

There comes a time in April and early May when elk and deer move up from the forests and brushfields in search of new forage at the same time most goats are moving down for it. They converge on a small number of rocky, south-facing sites that are more bare and warm and green than any other part of the high mountain valleys just then. With the first flush of root-stored nutrients in their sprouting foliage, grasses, sedges, and many of the herbaceous plants offer the grazers up to 15 to 20 percent protein—on the order of fresh cheese—and there is enough by then for all.

That is one reason the elk, deer, goats, and sheep all follow the retreating snowline upward through the coming months—to seek out nutrient-laden plants in the earliest stages of growth. In Glacier Park you can still find spring in late July, if you are willing to climb high enough. The elk and deer pass a good deal of the summer and early fall in alpine basins, and I found that bachelor groups of bull elk and buck "mulies" tend to have certain favorite high knolls that they use as resting spots, and also as retreats on hot and buggy days.

Elk are tall creatures, and bulls weigh up to 900 pounds. They coexist peacefully with goats most of the time if they happen to be feeding together on the same slope, but elk clearly make goats nervous when they approach very closely. At a common salt lick where I stationed myself for a time the elk easily displaced goats from the best licking spots while the goats in turn had little trouble routing mule deer.

Eight goats were bedded in a summer meadow just above a block of cliffs when a cow elk entered the scene in my telescope. As the cow walked toward the white climbers a nanny and a yearling closest to the elk's path began to paw vigorously in their beds. At the last minute they got up and displayed a few rampant horn tosses before grudgingly moving aside. The elk continued beyond them but soon hesitated and looked back toward the agitated goats. Hmmmm. Then she returned toward them, and this time her gait had a flounce to it. One by one the goats rose from bed as she re-entered their midst, and the excitement of the nanny and yearling, who were now bucking and whirling, spread through the band. Both yearling and nanny made mock charges at the elk, then hurried around to bed directly in her path as if to say: All right, let's see you make me move this time. And they pawed so hard in their beds they filled the air with dust. The elk pranced a bit herself and shook her head as goats war-danced on all sides. Finally she moved away—very slowly, lingering every few feet to view the riot she had incited. The yearling got up and followed her some distance, shaking its horns, and the rest of the band redirected their disquiet into chasing one another and squabbling over new bedsites.

Judging from my experiences with visitors in Glacier Park I would say that the confusion between mountain goats and mountain sheep, begun in frontier days, remains fairly complete. Those who stopped on the trail to peer through my telescope at mountain goats almost invariably told me how delightful these sheep were, and those who actually saw bighorn sheep often described them as mountain goats. (Mixing up two bovids is understandable. I don't know what to say about the tourist who got nipped by a tame hoary marmot he was feeding and duly reported to park officials that he had been mauled by a grizzly cub.)

Although they really don't resemble goats, wild sheep are justifiably renowned as outstanding climbers in their own right, perfectly at home on high, rocky terrain. So, from the standpoint of understanding the unique aspects of mountain goat ecology, the question becomes: exactly how much do the lifestyles of the two mountaineers overlap?

The fact that mountain sheep exist in many areas of North America where mountain goats do not, and vice versa, is a broad hint that the niche requirements of the two are not all that closely matched. Where they are found together it becomes evident that, like everybody else, sheep favor habitats that are less steep than those chosen by the goats. In typical mountain topography this places them on slopes that are lower in elevation as well.

Optimum habitat for sheep is a mixture of cliffs, broader ledges, fellfields and, most importantly, meadows. Their climbing skills are generalized. Possessed of tremendous speed and leaping ability, they don't have to rely on scaling rock walls to escape a predator; they can outrun it in elegant bounds across broken topography. By contrast, the goat is a plodder: short-legged, musclebound, stocky, and slow. Which only means, as discussed in Chapter 2, that the goat is almost wholly specialized for rockwork, able to ascend where none can follow.

In his book *Mountain Sheep*, Valerius Geist mentions that "[g]oats and sheep react quite differently to slipping in cliffs. Sheep which had lost a foothold jumped away and landed on a foothold below. Two goats that I observed slip instantly spread their legs apart, flattened themselves against the rock, and clawed for footholds as they slid down." The difference, I think, is revealing. Where the goats spend so much of their time, to jump away when they slip would be to find a foothold on nothing but pure mountain air. Sheep climb with agility up to a point, but mountain goats and mountain goats alone are the methodical masters of the near vertical.

Beyond this dissimilarity, sheep are less adept than goats at pawing through deep snow. Sheep are also specifically adapted to a diet of grasses, sedges, and herbs while goats—as we will see in the next chapter—eat a remarkable variety of plants, from lichens to trees and shrubs. In winter as in other seasons, the result is a segregation of ranges: goats to their icy, snow-laden cliffs, where the small bands exploit a patchy food supply; sheep to less sheer and less snowbound terrain, where the large groups typical of this species can find standard grazing fare for all.

The main reason sheep are absent from many coastal mountain ranges inhabited by goats is that the snow there often packs too deep and wet over the high country to blow away. While the bearded beasts can drop downhill and make a living on scattered outcroppings within the forest, the gregarious, open-meadow-loving sheep are simply out of business. Largely because they bear the brunt of many storms that arrive in Montana from the Pacific, the Swans hold no sheep either. But bighorn herds exist some 40 miles due east, just across the Continental Divide, where the country is more open, colder, drier, and windier than a Senate debate. This is also why sheep are confined to Glacier's eastern slopes until summer whereas the park's goats live year round on both sides of the Divide.

My estimate is that at most 10 percent of the general range area used by Glacier's goats overlaps sheep range, and seasonal differences in patterns of habitat use further reduce niche overlap.

To the extent that they do meet on the mountainsides here, the goats and bighorns seem to get along well, often feeding and bedding peacefully a few feet apart. I observed ewes with lambs make an effort to keep up with nannies and kids while grazing. The kids and lambs, fascinated by each other, would exchange nose sniffs and prance in tandem, though the nannies usually kept them from really playing together. Also, although the peak of actual breeding for sheep is in early December, one to three weeks later than for the goats, there is a fair amount of overlap between the general rutting seasons, and I twice saw bighorn rams pay court to nanny goats.

What if a billy had encountered one of those bold rams trying to make time with a nanny? A certain amount of one-upsmanship is practiced between the two alpinists in everyday encounters. It is almost always a subtle business; more subtle than goats, with their aggressive social hierarchy, practice among themselves and also less pronounced than rams show toward other rams. A clear winner—goat or sheep—is tough to pick.

A nanny–subadult band might yield the right of way to several rams or to a big band of ewes and juvenile sheep, but the same sheep might avoid a bachelor band of, say, five billies. In meetings between goat and sheep bands of similar composition in Glacier the sheep usually blinked first, if it came to that. This agrees with the more detailed findings of Colorado biologist Dale Reed, who is pursuing a study of the relationships between native bighorns and a goat herd introduced to that state in 1948. About 70 percent of the interactions between the two are neutral, according to Reed, and the goats prove dominant in the rest.

Except for the brawniest billies, goats are shorter and weigh less than sheep of equivalent age and sex. Why, then, should goats have the edge? For one thing, goats are simply not as inclined to tolerate close company —of their own kind or any other—and are easily aroused by what they consider a threat to their personal space. Sheep, being sheep after all, see nothing wrong with a crowd. And while overt aggression is uncommon among ewes, nanny goats are, if anything, more belligerent than billies.

These differences in social temperament might not mean much in goat–sheep encounters if both sexes of goat did not also possess two stilletos for horns. The horns of female sheep are no longer than goat horns and have blunt tips. The massive spirals of mature male sheep are highly evolved organs that serve as bludgeons in ritual battles and, more often, as ornaments whereby rams can judge each other's social status and so avoid wasting energy in unnecessary fighting. Goat horns are considered primitive by comparison. They are not ornaments. They are lethal weapons.

My purpose in taking an extra look at interspecific dominance is that among naturalists the question is sometimes asked as to whether sheep will push goats off a range or the opposite will happen. The answer: under natural conditions, goats are going to find food efficiently, avoid predators, survive, and reproduce best in habitats with certain qualities; the more gregarious sheep are going to do the same in habitats with different qualities; and nobody is going to push anybody anywhere very far until the environment changes. Where the niches of the two have a common edge goats may enjoy first choice in the matter of food and shelter at times because of their slight dominance. Following a series of good growth years an expanding goat population could possibly usurp marginal sheep range this way, particularly if wolves are missing from the ecosystem. We might go on to predict that goat herds transplanted to states where other predators—grizzlies, cougars, wolverine, lynx—are rare or absent as well may become serious competitors of sheep on the moderately steep slopes sheep would ordinarily have to themselves for pasture.

A final consideration in goat–sheep relationships is contributed by William Samuel and his Canadian colleagues, who have found the two mountaineers to have approximately a dozen parasitic worms in common. The parasites may be transmitted back and forth between species on shared feeding grounds and at salt licks, though the extent to which this actually occurs is unknown. One class of these helminths known as protostrongylid lungworms is associated with epidemic pneumonia and large-scale die-offs in sheep, but appears to have relatively little harmful effect upon the goats. Samuel and his co-workers have speculated that this ability of the bearded beast to harbor parasites potentially destructive to a bovid competitor might play a role in limiting the number of sheep that can coexist with goats in an area over time. The same might be said in the case of other disease organisms. For example, contagious ecthyma has been observed in both goats and sheep, but sheep appear to be the more susceptible of the two.

The Meat-Eaters

Fish and Game Department officials in Alaska told me they believed wolves were preying on some goat herds in the coastal mountains, maybe heavily enough to make inroads on the goat population, but they needed better information. Chiefly because so few other big prey species are available over wide, snowbound stretches of British Columbia's Selkirk Mountains, it is assumed that the wolves there regularly hunt goats. Reports of wolves killing goats anywhere else the two species are found together are few and typically limited to subadult goats.

Cougars are wonderfully quick, strong, stealthy predators, at home in rock-rimmed country. Evidence of the big cats killing mountain goats comes from a number of different investigators. Traveling through open stands of timber close to goat cliffs I found goat carcasses bearing unmistakable marks of the puma's work: deep tooth punctures in the neck from the cat's favorite killing hold, and shoulder meat cleanly removed by its specialized flesh-shearing teeth, the carnassials.

Grizzlies are omnivores, and it comes as a surprise to many people that the majority of the great bear's diet consists of grasses, roots, bulbs, pine seeds, berries, and small insects. Still, they do hunt animals of all sizes. The deceptively bulky beast can accelerate fast and cover 160 feet in three seconds once it is going all out. Most of the chases of goats and sheep by grizzlies that I saw were unsuccessful. They were also short, unless there were any weak, sick, or injured stragglers among the fleeing groups.

A grizzly in the Swans ambushed three healthy yearlings I was watching ramble away from the rocks; it very nearly caught two of them, powering through deep early snow while the young goats desperately floundered back toward the cliff. In Glacier, another grizzly sprinted out after a nanny in an alpine meadow right along the Divide and swatted her dead within seconds.

Black bears have been seen chasing goats in open country and also attempting to waylay them in thick vegetation. But black bears are neither as strong or quick as Real Bear (the Blackfeet Indian name for Griz). Nor do they frequent the high country where Griz is present. Grizzlies claim the alpine habitats as part of their territories and defend them against all other bears of both species. Indeed, grizzlies have been known to kill and eat black bears. So, having nearly as much to fear from Griz as mountain goats do, black bears tend to stay near forested areas, where they too can make an escape by climbing—trees, in their case. (Real Bear lose their tree-climbing abilities as adults because their claws become too long and straight to hook into the bark of trees and support their weight; black bear claws stay short and strongly curved.)

Goats show no standard reaction to bears. Nannies with young kids are understandably the most sensitive to disturbance, and I sometimes saw them flee straight away for a quarter of a mile upon sensing a grizzly in the vicinity. On the other hand, I noticed bands that appeared content to share a wide meadow with a grizzly as long as the bear was busy feeding and stayed in plain view. As a rule, the white climbers showed greater concern over the presence of a grizzly than over the occasional black bears they spied near the cliffs.

Eagles elicit strong responses from goats. Any sudden rush of air overhead, whether from an eagle or passing blue grouse, is likely to cause a goat to press itself against the rock face or squat with its hindquarters on the ground, a position that gives it maximum resistance to being knocked over. I too have crouched or even taken bellyflops to avoid a hurtling eagle, for the big birds of prey stoop (a term for their wing-folded dive) at intruders near their nest, be they huge elk or goatwatcher.

While it was not always possible to tell territorial defense from hunting attacks when eagles stooped on goats, I did see the birds attempt to snatch young kids from a nanny's side. They also tried to bat older goats from precarious footholds so they could circle down and feed on the broken carcasses, which is how birds of prey have been observed killing chamois in Europe.

None of the hunts I happened to watch was effective, but there are several reliable reports of both golden and bald eagles taking baby goats. And a naturalist in Glacier once came upon the bodies of a one- or two-year-old billy and a golden eagle together below a cliff, the eagle's talons still gripping the goat and the young billy's horns embedded deep in its assailant.

Scanning the Swan ridgelines for goats one day during the summer he assisted me, Steve Shanewise found a golden eagle closing upon a year-ling deer. The eagle used its momentum to lift its prey by the flanks and spill it heels-over-head. In an instant the bird had shrouded the deer with its outstretched wings, six feet from tip to tip, and begun tearing with beak and claws. The deer struggled up, was struck down again by the eagle, ripped itself loose again, and staggered away out of view with the eagle chasing it. According to raptor specialist David Ellis, eagles in Russia were successfully trained to kill wolves.

It is not hard to understand why even big billies on safe, gentle slopes may trot a few steps and toss their horns when the eagle's shadow brushes them. After a golden eagle landed in a nearby snag, one of my collared nannies and a second adult female charged toward the tree and then planted their forefeet up against the trunk as though they would climb it if they could. They kept pawing the trunk and shaking their horns until the raptor glided away. Other people have seen the same sort of behavior, and Brandborg recorded an episode in which it worked against the goat:

> At 4:15 a bald eagle flew by the cliffs on which two nannies, two kids, and a yearling had been feeding. One of the nannies crowded close to her kid as the bird circled 25 feet above them. The eagle then dove within a few feet to land on a pinnacle of rock ten feet above the cliff face. The nanny left the kid and started up the cliff toward the eagle and was within five feet of the bird when it jumped from its perch and flew over her, picked up the kid, and sailed out over the cliff. . . . The kid, which was only a few days old, probably weighed less than seven pounds.

Eagles are certainly the most visible predator in goat country and are really the only one that can harry the white climber at will within its rocky fortress. Golden eagles nest on the very walls and turrets of the fortress and rely upon cliff-deflected winds to carry them in search of unwary marmots, ground squirrels, and other quarry. There were six active golden eagle nests in my 120-square-mile Glacier study area, and bald eagles, which nested at lower elevations near lakes and river-bottoms, hunted the goat rocks from time to time.

Each fall in Glacier the handful of resident bald eagles are joined by southward migrating bald eagles for a feast on spawning Kokanee salmon (an introduced fish species) along McDonald Creek, a tributary to the Flathead River near the southwest edge of the park. The result is the densest temporary concentration in the lower 48 states of the birds we have chosen for our nation's symbol. At present between 500 and 1,000 arrive for the annual banquet.

I remember hiking along a crisp, reddish, late October trail in Glacier when the peaks of the Divide were holding back the surge of a storm-blue cloud bank from the east. The pass was filled with streaming mist, but through it, unerringly, through that tumult of winds and vapors, came eagle after eagle after white-headed eagle, wings partly folded for stability in the rush and lash of air. When they were through it, those wings would catch the western sun and open full. Each eagle seemed to pause and float for an endless moment over the center of the upper valley before trimming its wings again and beginning a long, effortless glide down toward the stream where salmon thickened the water.

I had work to do many miles down the trail that day. Yet by evening I was still sitting propped up against my pack, close to where I had seen the first eagle, and still eagles burst out of the storm, extended their wings, and drifted down through the late golden light.

I was able to learn about the goat's defenses against predators both by recording their occasional encounters with carnivores and by stalking goats myself in the Swans, where the herds were hunted by people and generally quite wary of me. Since each instance had its peculiarities it may be best to draw them together into a composite picture.

Let's start at the bottom, the predator's usual position on the mountainside relative to a goat. Ledges are visually broken habitats, and at times their arrangement can be employed for concealment. But predators using them usually choose the easiest, most open routes, where they are exposed to the sharp-eyed scrutiny of goats, which I often saw tracking my movements when I was at least a mile away across a valley. Nor is it easy for a predator to conceal its scent, because air currents swirl and shift through the tilted terrain, and a sudden blast of wind will set up eddies likely to carry its smell upward to the goat's nostrils even when the general wind direction is in the predator's favor.

An adult billy, most of his winter coat shed, on a mountainside in Glacier National Park.
All photographs are by the author unless otherwise credited.

Above: *A kid takes to the air during a play session with its fellows.*

Right: *Already at ease on steep terrain, this kid is about one month old. Pregnancy has delayed shedding in its nanny.*

On a flat meadow, a kid uses its nanny as climbing terrain. Karen Reeves.

A band of goats traverses one of Glacier's steep, stratified cliffsides.

Peaks and high basins along the Continental Divide reveal the sculpting action of glaciers past and present.

A wide-angle lens produced this view of a billy descending a steep slope.

A two-year-old female follows an adult female up lichen-splotched ledges.

A golden eagle, an occasional predator of goats.

Two white-tailed deer watch alertly as a grizzly forages nearby.

A Rocky Mountain bighorn bedded down in an insulating blanket of snow; Oreamnos *often does likewise.*

A mule deer buck with its antlers in summer velvet.

Molting from summer brown to winter white, a white-tailed ptarmigan is camouflaged against rock and snow.

A hoary marmot chooses to avoid further investigation by its large neighbor.

The normal activities of mountain goats are interspersed with behavior patterns that have developed as anti-predator devices. These include: the habit of raising the head to look around at intervals when feeding; a proclivity for walking on the outside edge of ledges and overhanging snow cornices to gain a better view of the situation below; pausing on high vantage points during feeding and traveling to gaze for long periods and test the wind before going on; the selection of bedsites that overlook the landscape and have a high wall behind them; a routine of carefully surveying their surroundings for several minutes before bedding down; and rising and turning every half hour or so to scan the terrain anew and then re-bedding to face a different direction than before (though this is probably for the sake of relieving stiffness too).

There is really only one major weak spot in the cliff-hugging goat's sentry system: The winter-colored beast pays remarkably little attention to what goes on above it. In the first place goats have slight bony ridges above their eyes, so their vision naturally encompasses less in that direction. Secondly, debris and larger rocks or hunks of snow and ice are constantly clattering down from above, and the goat learns to tune them out. If the wind held right I could prowl to within springing distance over their heads seven or eight times out of ten, in part because when I accidentally loosed small showers of talus and snow the goats paid little heed to them. Lastly, the goat, whose entire lifestyle is directed toward making it the highest large creature on the slopes at any given time, ordinarily does not *need* to do more than keep a sharp lookout below itself and a wall to its back that only it can climb.

Suppose a predator has made it through the goat's outer defenses and up onto the ledges, and the climber discovers that there is unwelcome company close by. Kids immediately rush to their mother's side or beneath her legs when still small enough. Other band members meanwhile draw tightly together. This gives smaller and weaker animals a certain amount of protection, because an attack upon them may be repulsed by a stronger goat which considers itself the intended prey.

If the hunter has not yet made its move the goat(s) may actually approach the enemy instead of running away. This seems an oddly inappropriate response. But the goat's chances of escaping depend upon its mountaineering techniques and familiarity with the local lay of the rocks rather than upon speed. It may only be one or two breathtaking steps and a leap away from safety. So it is to the climber's advantage to know precisely what confronts it and where it lurks. I could lure goats fairly close by shrinking behind a rock and waving a handkerchief or revealing just an elbow or a foot at a time. The same trick works well with prong-horn antelope, which are also given to approaching predators. I've watched them follow coyotes for a quarter of a mile. Fleetest of the continent's large mammals, pronghorn can sustain a speed of around 40 miles an hour and raise that to over 50 miles per hour for a brief time, if pressed. They know they can outdistance anything that doesn't take them by surprise, just as a mountain goat can outclimb anything.

Once satisfied that it knows the nature and location of the threat, the goat will walk away slowly and deliberately, as if it were in no hurry at all, until just out of view. Then it bounds and scrambles away at full tilt.

From playing with a cat or dog, you may have noticed that they are apt to stop stalking something and pounce or begin running after it the moment the object makes a sudden motion. Rapid movement such as the breakaway flight of a prey animal is a powerful stimulus for a predator to switch into full attack mode. This is why the best advice for someone encountering a bear at close quarters is, instead of stampeding away, to stand in place and then perhaps slowly back off. And it is why the goat acts so calm until out of sight. Slow, steady movements are an attempt to avoid triggering the chasing response and thus gain a few precious seconds and yards, once the sure-footed climber has decided upon an escape route. I'm not sure whether this behavior is wholly instinctual or partly conscious and learned.

Then try and catch it. You aren't sure whether the goat has gone ahead, straight up, or half-leaped, half-fallen down some seamless chimney. Its first jumps may have placed it among stone facets so sheer and blocky you can't see more than a dozen feet. The goat may suddenly appear directly overhead, then vanish again like the mountain spirit it is. Again you have few clues as to which way to follow. The predator's nose might be able to indicate the general direction, but a goat in its home range knows every shortcut.

Suppose that despite all its maneuverings the goat finds itself cornered, or that it discovered its enemy too late to run and climb. Or that it elected not to flee at all. The goat is a formidable enemy itself. I once made the mistake of assuming a 14-month-old yearling billy in my trap would be easy to throw and collar; he stabbed me three times before I got a hand on him. A half-dozen different times when I surprised an adult goat at close quarters on the cliffs it turned on me at once with lowered horns. A couple of the billies assumed tensely arched threat postures and began stamping in my direction.

Hunting guides in the Bob Marshall—who, in my experience, make their living partly by their skill in finding animals for their clients to shoot and partly by their talent at spinning good stories when they can't come up with the animals—told me they have seen pairs of wolverines working together to kill young goats. I've no doubt the wolverine does deserve some of its reputation for ferocity. One ran me into a lake in Glacier. Another chased a park employee off a roof he was shoveling. The great naturalist Adolph Murie, who spun stories you can believe, tells of seeing a wolverine chase an Alaskan grizzly off a carcass.

Yet I several times saw one or two wolverines approach goats with the following results: the little goats shouldered up against the big goats; the big goats lowered their rapiers while snorting and stamping, and then began marching toward the wolverines; the wolverines left to try their luck elsewhere. It was the same each time I saw a pair or small family of coyotes confront goats. The Canadian naturalist Claude Guiguet described a wolverine one minute chasing a goat band and the next being lifted on a horn and tossed down the mountainside. The strength a goat possesses in its neck and shoulders is suggested by the ability of one adult to lift another and more or less throw the animal over its back. Both Hutchins and Stevens saw this more than once among goats contending for salt in Olympic National Park.

A lynx I saw stalking a billy made the right move coming from above, and reached a position from which it could pounce, still undetected. But it hesitated, perhaps unwilling to risk anything but a perfect opening, because the billy was three years old, nearly full size. The cat shifted its weight, and the billy saw it. At first he backed up against a corner. Then he returned and began stamping. Soon he was jumping up and hooking the air below the cat. The lynx settled for dangling its paw here and there over the ledge for a while and then ambled away with its curious high-rumped walk.

Brandborg, Seton, and various others mention mountain goats killing dogs. I was told by a reliable woodsman and expert bowhunter, Jack Whitney of Bigfork, Montana, about a Swan Mountains billy attacked by hounds originally on the scent of a cougar. The billy made his stand with his back against a cul-de-sac, and by the time the dogs' owner arrived on the scene nearly all of his pack had been skewered. It stands to reason that an adult goat or a band containing adults is not entirely at the mercy of a wolf pack. Early in this century the eminent naturalist William Hornaday described an incident in which a goat mortally punctured a grizzly, and similar accounts—some more believable than others—keep cropping up every so often.

Hooved animals are typically most susceptible to predation during late winter, when they are confined by deep snow and many are in weakened condition, and during the birth season. But most mountain goat herds are on fairly steep cliffs fully 90 percent of the time throughout winter. And in the birth season that figure may reach 100 percent for the vulnerable nannies and newborn kids.

I never saw any predator habitually combing the goat rocks except, of course, eagles. Hundreds of hours of goatwatching would pass without my seeing even a single four-footed goat enemy there. Moreover, I would go weeks at a time in winter without picking up any big carnivore track in the snow among the ledges (which also told me that nighttime hunters weren't working the area either).

Apart from the still undefined impact of wolves on goats in parts of Alaska, no one has yet reported evidence that any predator does look regularly to the mountain goat as a source of protein. Any predator that did would be unlikely to keep its stomach filled with much besides hunger pangs—assuming it didn't get the end of a horn there first. This is not to dismiss the combined impact of the various high-country hunters that will snag a goat when a good opportunity presents itself. In many regions those opportunities come chiefly during the snow-free months, when the goats' use of non-cliff habitats such as meadows and talus slopes for feeding and traveling increases markedly.

The goats themselves tell us that the farther they stray from the ledges, the greater their risk of getting hit. Watch a solitary nanny cross an old glacial moraine grown up into a rolling meadow with copses of wind-warped fir. Her customarily steady pace is replaced by a skittish half-trot, interrupted by abrupt halts and reconnoitering. The least disturbance—a bird call or the scurrying of a marmot—causes her to jump. Her tail is out now, and she trots on, spurting into a full gallop as she shies around a tree clump full of shadows. The rare goat in a closed forest has all the self-assurance of a child in a haunted house.

With this last sentence it becomes clear that I've been generalizing for a couple of pages at the expense of the forest-wintering coastal goat ecotype. These seaboard populations could hardly afford a phobia about dense trees. As discussed in the preceding chapter, their low-elevation winter ranges, while generally plenty steep and rugged, often lack broad, continuous, open cliff exposures. The animals then have to make do with less secure fragments of rocky escape cover and carry out more of their activities under a closed forest canopy. The deeper the snows, the farther the goats may have to descend into marginal terrain, and the more they probably constitute an important exception to the white climber's relative isolation from carnivores such as wolves and cougars over the cold months.

To be able to measure predation, the field biologist usually has to decide how much weight to give secondhand or circumstantial information. Cougar and lynx prefer fresh meat to carrion, but many other carnivores, including the noble eagle, are dedicated scavengers. So, does the small white leg hanging over the rim of an eagle nest mean the kid was carried off alive, or simply that it was lying crumpled and unmoving when the bird spotted it far below some seamless slab that the young goat had tried to force a route across, making its first and last bad climbing judgement? Long white hairs in coyote droppings told me only that these "brush wolves" had been feeding upon a goat, not whether they had killed it. If anything, an abundance of fur in the feces points to scavenging, because most carnivores are satisfied with the meat and fat from a fresh kill.

Possibly as a legacy from our own scavenging past, the human nose is amazingly sensitive to ethyl mercaptan, the essence of rotting meat. Our otherwise undistinguished organ of smell can detect one four-hundred-billionth of a gram—a few molecules—of the compound in a liter of air. Several times I sniffed my way to a dead goat only to discover that it was accompanied by a grizzly; and, with the bear straddling the corpse and pointing its nose my way, I had no choice but to backpedal and write down: "Refused permission to make close investigation." Griz will drag a carcass some distance to a convenient spot where it can rest and feed at its leisure, concealed from other scavengers. So, sometimes you can't even be sure of where a goat died, much less of what did it in in the first place.

Taking direct and indirect evidence together, it appears that predators have more than a negligible effect on mountain goat numbers, but not very much more in most regions. The picture could change somewhat as data from radio telemetry studies accumulate. The little, light-boned carcasses of first-year goats—the class that experiences the highest mortality—have a way of vanishing without a trace, and it might be especially revealing to monitor a large sample of kids by radio. Nevertheless, I would not look for the overall picture to change very much.

In the course of its evolution *Oreamnos* climbed away from most of its hunters, and it escaped them fairly successfully, as it did most of its competitors. With the possible exception of the musk-ox, I can think of no North American ungulate species that is less subject to predation and competition—or, it seems, to serious disease—than the mountain goat.

In leaving so many of its large neighbors below, the white goat came face to face with the unyielding cliffs and the extreme weather conditions of the upper elevations. It is a narrow niche, and such predation and competition as goats still experience act to keep them there, between the rock and the mountain winter. We saw in Chapter 2 that the goat's anatomy and climbing skills are a match for these rocks above the angle of repose. In our search for the natural factors that most effectively control the increase or decrease of mountain goat populations, therefore, we have narrowed the list toward the subject of the next chapter—the long season of snow and cold.

A Lost Tribe

So closely have some of the large, powerful wild beasts of our continent become associated with the mountains of the West and the wildspans of the Far North, it is all too possible to forget that little more than two centuries ago—a microsecond on geological and evolutionary clocks— there were wolves in St. Louis. A little over three centuries ago, there were bison in Washington D.C. Millennia after the empires of Egypt and Greece had flourished and decayed, the Great Age of Mammals continued in North America. The Indians lived within it. And in that epoch, so few generations of Americans ago, when a rainstorm could pass across miles of a single herd of bison and many more miles of that herd would be dry, cougar stalked the tall grasses of Georgia, elk grazed the banks of the Mississippi, and Griz ambled through Kansas and would gather by the score on the beaches of California to feast upon a beached whale carcass.

They and lynx and wolverine are not the species they were a short time back. We have changed their evolutionary course overnight, making them mountain and northern mammals by default. We did not, as some say, "push" them there like refugees. We exterminated them and disrupted their natural habitats everywhere else, leaving those small fractions of continental populations that had been living in places like goat country all along. It is worth keeping this in mind when thinking over the subject of neighbors, the more so when you consider that goat country too is now changing lightning-fast on the geological and evolutionary clock, due to intensified resource development.

A perfect example of a beast missing from so much of its original homeland that we have forgotten where it really belongs is the final mountain goat neighbor I want to introduce in this wide-angle chapter —the mountain race of woodland caribou.

Reindeer and caribou belong to the same holarctic species, *Rangifer tarandus*. North America has five native caribou subspecies, all of them closely tied to habitats with abundant lichen, their chief food source. Four of them live in tundra regions of the arctic. The fifth is the woodland caribou, largest, darkest, and least sociable of the subspecies. It finds its lichen in boggy, old-growth forests of the boreal zone, which stretches across Canada and down into the northern tier of states.

Before the turn of the century viable populations of woodland caribou lived year round in Washington, Idaho, Montana (including the Glacier Park and Swan Mountains areas), Minnesota, Michigan, Wisconsin, Maine, New Hampshire, Vermont, and possibly upstate New York. Unrestricted shooting, together with clearing of mature forests for timber and agricultural use, eliminated the last caribou from New England by 1910 and from the Great Lakes by the 1940s.

A related factor may have contributed to their demise. In somewhat the same way that mountain goats harbor parasites that afflict sheep more seriously, seemingly healthy white-tailed deer carry a protostrongylid worm that is deadlier than wolves to a caribou, affecting membranes around the brain—the meninges. As the old-growth forests were cleared, meadows and brushfields grew up in their stead and provided plentiful habitat for the white-tails, which are adapted to transitional plant communities. Deer populations boomed, and with them burgeoned the parasite fatal to caribou.

The caribou of western forests are recognized as a distinct race, being still darker than other woodland caribou and even less gregarious, traveling in small family-sized bands or as solitary individuals except in the fall rutting season. Their common name of mountain caribou derives from their preference for mature spruce–fir or cedar–hemlock forests above 4,500 feet or so.

They stay there year round. I've caught up with them at 6,500 feet in late winter on a snowpack ten feet deep. They cope with such an environment by snowshoeing across an extensive range on their huge, widespreading hooves (all caribou have this sort of footgear). Their food? Lichens, as usual, but in this case arboreal lichens, the thready wisps and nets that hang from tree branches and are often called old man's beard or—erroneously—tree mosses.

Their thoroughly unique and fascinating lifestyle occasionally brings them into contact with mountain goats and sheep where the subalpine forests adjoin steep and rocky winter ranges. These different mountaineers are likely to meet again in summer when all three are foraging in alpine meadows.

British Columbia holds the largest number of mountain caribou, but populations have dwindled throughout the province as a result of overshooting, backcountry roadbuilding—which makes them more accessible, and clearcut logging at high altitudes—which does away with essential caribou habitat wholesale. Alberta has some mountain caribou as well. And though not one person in a thousand realizes it, so do the contiguous states.

The caribou populations native to Washington, Idaho, and Montana—naturalist Olaus Murie collected a report of caribou in northwestern

Wyoming in the late 1800s—have shrunk to exactly one herd of at most 25 to 30 individuals roaming the Selkirk Mountains, where a mountain goat population is also found. At any given time, slightly under half of this caribou group will be in the northern Idaho and northeastern Washington portions of the Selkirks and the rest will be in the British Columbia portion. In other words, we currently have an average U.S. caribou population (outside Alaska) of about 10, according to Idaho biologist Donald Johnson, who has directed most of the studies on this herd. When delighted biologists discovered new colonies of black-footed ferrets in Wyoming during 1982, the caribou assumed the distinction of being the rarest native mammal in the lower 48 states.

As late as the 1960s the estimate for caribou on the U.S. side of the Selkirks stood at 50 to 100. Our last herd is clearly in trouble. Yet virtually no one knows about it. At the mention of caribou today our imagination leaps aboard a dogsled and goes mushing away to the frozen North— missing our homegrown group by a couple of thousand miles. Year after year, more roads and clearcuts penetrated the high, old-growth forests left to this herd, while official protection and funds for research and management remained meager.

In January of 1983, as I was revising this book, the Interior Department at last threw the caribou of the lower 48 a lifeline: emergency designation as an endangered species. Now we will see if these mountain goat neighbors still have the strength to grab it.

CHAPTER FIVE

The Yearly Ice Age

SOMETIMES THE BEST thing you can say about a winter day is that it was short.

Beth and I were carrying a load of gear the final miles uphill toward our Little Creek outpost in the Swans. We had been gone from this camp nearly three weeks and were anxious to catch up with the lives of the members of the goat herd wintering across the valley. It was January. As seems to be usual for this part of the Rockies, the first real thaw had arrived not long after the New Year and begun to settle the waist-deep powder that had been stacking up, loose and light as eiderdown, since October.

Now at last there was a good base for skiing. But halfway to camp all the warm clouds from the west piled together into a soggy, concrete-colored mess and sank to ground level. Soon rain was leaking steadily through our parka seams and down our necks. Day turned to dusk before 4:30. We pitched a pup tent along the logging road that was our trail and fell asleep to the drear, muffled sounds of water drops pelting snow.

When we awakened in the morning our tent fly was stiff as tin. So were our boots; we had to pound the leather to get them on and step outside. Outside stung. Outside had become 10 degrees (F) below zero and was clearly on its way to something colder.

It was nearing evening and −25 degrees before we reached the Little Creek outpost. Here stood an eight-by-ten-foot canvas tent stretched over a lodgepole frame and covered by plastic sheeting, which helped keep wind and weather out while holding heat from our small woodburning stove in. Around the stove were a lodgepole table, a lodgepole bed with a mattress of dried grass and spruce boughs, metal chests full of grub, a gas lantern, books, cards, and a cribbage board. Here, in short, stood the most splendid luxury in many a tall, frostbitten mile. Except that we could not find any of it.

Although we had shoveled the campsite right down to frozen earth before departing, less than three weeks of storm and drift on the mountainside had completely covered the eight-foot-high tent, leaving us to stare across a perfectly smooth, blank slope. In the northern distance the last pale arctic light evaporated from the peaks of the Great Bear Wilderness.

We cut a long pole and began probing beneath the surface of this landscape where everything was familiar yet everything was changed. Beneath the surface of my consciousness I felt that the tent's burial was a message: You are not welcome back. You don't belong up here. But sometime around −30° the probe struck home. Once the stovepipe was shoveled free we tunneled down like weasels and slid in through the door. The sagging tent was a frost palace, rimed with crystals, and we cooked a royal dinner while candlelight skated over the melting ice. That night, 24 hours after the rainstorm, the temperature reached 40° below.

Minus 40 happens to be about the lowest temperature natural antifreeze compounds in woody plants can counter. The trees and shrubs found in subarctic and subalpine regions are those that are able to remove much of the water from cells in the vital cambium layer, where growth and nutrient transport occur, and store it in intervening spaces. This way, when supernumb weather does crystallize the liquid, causing it to expand, cell walls will not be burst from within.

The boreal species endure when the mercury contracts toward the bottom of the thermometer, but not without a lot of cracking and banging as water in other tissues and in dead heartwood freezes up. The vast silence of a winter forest is overtaken by an eerie sound rather like running gunfire from an unseen enemy.

The air itself smells brittle, foreign. You realize that it is, after all, 78 percent nitrogen and laced with helium, argon, ozone, and neon, among other gases—and is 138.6 Fahrenheit degrees colder than your body. When you can spit and see your saliva turn to frothy ice before it hits the ground you also realize that the margin for error has grown awfully small. There is no slack left in anything. You are not going to get to screw up very seriously and still stay liquid.

The nearest plowed road from our Swan outposts was 25 miles or so west and across the wrinkled Swan divide. The closest human habitation in any other direction was about 60 miles distant. We had no radio contact; the topography blocked transmissions. We did have a snowmachine, a tremendously noisy tanklike affair we sometimes used to transport stores of food and equipment over snowbound logging roads. It could conceivably have taken us the 70 or 80 road miles down the South Fork of the Flathead to town in an emergency, though its top speed was about ten miles an hour under the best snow conditions, and it had days when it didn't want to go anywhere.

From time to time Forest Service rangers came into the country to run a snow depth survey or mark timber, and stayed over at the Spotted Bear station, which was only 15 to 30 miles from the various cliffs we were working. We saw them three or four times between late fall and spring. They were the only people we saw.

For the most part we were completely alone and dependent upon ourselves. I worried about safety. I still do. I worry more that it will become harder and harder in this nation for any person to enjoy as much sparkling freedom over as wide a stretch of uncrowded backcountry as we did that winter. The only things we really could have used out there were a few more calories of heat.

Despite our elaborate camping gadgets and clothing, a few days' stay on mountain goat range during ice-gripped windy weather is so exhausting for us naked apes that we have trouble getting any sort of intuitive sense of how the white climbers can contend week after week with still more demanding conditions.

The first thing to bear in mind is that the goats, like most mammals, are operating with a somewhat different engine than we are. They breathe faster. Their heart beats more rapidly. Their body temperature is approximately four degrees above ours, which means certain chemical reactions are proceeding at a much livelier pace.

In addition to metabolic heat generated by its muscle tissues and internal organs, a goat benefits from what is known as heat of fermentation. This comes from the processing of food by the bacteria and protozoans in its ruminant digestive track, particularly the vatlike rumen itself. Anyone with a compost pile is aware that microbial action can put out a considerable amount of thermal energy. In effect the beast is cooking with gas, enjoying a measure of free heat while you shiver and hop around rubbing your arms, wondering how it can just lie there in this blue norther of a cold snap.

Meanwhile the long, plush double coat of fur with its countless dead air pockets is greatly slowing down the flow of that body heat away from the goat via radiation, convection, and evaporative cooling. The thick hide plus subcutaneous fat deposited during late summer and fall form another layer of insulation.

Our thin, naked skin, by contrast, seems to have been originally designed for unloading heat in a hurry, primarily through the evaporative cooling of perspiration. We have such an abundance of sweat glands and pores that our skin remains moist even when cold. Continued evaporative cooling is thus the main contributor to the wind chill factor that turns the breeze we welcome in summer into a bitter enemy in winter.

With just a ten-mile-an-hour wind, −20°F becomes the equivalent of −45°F on the surface of our flesh, −30° equal to −58°. A 50-mile-an-hour gale such as blows across the high ridges makes −20°F effectively −88° while −30° becomes an outer-galactic −103°, and so on. Remember, though, that these figures, announced so dramatically by weather forecasters (someone once said wind chill is ordinary cold with a press agent), apply specifically to the exposed hide of man. They mean relatively little to a mountain goat, which has very few sweat glands and whose dense fur covers everything but its muzzle and hooves.

What about those hooves, however? I could mentally wrap myself in a goat coat and feel reasonably comfortable, but I could never imagine how *Oreamnos* or other mountain ungulates manage to keep their toes and slender, bony lower legs warm. As it turns out, they don't.

Neither the hair on the leg nor the horny nail material of the hoof itself nor the thick epidermal sole of the traction pads is actually living tissue, any more than are our hair, nails, or flaking, outermost skin. Consequently, no harm is done to the exposed surfaces of the lower leg when they come in contact with freezing rock, snow, or air. Inside, there is less muscle around the foot bones than tendons, cartilage, and ligaments, all built of fibrous connective tissue. This is tough, fairly dry, gristly stuff and can do its mechanical work warm or chill.

Not having twenty pulpy, sensitive primate fingers and toes to worry about, the hooved animal opts for chill. Its circulatory system delivers just enough blood to the lower limbs to keep them alive. The rest is rapidly returned to the hot body cavity via anastamoses—connections that shunt blood directly from arteries to veins, bypassing the small and more sluggish capillary network. The result is a substantial savings in heat that would otherwise be lost through the extremities. Wading birds and members of the penguin family, among other creatures, conserve warmth in like fashion. Consider the example of the emperor penguin: without anastamoses to short-circuit the blood flow to its big, naked, webbed feet the creature would soon have all the fire drawn out of its body by the ice it stands on.

Certain kinds of behavior assist anatomy to minimize heat loss. Snow itself is a good insulator against subzero temperatures. Montana's grizzlies typically hibernate on north-facing slopes at high altitudes, where a deep, lingering snow cover will form an extra thermal barrier for their earthen den. Mice, lemmings, and the rest of the goat's small neighbors that remain active at upper elevations through the winter suffer heavy losses in the rare years when there is little or no snowpack to burrow into for shelter.

If you want to burrow into a hillside, you will find that, no matter how polar the conditions outside, a snow cave stays about 35° to 40°F with you in it—a bit clammy but always a handy emergency bivouac.

Mountain goats paw a deep bed in the snow at times for protection from the weather. They also use natural caves and clefts in the rock for shelter, and often bed wedged beneath a low, overhanging ledge. When I went looking for a place to hole up on the cliffs, the refuge I found would more often than not be carpeted with a deep accumulation of goat pellets.

The white climbers characteristically bed with their legs tucked up against or under the warm body in winter, whereas in warmer weather they assume more sprawling, heat-dissipating positions. And yet a goat occasionally surprised me by casually stretching out on an open point in the teeth of an arctic storm. Overall, I was impressed by how seldom the goats altered their daily routines as a concession to blasting wind or crackling cold.

Given its physical specializations, *Oreamnos* can function at full capacity in all but the very worst weather that comes its way—as long as it can keep its engine stoked with adequate food. The availability of food depends upon the other major aspect of the high country winter, the one that buried our tent. It is snow depth that exerts the most profound influence upon mountain goat behavior and survival. Wind and temperature should be regarded more as accessories, important to the goat chiefly as they add or subtract snow from various parts of the mountainside.

Winters and summers in the high mountains are like brief re-enactments of the advances and retreats of the glaciers that shaped the bearded beast. Goats typically spend the warm months dispersed over the uppermost rocky reaches of drainages and then, while autumn snow deepens, contract toward a few generally south-facing cliffs as far down the valley as sufficiently steep outcroppings can be found. For some herds this may involve a migration of up to 10 or 15 miles. For others it is simply a straight drop down the same slope. The seasonal move takes most of them from the alpine zone to other cliffs nearer treeline or farther down into the forest zone.

Warmer air temperature is the main advantage of heading downhill. A

3°F gain for every 1,000-foot decrease in elevation is the rule of thumb. This translates into both less total snowfall and more frequent melting of the snow that does land. In the Pacific region, where the climate is moderated by the ocean, both the coastal goat ecotype and some of the herds living farther to the east can climb down completely below snow line during a mild winter to cliffs receiving only sleet and rain.

South-facing exposures are almost always more thawed out than other slopes as a result of direct solar heating. The steepness of a cliff also significantly influences its snow-shedding capacities. The closer it tilts toward vertical, the narrower its ledges, the less room there is for snow to build up, and the faster wind, melting, and sheer gravity carry away whatever snow tries to cling there—just as they do any other loose material above the angle of repose. Moreover, proportionately greater areas of bare, vertical rock surface are exposed to absorb solar radiation.

I can recall watching a coat of mine—a very nice, warm, expensive coat of mine—sail three miles up and over the Continental Divide. For all I know it finally settled onto the head of an Iowa farmer, who now believes in miracles. I've run into still stronger waves of mountain wind that toppled me backward like a shallow-rooted tree and made waterfalls cascade uphill. Pacific-spawned air masses intercepted by Glacier's ramparts are forced up the west slopes, cool as they rise, then sink down the east slope in invisible torrents, periodically raging up to 100 miles an hour —hurricane force.

Winds like these clearly have a lot to say about where snow collects and where it doesn't. Swirled and funneled by local topographic features, they might whisk most of the snowpack off an entire mountainside or bare up just one piece of one promontory while heaping drifts over the rest. The treeless upper elevations tend to get smacked the hardest, with the curious result that a few high cliffs and ridgelines and occasionally the very summit of a peak or plateau may be left virtually snowless when all the world below seems to be drowning in white flakes.

The importance of such windblown sites as feeding areas for many herds breaks the rules about what sort of slope you can expect the white climbers to choose during the cold months. That's fine—it means they have more options for survival. A few herds end up wintering as high or higher than they summer.

Every so often Beth and I would take climbing rope and ice axes and work our way up the cliffs to have a close-up look at goat winter range. Beth was the botanist; she collected all the local plants in summer and spent weeks tweezing them apart under a hand lens next to an assortment of identification manuals.

In case you've never experienced one, a technical plant identification book is organized as a series of multiple-choice guessing games that you almost always lose. Does it have a this? No. A that? No. A them? Yes. Go to 42a. "Spikes 7 to 9, androgynous; perigynia unequally biconvex." Is it? No. Are they? No. Spikes 12 to 16? Yes!! Now, only half an hour into this specimen, you are ready to choose between 78 f, g, and h. "Corolla campanulate; filaments pilose-appended at base." Hah! Yes again. "Stem tall, solitary, 4–10 cm high; peduncles strict." Can it be, at last? I mean, talk about your strict peduncles. (The ruler trembles in your hand.) Amazingly strict! By the hair of the Jolly Green Giant, it's . . . it's . . . *Phyllotaxus obscurum!* Oh Joy! Oh Science! Oh Wait a minute. The rootstalks are supposed to be glandular-puberulent. Well, maybe . . . Ummmm. Says here *Phyllotaxus* doesn't much grow outside the Mojave Desert . . . and so on.

Beth eventually cornered the proper name of each species, though, and through her eyes I began to recognize key plants on the goat cliffs, then the make-up of plant communities. A time came when I ceased to see the vegetation in static terms and could sense slopes in transition, the flux of invading species in disturbed habitats, the dynamic balance of forces in a climax forest or alpine tundra—not expertly, but well enough.

One of Beth's specific projects was to find out which kinds of food were available on different parts of the winter range and which the goats were actually selecting to eat.

Where the angle of a ledge-tiered slope was moderate the snow was generally deep: knee-high on the flatter sections, chest-high and ready to avalanche in the ravines and couloirs. Mountain goats, with their massive forequarters and wide-spreading hooves, are strong pawers willing to take on major excavation projects. Given their niche, they have to be. They stomp, rake, push, pull, and throw snow aside with their feet, shove it aside with their muzzle, and dig it out from under the edge of icy crusts.

Following fresh tracks from feeding crater to feeding crater we found mostly snipped clumps of various grasses in the bottoms. Sedges, which stay green under the snow, were not as abundant on the ledges, but once the goats struck part of a patch, they went out of their way to uncover the rest of it.

That symbiotic relationship between mammal and microbe that we call the ruminant digestive system has a genius for manufacturing many of its own energy-rich fatty acids, carbohydrates, and even B-vitamins from little more than dry cellulose. Many human cultures and a whopping part of their economies are based upon this symbiosis, this natural economy. Nevertheless, both our domesticated ruminants and, to an even greater degree, wild ruminants need some ready-made nutrients from their forage to maintain the bacterial colonies that in turn maintain the mammal in good condition. Thus, fresh green plants high in protein and minerals, such as sedge, are especially valuable items in the winter diet.

We could see that the goats had also snipped off the outer twigs, or "leaders," of mountain ash, serviceberry, chokecherry, and mountain maple bushes, all of which are good protein sources. Shrubs generally grow best on broad ledges and talus fields around the cliffs. These sites offer deeper soil suitable to woody plant growth, but by the same token they collect a thicker snowpack than the narrow ledges. Although the leaders protruded above the snow, it was even harder work for man and beast to plow from one bush to the next than between feeding craters, unless weather conditions produced unusually firm snow or crusts. Sooner or later, then, the hoofprints we were following would lead us on toward steeper, less snow-muffled cliff sections.

Now we were in prime winter goat range, where increased climbing risks bring the rewards of a better exposed food supply. In a niche with a six to eight-month winter regime, this is the fulcrum of the bearded beast's ecological balance.

Roped together, we inspected feeding sites near the outer rim of ledges. The snow was thinnest here. Melted back a bit from the rock face below it and tapered down by winds, the snow was only about six inches deep altogether, while far below in the mountain valleys the elk and deer waded through a snowpack already several feet thick.

From the tracks we could tell where a goat had briefly pawed, fed, and then braced its padded feet to lean out over the sky and pluck bunchgrass stalks from a cranny just below the rim of the ledge. Soon afterward the goat had turned around and nibbled a small fern from another cranny, this one in the rock face above the ledge. At one point the beast reared up and pawed loose a cushion of club mosses (*Selaginella*—not a true moss, but a primitive vascular plant) from the edge of the upper ledge, seeking the green inner fronds. Then it was back on all fours pawing through a foot of snow for more grasses and the occasional sedge or dried herb.

A belay and an ice-axe crawl farther on we found a few smallish serviceberry bushes with a grim roothold on the rocks. The story told by their ragged tips was that the shrubs had been worked over once earlier in the season, and our guide had cropped them again and stripped the bark off some larger stems as well.

No matter how severe the angle of an outcropping, there will come whiteout storms that inter its ledges with foot after foot of fresh powder crystals. Or there will come thick, moist, sticking snows, and then crusts like plaster to lock up everything beneath them. It may be days or weeks before any of the stormpack starts to loosen and slip away.

In the meantime the goats are faced with as much or more digging and

active, following a long mobile snout under the snow toward its next meal. As it happened, El Gordo's snout led it through the tent one day and over to the food dish of Kobuk, the Finicky Malemute, our semi-loyal dog. Nirvana! Whether Kobuk had lain and watched snowflakes all day or mushed ten miles behind us carrying his dogpack, he never once finished what was put in his bowl.

For weeks thereafter the Return of El Gordo to the trough was prime-time entertainment in the goat camp. Shrews have a metabolism like a miniature nuclear meltdown and need to eat their weight in one thing or another so often they would starve to death if they stopped to catch a few solid hours of sleep. The number of overweight shrews in the world is therefore limited, which tells you something of the devoted effort required on El Gordo's part to inflate to squash ball proportions before abruptly disappearing, never to return.

By way of other diversions, we always had snow to shovel to keep the tent and woodpile clear. We built snowmen, snow goats, more snowmen, and had approximately 5,000 snowball fights, some inside the tent for variety. Just as terminal numbness and boredom was approaching whomever had telescope duty, a timely snowball would arrive in the back of the neck, and the chase was on once more.

Sliding like otters downhill in our slick snowsuits was a popular sport, with points given for distance and form. Once in a while we lubricated the slide with a snort of blackberry brandy. It was probably a good thing we were never able to carry in very much of the stuff. As it was, the goats would have been hard put to classify the behavior going on across from their cliffs the year Beth and I spent the entire winter in the Swans.

To climb the Little Creek cliffs or travel to survey other winter ranges amounted to a vacation for us. Our second key outpost was at Bunker Creek. On the way to it we usually stopped to resupply from our base camp at Meadow Creek, near the chief northern entrance to the Bob Marshall Wilderness. From Meadow Creek we retraced our steps across the footbridge over Meadow Creek Gorge, where the wide South Fork of the Flathead narrowed to no more than two dozen feet and smashed malachite-colored rafts of ice against walls that were millions of years of limestone strata below us. Then we turned west and after five miles reached the mouth of Gorge Creek, the long cascade out of Sunburst Lake and Swan Glacier. An elk herd and, higher up, an occasional billy or two wintered on the rocky hillside across from Gorge Creek, and it was one of Kobuk the Wolf-Blooded Malemute's favorite places for howling back to the coyotes. Another four miles or so westward, and we were at the junction of the North and Middle Forks of Bunker Creek.

Our outpost here was a cabin built by one Soup Creek Jack, said to have killed a man directly before coming to this neck of the woods for some much-needed solitude decades ago. Jack was good with an axe; the little place was a nice hand-hewn piece of work. Unfortunately, the sill logs had rotted in the years since he had trapped and hunted out of the cabin, and the structure now tilted at an improbable pitch. We were never sure a fresh snow load wouldn't collapse it on our heads in the night, despite a couple of temporary props. Still, it looked pretty good to us at the end of a snowy day on the goat cliffs up Bunker Creek.

A short walk from the door flowed the North Fork of Bunker Creek, making ice sculptures and music. More music came from the ouzels, birds also known as dippers, which walked under the water and ice at all temperatures, probing for aquatic insect larvae. They are slate-grey creatures, matching the water beneath a low storm sky. But they are always in bright motion, bobbing—some say this helps them judge the depth of submerged objects, shaking trickles of water off their backs, and rocketing up and down the streambanks in flight. Sometimes their song is the only one in a mountain valley besides a jay's calls or a raven's bells and croaks, and it is pure silver, like those days when you are skiing into the sun while sudden showers of powder snow spill off tree branches. With ouzels in the country there is really no such thing as the dead of winter.

As the yearly ice age progresses, the snowpack keeps rising, available goat range keeps shrinking, and the food within that range keeps getting more and more used up. Yet the energy equation for survival never varies: intake must equal outflow.

A goat at rest is burning energy simply to stay warm and maintain vital body functions. Much more is burned in the search for food, shelter, and safety, and in social interactions. If fuel in the form of fodder can not be found as quickly as it is being expended, the animal can counter the negative energy balance for a time by burning fat reserves. When the fat stores are used up, however, muscle and other tissues begin to be metabolized to make up the deficit. The embers are kept aglow, but the beast is starving. Weaker, it becomes less able to find food and defend what it does find against other herd members; thinner, it is less able to fend off penetrating cold.

It is a downward spiral toward death in the form of freezing, or caused by the collapse of basic physiological processes—though an animal in poor condition may be easily claimed by other agents of mortality first, with a predator, parasites, disease, or a climbing accident administering the actual *coup de grace* to a victim condemned by starvation.

Most of the mountain goats that die in a given year do so between the start and finish of the snow season, and the best evidence to date points to starvation as the primary cause. As might be expected, the losses include the old, the injured, and those with other infirmities, like the billy with badly formed teeth whose carcass I examined. But by far the heaviest toll falls upon the young.

An orphaned kid was dragging an injured leg as it moved along a powder-covered stretch of Glacier's cliffs in November. Soon it stopped to bed in a sheltered nook, and it was reluctant to get up again even as I walked toward it with Karen Reeves, to whom I have now been married for six years. Karen and I had kidnapping on our mind. This youngster obviously was not going to last on its own much longer, and our first impulse upon seeing its condition was to take it home to our cabin for winter. Glacier has rules that forbid even feeding the ground squirrels; it would have amounted to high crime to steal a goat. In the end we obeyed the law, because the fundamental law in the park, from which all others spring, is to leave things as you find them. There are not that many places like Glacier where we can learn how nature—intact, full-bodied nature—rather than man defines the meanings of life. We left the kid to be the predators' way of living, the scavengers' way of creating more of themselves, the goat herds' way of preventing overcrowding. It was the right thing to do, and we felt lousy about it.

Even when it is in perfect health and has a mother to care for it, a mountain goat kid almost qualifies as a different species than an adult goat when you compare abilities to cope with the winter regime. To begin with the kid weighs only a third as much as a *small* full-grown animal, and stands between one-half and two-thirds as high at the shoulder. In snow chest-deep to an adult, kids practically disappear, and I often watched them flailing across thick powder like dog-paddling swimmers. Nor can a kid bring to bear anything like an adult's strength when it comes to pawing away snow or breaking apart crusts to get at food. As in traveling, they use up more energy than their elders with less result. I would see them hammering fruitlessly at icy surfaces with their small hooves while older goats fed busily nearby.

As an animal grows larger, its mass (or volume, or however we want to define bulk) tends to add up at a disproportionately faster rate than its total surface area. Mass, being three-dimensional, increases cubically (M^3) while surface area, being two-dimensional, can increase only as a square function (A^2).

The point of these physics is to show that although mountain goat kids and adults have the same basic shape, their surface-to-mass ratios are not at all equal. The smaller kid owns a much greater surface area relative to its mass. Because the surface area is where an animal's heat is lost, and the body mass is its reservoir for heat storage, this means that the kid is the more easily drained of precious heat. Put another way, kids are bound to have a more difficult time balancing their energy budget through the cold months, even apart from their problems contending with deep snow and crusts.

Lastly, kids have less fat and other stored food to burn as emergency fuel than adults do, in part because so much of their food energy in summer and fall is committed to growth. It is not unusual for northern ungulates to drop 15 or even 20 percent in weight over a winter. For a kid this can amount to a deadly serious reduction.

Reviewing the various studies done thus far, annual losses of between 40 and 60 percent of the kids in a herd are typical, and losses as high as 80 percent are not uncommon. The great majority of this mortality occurs between late fall and spring, and the total clearly varies with the severity of winter conditions; an easy winter can double the number of kids left to see the bushes leaf out.

First-year mortality is high for many hooved species, though generally not quite as high on the average as for mountain goats. Animals in their first year of life are almost always the most vulnerable single age class in a population. As a rule, other artiodactyl young suffer more from predation, especially in the helpless weeks just after birth, and fare somewhat better against the threat of starvation, being larger and stronger than goat kids. No other wild hooved animal in the northern latitudes of this continent is as small in either height or weight its first winter as a goat kid.

None is quite as small its second winter as a mountain goat yearling is, either. The other North American Bovidae (musk-oxen, bison, and mountain sheep) are similarly slow to grow and mature, but are bigger to begin with. North America's Cervidae (white-tailed deer, mule deer, elk, moose, and caribou) and pronghorn all reach more or less adult size before two years of age.

With a winter weight averaging between 60 and 70 pounds, the goat yearling is about half again as large as a kid but still only about half the mass of a smallish adult. Moreover, any gains in size and strength from the first year are largely offset by the fact that it is now on its own. No longer can it bed against its mother's side for warmth and shelter from the wind. No longer can it follow directly behind as she plows the trail or feed nose-to-nose with her in the bottom of the crater she has pawed. Formerly, its nanny not only assisted its access to prime food and shelter, but aggressively defended that access against competing goats. But the kid-become-yearling has also become one of the most consistently low-ranking members of goat society. Now unprotected, it is threatened and chased away by all older animals in female–subadult bands—including its mother, and by any more dominant yearlings as well.

If you reason things out this way it becomes apparent that a mountain goat's probability of survival through its second year might not be very much better than during its first year. Yet until the 1970s not enough data existed to conclusively prove or disprove the matter, for the simple reason that I mentioned in the Introduction: the difficult problem of distinguishing kid, yearling, and two-year-old age classes while censusing a large population from one year to the next.

In the late 1940s and early 1950s, Brandborg had picked up enough evidence to at least suggest fairly heavy mortality throughout the first two years of life. Two decades later while carrying out the first major radio-tracking study of of the bearded climber, Chester Rideout managed to produce practically complete counts for all three subadult age classes in Montana's Sapphire Mountains. After the hard winter of 1971–72 he discovered 73 percent of the kids and 59 percent of the yearlings gone from the population. The following year, 1972–73, brought an extremely easy winter, and Rideout found nearly three-quarters of the kids and practically all the yearlings still there at the end of it.

The Sapphire herd happens to be a transplanted one, introduced to atypical terrain and characterized by a higher than average birth rate. I was eager to find out exactly how (or if) Rideout's intriguing figures would fit a good-sized native population, and for that I had to wait until I reached Glacier.

During the first year of traversing the park's valleys, crossing and re-crossing the long pointed shadows of the peaks along the Great Divide, I got all the population counts I could have hoped for, and at first glance they were more puzzling than enlightening. I've put the relevant figures in a brief table below (Table 2).

Looking first at the results for 1974 alone, which show exactly the same proportion of two-year-olds as yearlings in the population (36 per 100 adult females) it appears as though yearlings are invulnerable. Which is curious. That same year, Ursula Bansner, a remarkable woman who has since gone on to study grizzlies, wolves, and eagles, was observing goats at a heavily used salt lick near the park's southern boundary, and she was getting *more* two-year-olds than yearlings in her counts. Which is downright suspicious.

What we were seeing, Ursula and I realized, was a special type of population structure. The high proportion of two-year-olds in 1974 was a holdover, the legacy of exceptionally good kid survival during 1972–73.

TABLE 2. *Winter Mortality in Subadult Classes, 1974–76*

Age Class	NUMBER PER 100 ADULT FEMALES				
	1974	Moderately Heavy Winter (% Loss)	1975	Very Light Winter (% Loss)	1976
Kid	56		55		57
		41%		27%	
Yearling	36		33		40
		44%		15%	
Two-Year-Old	36		20		28

This was the same light winter that barely scratched Rideout's juveniles in the Sapphires. (I remembered it because it had been a good one for two orphaned kids in the Swans and because it led into a cloudless, tinder-leaved summer full of dry lightning, when I had hiked right off a goat survey and onto a fire crew to help fight a blaze searing a drainage known as Goat Creek.)

So, while 1974's surveys provided some useful information in themselves, the telling data came the next year when I could compare them with my best counts of each age class in the 1975 field season. In the interim had passed a slightly heavier than normal winter. As the table shows, 56 kids in 1974 (all the figures are on a per 100 adult female basis) became 33 yearlings in 1975, a decrease of 41 percent in the kid class. Meanwhile, 1974's 36 yearlings became 20 two-year-olds in 1975, revealing a *greater* decrease (44 percent) in the yearling class.

Frank Singer, a Glacier researcher observing goats at the same salt lick Ursula Bansner had surveyed the previous year, came up with almost precisely the same proportions of yearlings and two-year-olds in the 1975 population that I did.* Since Singer was sampling an entirely different

---

*These salt lick studies were part of a joint effort by the park and the Federal Highway Administration. Its purpose was to determine the feasibility of constructing an underpass for the goats so that they could continue crossing a highway en route to the traditional salt source nearby, after the road was upgraded for higher speed automobile travel. The world's first mountain goat underpass was finished not long ago, and I am happy to report that it works like the proverbial charm.

Everyone knows salt is important to many mammals, and frequent use of mineral sources has much to do with the movements and daily activity patterns

segment of Glacier's goats, I knew my results were not being skewed by some local variation in topography, weather, or any other factor. They were on target, and amounted to firm evidence that a mountain goat's survival during its second year is indeed not necessarily much better assured than during its first year, the mortality being concentrated over winter in each case.

Then came the winter of 1975–76. It was a markedly short, benign season, and both kids and yearlings thrived, declining only 27 percent and 15 percent, respectively. The significant thing to note is that a 15 percent decline in the yearling class would be considered quite high for other types of hooved animals. We wouldn't expect to see that sort of figure for them except possibly after a very bitter, long winter.

I keep pointing out that the coastal goat ecotype descends farther and farther toward the sea to escape the glacierlike extension of a sodden snowpack downward from the peaks. What does it do if this yearly "glacier" reaches right down to the ocean, as happened in southwestern British Columbia during the winter of 1978–79? In that season, storms twice dumped over 3 feet of snow on the beaches in less than 24 hours. Hebert had been keeping track of two herds there for several years. Each had increased steadily through a series of easy winters. By the time the 1978–79 winter melted away into the surf, between 80 and 90 percent—not of the juveniles, but of each entire herd—were missing. They just plain got shut out of existence.

If we are searching for the natural influences that regulate mountain goat populations, we need not look too much further. Good winters—good survival of kids and yearlings, yet the kid mortality will still be slightly higher and the yearling mortality substantially higher than other North American ungulates experience. Heavy winters—very heavy

---

of mountain ungulates from spring through at least late summer. But no one knows precisely why salt is so important to these animals, or precisely which mineral salts the animals are after. Explanations range from the "they're just sort of crazy for the stuff" theory (which assumes that they, as we do, like to titillate their palate with more salt than they really need) to exceptionally complicated physiological possibilities. I'll summarize the two different prevailing theories. The first and traditional one is that the animals using licks are replacing stores of calcium, potassium, sodium, sulfur, and other mineral elements depleted over winter as these herbivores subsisted on dry, mineral-poor forage. The second theory postulates that the imbalance actually is created by the fresh, succulent, and slightly acidic spring and summer forage. This type of food passes rapidly through the gut, and the process of digesting it uses up certain minerals (notably sodium) faster than the plants themselves (often low in sodium, especially on typical goat range) provide.

losses in both juvenile classes, with the brutal years that eliminate up to 80 percent of the kids being likely to take 40 to 60 percent of the yearlings, if not more, plus a higher-than-average percentage of older animals.

Thus, despite all the cold-proofing and adjustable feeding habits the species has evolved to meet winter on the high mountainside, the cold season strikes hard at the point of least resistance: the small, slow-growing juveniles. (I suspect two-year-old survival is distinctly poorer than for adults as well, but couldn't consistently pick out three-year-olds in general surveys well enough to be sure.)

The susceptibility of the kid and yearling age classes to extreme winter environments not only acts as an effective check on population increase, but may be one reason *Oreamnos* is not found in the arctic beyond the southern third or so of Alaska, even though mountainous habitat continues all the way to the northern edge of the state.

And winter is not done with the white climbers yet. In March and April warming midday temperatures followed by nighttime freezing begin regularly setting up crusts. Skiing and snowshoeing atop the firm snow, I breezed over rubble and blowdown timber as though on an endless smooth carpet. Once the crusts are strong enough to support a goat's hooves as well, the climbers' mobility takes a quantum leap. Even as forage in the picked-over cliffs becomes harder to paw for, many herds are able to travel into adjoining areas to browse exposed shrub and tree branches. Or they may move on to other outcrops with newly melted-out ledges. For some, the growing freedom of movement is a nick-of-time rescue from starvation. For others it is too little too late. No goat can really count on it anyway, for March and April also may lay down more fresh snow than ever.

What you can count on in March, April, and May, and—in some years —June, as temperatures zig-zag across the freeze/thaw point, is avalanches. Count on them in early spring; look for them from early winter until early summer, under all conditions, including subzero. Where? I wish I could say. You only know what the long open stripes and fans down through the trees tell you. But each year brings new swaths. A cornice breaks loose, falls, shocks a few square feet, fracture lines laser across the snowpack, and an unexpected part of the mountainside is suddenly in chaotic, all-consuming motion.

A fresh powder snowpack is up to 90 percent air, and the avalanches it engenders are among the least predictable and most explosive. The downrushing mass creates cyclone-strength winds which snap and flatten trees that the snow itself never touches. I've seen this cold-weather breed of slide as early as November and marveled that glasslike stars so fine and fragile could tear apart a forest with such fury.

There is a growing body of knowledge about the myriad combinations of conditions that compress sharp-edged crystals into a pile of tiny ball bearings, or dissolve the bond between a particular snow layer and the one beneath it, or cause a moderate slope to spill loose while a steeper one holds fast. After reading reports on the slip, slide, and tumble physics of a snowpack I felt that I knew a great deal more—about why you never know where and when the next avalanche will hit.

The Blackfeet Indians on the plains east of Glacier said spring is the time the mountains are talking. Meltwater trickling everywhere lubricates the contact between rock and snow, and the roar and thunder and echo of slides and icefalls in a big valley becomes a continuous conversation on a sunbright afternoon. Warm rains bring the mountains' mantle of snow smashing downward too. Then, toward evening, the meltwater that has trickled into rock seams freezes again, expanding, splitting away small chunks of stone, sections of ledges, sometimes a great slab of cliff, and the mountain voices talk on at a different pitch far into the night.

On spring days I tried to cover as much ground toward my destination as I could early in the morning, while the shadows and crusts still held things in place. After the temperature dropped enough in the evening to tighten up the snow—though not the rocks—again I headed back to camp, almost always crossing fresh avalanche rubble over the morning's trail.

It is a measure of the frequency of snowslides in spring that goats often cease to pay attention to the cracking and booming on all sides of them. It generally takes an overhead rockfall or avalanche sound aimed their way to produce a startled reaction. The ears go back and the tail up, and they are on their way at a gallop. If they are already on a steep section of cliffs they will seek a protective overhang. Lacking that, they pace and stamp and, as the sound rumbles closer, crouch. And then, when the ground starts to vibrate, they squeeze tightly against the uphill rock as if trying to press themselves into a crack. Or (each animal makes its own decision) the goat may break and run at the last minute.

Like other goatwatchers, I saw avalanches crash by narrowly missing goats. I saw them split herds. I saw goats trigger avalanches as they walked across a slope. I saw one adult nanny pace back and forth in her bedsite for two hours as one slide after another passed like monstrous locomotives on either side, while I huddled or paced beneath an overhang across a little couloir from her. But I never saw a goat die in an avalanche, just as I never saw one fall to its death. Like other goatwatchers, I can speculate that avalanches account for many goat fatalities, but I can't pin down how many. More to the point, the question of whether the objective dangers in mountaineering—snowslides, plus rockfalls, icefalls, and landslides—add up to an additional limiting factor for mountain goat populations remains open.

Over 60 percent of the 30 carcasses I have found so far were in avalanche debris. Rangers, road crews, and other Glacier personnel reported 26 additional carcasses to me over the years, 24 of them almost certainly killed by avalanches. Taken together, the existing studies of mountain goats show avalanches being responsible for more corpses than predators, disease, or any other single culprit, including climbing accidents. But all this really tells us for certain is that avalanches bring more goat bodies down to the base of mountains, where people can find them, than other causes of death do.

They bring enough, however, to produce some noteworthy patterns on the part of scavengers. John Holroyd mentioned that in British Columbia's Kootenay National Park, coyotes and lynx regularly patrol slide areas beneath goat cliffs in the spring. I noticed grizzlies systematically checking the same sort of places soon after coming out of hibernation each year in Glacier. Perhaps the scavengers are telling us indirectly that avalanches—combined with climbing accidents—are an extra limiting factor. There is little doubt that in certain unlucky years the number of deaths in a particular herd from avalanches alone will exceed the number of births. Nor is there any doubt that the drain on mountain goat populations from avalanches and related objective dangers is uniquely high among North American mammals. And this drain, which cuts randomly across all age and sex classes, combined with high kid and yearling mortality and losses in older age classes due primarily to food shortages, surely makes winter all the more pre-eminent as a controlling influence on the white climber's population dynamics.

Karen and I stopped at the spot where we had once contemplated kidnapping the orphan. It was early spring in Glacier now, and we were on another survey. Of course there was no sign of the young goat. The mountains were talking, and we knew we shouldn't stay long here below the sawblade crest of the Divide known as the Garden Wall. I wanted to get around one more bend to have a quick look at the cliffs up the valley. Karen stopped to put fresh wax on her skis first. She finished, and we started on—and a massive flood of snow, ice, rocks, busted brush, and little trees poured over the ledges precisely where we would have been had her skis kept their wax a bit longer.

The only slides that ever trapped me were two quiet slumps that took me a couple of dozen feet downhill and clotted up without further ado. Sometimes if I get that feeling that the odds are in favor of the house among these peaks, I remind myself that when I am climbing or skiing I am not driving a car, or walking the streets of a big city at night, or hating in my heart and arteries to get up and go to work in the morning, to name just three more dangerous enterprises. But I would rather talk about green-up.

A day comes in early spring when, avalanches notwithstanding, you know the earth's axis has turned. You feel it in your pores, the relaxing; you can let down your guard against the cold. The worst it can do now is make you uncomfortable. You sense a common bond with all the survivors and a gratitude you will never be able to put into words the way you want to. Gratitude not just for being alive but for the existence of such a thing as this season, forever coming to renew and replenish.

All winter long an odd insect called the snow scorpion, related to water striders in the family Gerridae, has intermittently appeared atop the snow. It is a cold-blooded creature and therefore supposed to be immobilized by the temperatures it crawls around in; but antifreeze compounds similar to the ethylene glycol we put in our car radiators (similar, too, to the compounds in boreal forest trees) are part of its constitution. Now, in early spring, these snow scorpions are more prevalent than ever, out eating snow fleas, primitive wingless insects belonging to the springtail order Collembola, which collect on the snow in teeming masses, turning parts of it black. The snow fleas are feeding in turn on fungi, spores, and pollen, and on the algae that grows directly on the slightly dirty surface of spring snow, coloring parts of it red or pink. On the snow itself, then, begins one of the first food chains of spring growth.

At the same time, seeping meltwater has stimulated mosses on the sun-heated rock walls to put forth a new, almost fluorescent green. Miraculously, butterflies float over vast snowfields, stopping to lap sap exuded from swelling buds on the bushes. And where bare ground can be found, you, the winterkeeper, crawl on hands and knees over the brown, matted grasses like a pilgrim to find and cherish a single green blade of grass; a frond; a spore capsule; or a spear-tipped shoot of an avalanche lily just erupted, with damp soil particles clinging to the rising stalk; and to smell the fragrance of the earth itself, realizing suddenly that the air has had no sweetness for a long time.

Perched on a snag bleached the color of raw silk is, all at once, a mountain bluebird with acres of sky from a summer's day condensed upon its back. Fast-moving weather blows past, a procession of sun, hail, the puffed, round-edged clouds you have not seen in months, sun again, rain. Thunder stalks back into the country. The wood ticks are out. Goat pellets dissolve to nourish new grasses. Wedges of Canada geese and silver lines of whistling swans fly northward through the passes. Hawks migrate by soon afterward, and eagles return, searching the cliffs for carrion. The first mottled signs of molting appear on the goats' fur. As the creeks open up the first bear tracks appear. You forgot how huge Griz's were. Melted out a day or two by the time you cross them, they look even bigger. The goats descend about as far as they will all year, to meet the upward-spreading green.

Above 5,000 feet, some years, May still looks like winter. Other years it qualifies as flood time. Small creeks become brown and gray torrents spilling over their banks as they carry meltwater from the Swans and from the west and south sides of Glacier to the Columbia River and the Pacific; from the east side of Glacier toward the wide Missouri, the Mississippi, and the Gulf of Mexico; and from the northeastern side of Glacier toward Canada and Hudson's Bay of the Arctic Ocean.

Melt, compact; melt, compact; and at last the menace of snowslides is minimal. By then it is the last third of May and the beginning of the goat kidding season. And yet winter is still not quite finished with the white climbers.

Adult goats may be able to outlast the winter cold, food shortages, and consequent weight loss that combine to kill juveniles, but the adult nannies may do so at the expense of the smallest goats of all—the growing fetuses they carry within them. If a nanny goes too long without adequate nutrition in winter, she can no longer meet the additional energy demands of pregnancy, and the fetus will die and be absorbed back into her body. The harsher and longer the winter, or the more marginal the quality of a herd's winter range, the fewer the nannies that are able to carry a fetus the six months to term. In a typical range in a typical year not many more than 50 to 60 percent of the mature nannies of a herd give birth, with less than five percent of those nannies producing twins.

Given their relatively small size compared to fully grown nannies, pregnant two-year-olds may have particularly poor success in completing gestation under adverse circumstances. Pregnant three-year-olds also might be expected to produce proportionately fewer kids than older nannies. Harsh winters or marginal winter range quality can also retard growth and the onset of maturation, so that nannies are not even capable of successfully mating until age three-and-one-half, or possibly age four-and-one-half. Judging from his research results, Christian Smith feels this may be the rule, rather than the exception, among many native coastal goats in Alaska. Delayed maturation has been noted in several nonnative herds after those populations filled their new ranges to capacity.

Next there is the possibility that kids born to nannies whom winter has left in poor condition may be smaller and less viable than normal, less likely to survive the critical first hours and days. This is known to be true for other wild ungulates and many domestic ones and has recently been documented among Olympic National Park's mountain goats. The first hours are crucial even for robust infants born in foul weather, for they are in danger of hypothermia until their birth-fluid-soaked coat dries, with the help of the mother's licking.

Finally, Victoria Stevens's work with the nonnative Olympic goats has revealed that the severity of a winter may even affect reproductive success one-and-a-half years later. The deeper the snow, the longer it takes to melt, and the less time females have to recover through spring and summer and be in good enough condition by autumn to ovulate—that is, to become fertile; hence, the poorer their chances of producing a kid the following spring. This relationship may not be as noticeable in less crowded, natural populations, but we should look for it to be operating at some level.

It is early June, the height of the birthing season, as I write this. The 1982 Memorial Day weekend has just come and gone. For three days fresh snow has been falling across Montana, and there is three more feet of it in the high country than there was before the storm began. I really can't tell you just when winter is finally going to yield its grip on the goats this year, and retreat back up the mountainside to wait in the crevasses.

CHAPTER SIX

High Society

THE VERY FIRST mountain goats I saw in the Swans were pawing through crusted March snows for food. All right then, in the format I had designed for recording goat notes I checked off "Feeding." I had two other possibilities listed under the heading of Behavior: Bedding and Traveling. I did not envision the cloven-hooved beasts doing very much else, though I had reserved a fourth column I labeled "Other" to take care of play among kids, licking salt, escape from predators, and so forth.

But something else was going on now among that first group, and it set me scribbling cramped paragraphs in the space beneath "Other." In the half hour I was able to watch the four members of the band before a snow squall hid the cliffs, several fights broke out between different individuals, and one chased another along a dangerously steep section of ledges and over the slippery top of a frozen blue waterfall.

Beth and I saw some single goats and a nanny and kid during the following days, but it was not until we crossed to the other side of the Swans to survey that we encountered our next band. We began that April day atop a ridge on a snowpack so deep it submerged the lower third of tall whitebark pines. From there we slid down the mountainside into emerald spring, stopping on a cozy ledge, where we slept on lily shoots for an hour in a patch of sun. We awakened to find eight goats feeding together not far above us. An even more surprising number of battles took place between them than within the first band we had seen. One confrontation led to a young goat being butted off a 15-foot drop by an adult nanny. During another quarrel a different nanny slipped while pursuing her opponent and began to hurtle headlong downhill. Only an incredible slapdash fandango of leaps and lightning-quick half-steps checked her momentum and saved her from a broken leg or worse.

Shortly afterward, on the slopes of the same valley, we spied two billies together. It was our first sighting of a male association, as the other billies we had found were all solitary. Concealed behind a boulder we watched as the pair began dustbathing. I duly jotted that down under "Other." I knew the dirt they were working into their fur and skin would be useful in discouraging insects from biting, which is one reason dustbathing is a common activity among many mammals. (Some African tribespeople daub their skin with mud for the same reason.) But wait. The billies' pawing was turning into what looked like a contest to decide which one could move the most dirt. Then they reared up and began dancing around one another like shaggy satyrs, giving violent flourishes of their horns.

With more days and observations it quickly became apparent that we were not chancing upon isolated or unusual events. Such aggressive encounters accompanied nearly everything else the goats did. In bands with more than eight or ten members a single animal might be involved in as many as one or two dozen fracases in an hour.

The earliest analysis of mountain goat social behavior was done by Valerius Geist in 1964, in a paper dealing with the rutting season. Elmer DeBock and Chester Rideout had added valuable details since then. Yet nothing I had read about the bearded beast, nor anything I had seen among other hooved big game in North America quite prepared me for the constant high levels of hostility I was witnessing among these goats, even outside the rut and away from salt licks. Nor could I think of any obvious cause for all of it. Didn't the climbers have a tough enough time keeping their balance on the precipices without warring with each other?

It stood to reason that, however foolhardy this business of feuding on sheer-sided crags might seem to us, the goats would not be investing so much time and energy in it unless it served an important purpose. And if I were ever going to fathom this high-altitude society the first thing I needed to understand was its language. So I chucked away my rudimentary Feed/Bed/Travel/Other expectations, looked more closely at what Geist, DeBock, and Rideout had deciphered, and set about learning to speak Goat.

The bleating sound the climbers make was known to every goatwatcher. It is, after all, a call designed to carry across the cliffs and attract attention—a nanny's attention to the kid who utters it or vice versa, especially if the two should lose sight of each other amidst the rocks. That was thought to be about the extent of the goat's voice until Geist noticed billies making roars and buzzes in the rut. Then Rideout came back from a close-up look at goat behavior near a Glacier salt lick, and the tape recordings he carried held an unexpected array of humming, grunting, and snorting noises made during battles. These vocalizations hadn't been reported before because they are largely private communications audible for only a short distance, and the goats don't necessarily produce them every time they perform a certain behavior pattern.

It is the behavior patterns themselves that convey the essential information, though. To speak Goat is really to speak a body language, a vocabulary of specific postures and movements expressed with any number of subtle variations in form and intensity. The noise aspect of the language is secondary.

Sheep, elk, and many other herd-living ungulates will associate shoulder to shoulder for long intervals without any overt show of animosity. Mountain goats, however, continuously defend their mobile personal space, a sort of sphere of influence extending about six to eight feet from an approximate center at the goat's head. Whenever one sphere rubs up against another, either in the course of normal activities or because one goat is forcing the issue, somebody has to move. The social dialogue has to do with whether one of the goats will move on its own accord, or whether threats and possibly a fight will be necessary to decide who stays and who goes.

The conversation goes on at a given level within every group, and the arrival of one or more newcomers from another part of the range causes a burst of more heated physical discussion. Rarely does any goat join a band without a tussle. Though it usually takes place right away, I might find newcomer and band members interacting by elaborately ignoring each other instead—a social complexity practiced among our own kind. But even then, there is an aggressive stiffness to the goats' movements as they walk and feed, and the gap between their personal spheres is steadily and purposefully closing toward the inevitable clash.

A newcomer joining a group of, say, five goats will have at least four or five agonistic encounters within the first fifteen minutes or so, as it tests and is tested by every member of the band in lively succession—even by those which wouldn't have the slightest chance of forcing the newcomer to give way when they meet. Now imagine seven goats joining that group of five: pandemonium. And a goat is usually treated as a newcomer even if it has associated with the others just a day or mere hours earlier.

Depending upon how strongly motivated it is, a mountain goat challenging another may stare, walk, trot, run, or leap at its opponent. It may deliver a quick upward stab of its horns at the conclusion of its forward movement. On the receiving end, a goat may turn its head and look away, or walk, trot, run, or leap away, depending upon its own motivation. If hard pressed and threatened with horns, it may crouch or slink away, lowering its rear end most of all, for the rump is the usual target of hooks and prods. In extreme cases, as when a goat is cornered on the rocks by an angry aggressor or caught between two oncoming goats, it may go from a crouch to a squatting position. This eliminates its rump as a ready target and sometimes seems to halt further attack. On several occasions I saw nannies in desperate social straits not only squat but urinate, which caused the aggressor (if it was another nanny) to squat and urinate as well thereby breaking up the pursuit—at least temporarily.

Thus far the activities I have described are mainly goatish versions of some very generalized agonistic behavior patterns: approach and withdrawal; attack with weapons, and avoidance of blows. It is not surprising that one animal can cause another to flee by coming rapidly toward it, and the goat's rush-threat is sometimes accompanied by an impressive snort or grunt while the hooves are slammed down at the end of a forward jump. Interestingly, a hard stare can achieve the same result. Through its eyes alone one goat can make another uncomfortable and control that animal's actions to some extent.

Notice the yearling nanny coming perilously near a two-year-old billy at a salt lick, the scene of continuous rivalry. The yearling is aware that she is pressing against the limit of his personal space. She is already crouching and has her tail up. But the craving for salt is a powerful one, so she persists, keeping a close eye on the bigger goat as she hesitantly edges forward. Another step, and the billy lifts his head and fixes the yearling with his gaze. Instantly the younger goat crouches further, then backs up and glances behind herself, at the mountains crumpling the far horizon, at her hooves—anywhere but at the billy—and she starts scratching herself hard on the shoulder with a hoof.

To us, the yearling, who is clearly nervous, seems to be trying to appear casual and uninterested, as if sneaking in to lick salt at the spot monopolized by the billy were the last thing on her mind. Maybe the reason a human observer can easily put himself in the goats' situation here is that we too, like wolves and many other mammals, use the stare as a low-key way of projecting our influence. If you get on a subway and find some tower of power glaring at you—his leather jacket has his gang's name, the Manglers, stitched across the back—you carefully study the advertisements and the floor while you pick at your sleeve or clear your throat and wind your watch. In elevators—the classic setting in which people are crowded beyond their normal personal space requirements—everyone takes a terrific interest in the ceiling or shoes, because to look directly at someone from so close a distance would be mildly threatening, or as we call it: rude.

What happens when one goat stares or advances toward another and the other refuses to give way? Now the climber's most formal aggressive pose is elicited. The goat being approached turns sideways to the oncoming goat and stiffens its legs, stretching upward and tensing its shoulders and back while the belly is drawn in. The head is pulled down and toward the chest; or it may be pulled low and slightly away, and twisted so that the horns are pointed toward the other goat, cocked back like a fist for a sudden strike. The tail is tucked down.

Termed the present-threat, this posture is, again, a goatish expression of a behavior pattern common to quite a number of different animals. It is a display designed to let an animal reveal its maximum size, which is an indicator of its strength. The manner in which the display is performed also says something about the animal's willingness to stand and do battle, a measure of confidence that is hard to fake for long. Some animals make a head-on presentation, but most appear larger when viewed from the side and so, like the goat, make a broadside, or lateral, display. The goat's wide pantaloons add to the effect, along with the dorsal ridge of hairs, which the displaying animal may partly raise like hackles. It may also begin making rumbling, growling, or low humming noises, particularly if it is a male.

An approaching goat may be so intimidated by the present-threat of its

13. *A subadult female making a rush-threat, and an adult female responding with a present-threat.*

14. Typical fighting posture: two goats circling antiparallel in a mutual present-threat.

antagonist that it stops and turns away without much argument. One thing it will almost certainly not do is continue on to actually strike the goat giving the present-threat, because the lateral display appears to operate as a signal that inhibits direct attack. The adversary might make a couple of short leaps and horn threats toward the laterally displaying goat, but this is often a sign that the adversary is losing the encounter and will soon turn tail. If this attacker is not discouraged and remains intent upon driving the displaying goat away, it will usually exhibit a present-threat of its own.

The antagonists then begin to circle one another head-to-tail with stiff, stamping steps. On slanted ground each strives to keep in the uphill position as long as possible. Should neither give way, the antiparallel circling becomes closer and faster, and one or both may be emitting growling, roaring, or humming sounds. Each may begin hooking its horns toward the other's rump and flank while wheeling its own hind-quarters away from the opponent's horns. As during a rush-threat, the thrusts typically stop short of actual contact. The duel continues until one gladiator loses its nerve and flees. Just before bolting, the defeated goat may make a wheezing sort of snort or a high quavering hum almost like a whine. These noises are possibly a message that tells the winner: "I've nearly had enough" and thus saves the loser from a damaging assault just as it prepares to let down its defenses. The victor of a circling encounter seldom bothers to chase the vanquished goat more than a few feet, if at all.

Fighting among mountain goats plainly is a ritualized affair. From start to finish, aggressive interactions proceed according to mutually understood rules and customs. As rivals select one behavior pattern or another and perform it with one degree of intensity or another they are communicating—continuously sending and receiving information about abilities, mood, and intentions.

Most vertebrates and many of the so-called less complex animals have evolved ways of settling their differences short of all-out destructive struggles. The mammals make particular use of their intelligence to achieve much the same result with still less risk and expenditure of energy. Haphazard battling would be next to suicidal for the sharp-horned goats since a single puncture anywhere could lead to serious infection, and a thrust into the chest or thin-walled belly could mean quick death. Winners as well as losers would suffer unacceptably high rates of injury from no-holds-barred matches; no population can thrive with too many of its members among the walking wounded.

Yet bringing heads and horns together in the sort of formalized collisions or pushing contests practiced by sheep, ibex, bison, and most other bovids, won't work for the goat either. It would bring the primitive, wickedly pointed rupicaprid horns into contact with the face and its sense organs—the eyes being the most vulnerable—and with a skull that is thin-boned and fragile by ungulate standards.

I often come across the common expression "butting" used to describe what mountain goats do with their horns. I find myself using it too, telling someone that "A nanny butted a young billy that was feeding too close to her," for example. The expression is misleading. Strictly speaking, a butt is a ramming blow with the curved front of the horns. Sheep butt. A domestic billy goat will give you a butt. Cartoon mountain goats gallop toward some unsuspecting human climber and butt him off into the blue yonder. *Oreamnos* mountain goats, however, tuck their chin down and then jerk up with a prod, a stab, a piercing hook. Once in a great while a mountain goat will merely push another with the blunt curve of its horns. The rest of the time it is the point of the weapon that is used, an altogether different and more dangerous matter than a butt.

The mountain goat's system of fighting therefore orients weapons away from the head, while substituting intense threats for actual contact.

In over 95 percent of the thousands of conflicts I recorded, the goats were able to decide whose personal space was pre-eminent without touching one another. That's good communication.

And the other five percent? Naturally, pointed threats would not be nearly so effective if the daggers were not brought into action every so often. Here too there is a safeguarding device, though. If you were to examine the hide of a mountain goat you would find it becomes exceptionally thick in precisely those areas to which the goat fighting code directs most of the blows—the rump and flank. Called a dermal shield, this posterior section of the skin is so tough that some Indians are said to have fashioned it into breastplates for deflecting arrows. The bearded climber's natural armor probably evolved apace with its fighting style.

Kids and yearlings strike each other so frequently in the context of play that I didn't bother to count their contribution when adding up blows delivered in goat social interactions. The juveniles even neck-wrestle and joust head-to-head at times, which could be a vestige of some ancestral fighting pattern. Whatever the case, juveniles can afford to swing freely. Their horns are short and the power with which they wield them is limited. Besides, it is a good opportunity to practice using their weapons for the time to come when King-of-the-Mountain will be more than a game.

As yearlings approach two years of age they grow less playful and noticeably more formal in their aggressive poses, and consequently are less prone to strike. But when they do—when any goat older than 16 to 18 months does—the possibility of serious injury exists, rules and padded hides notwithstanding. Although the majority of horn contact I saw involved prods in the rumps of fleeing goats, I did observe some hard, penetrating thrusts during chases. And if the goats did come to actual blows while circling in mutual present-threats, they were solid hooks, and not all of them landed on the dermal shield. The closer I was able to work to the climbers, the more I noticed occasional puncture wounds on the side, shoulders, and even the neck that looked to have been caused by stabbing. Though the data are limited, other goatwatchers have reported puncture wounds in every age and sex class. And the chamois, the only other rupicaprid whose behavior has been well documented, engage in still bloodier head-to-tail contests, hooking each other in the underside.

Both DeBock and Geist described serious injuries and death resulting from fights between rutting males, and Montana biologist Bart O'Gara sent me this note on the subject: "I have had three billies brought to me by hunters who wanted to know if the goats were fit to eat. All had horn punctures in the flanks (and into the abdomen) that were becoming infected. I doubt any of them would have survived the winter." Mortal duels between rival suitors in the animal kingdom is the type of macho stuff that keeps outdoor writers in business. We humans relate to it so well we sometimes fail to remember that it is very much the exception rather than the rule for hooved animals, *Oreamnos* included. Here we have a case of goats so aroused by breeding urges and probably so equally matched in size and ambition that neither wants to give way, even after its attacker's wrath has led from threats to blows. I'm going to save most of the rutting season for the next chapter, but this is a good place to point out that the majority of horn contact I witnessed over the fall breeding period was not between rival males; it was delivered to the billies by the nannies they were trying to woo.

Some of the hard blows between goats come as a result of an animal not being able to give way even when it wants to. As an example, I once saw a two-year-old nanny continue to harass a kid after the kid's mother had twice chased her off for the same offense. The third time, the mother ran at the two-year-old without warning. The younger female bolted, but the route she hastily chose for escape led instead to a blind alley; the ledge was sheared off by an impassable fault. The crouching two-year-old was hooked four times by the relentless mother and might have been worked over some more had she not risked a jump to a faint trace of a ledge below.

Among the very first captive mountain goats displayed to the public were two kids sent to the Bronx Zoo in 1902. As the pair grew older their horns had to be removed to keep them from injuring each other in the confines of their cage. I can think of half a dozen instances in which game managers who had trapped goats for transplanting relearned this lesson; many of the animals they had captured and kept restricted in close quarters were found dead from repeated goring.

A magazine account by one observer tells of older goats helping a kid learn to cross difficult terrain by prodding the youngster. As he interpreted things, the big goats had the little one's best interests at heart. More likely the kid was learning the hard way to keep out of the path of older goats.

While trying to come up with an estimate of the danger inherent in the winter-colored beast's normal climbing activities (see Chapter 3), I said that in 4,400 goat-hours of observations in the Swans I saw just 29 missteps that threw the climbers off balance and that only five of these were on dangerously steep slopes. I reserved for this chapter the fact that in those same 4,400 goat-hours I tallied 291 agonistic social encounters in dangerously steep climbing situations. And *thirty-nine* of these resulted in a goat losing its footing and falling; of these, 18 were directly pushed, prodded, or knocked over the edge; 18 others were forced to make a frantic leap to escape and lacked adequate footing to land on; and the remainder were either innocent bystanders bumped off a ledge by battling goats, or a case of the aggressor slipping in its haste.

I saw the same sort of aggression-related climbing mishaps in Glacier, including an incident of one goat knocking another down into a fast-moving river near a salt lick. Far back in the Mackenzie Mountains of the Northwest Territories, I recorded rates of agonistic encounters among resident goats for a few days. The results matched those from Glacier, and in one instance a yearling almost fell into a chasm it had been compelled by a nanny to jump. And from Montana's Bitterroot Mountains, Bruce Smith reported, ". . . goats forced subdominants during agonistic encounters off cliff ledges with falls up to 20 vertical feet. . . ." We are dealing with a phenomenon common to *Oreamnos*, not just to an exceptionally ornery population or two. Aggression among the beasts leads to injuries from horn weapons and, perhaps to a greater extent, from climbing spills.

The dominance, or "pecking," order among the climbers is fairly straightforward up to a point: big goats lord it over smaller goats. Because body size, horn size, and strength tend to keep increasing with age, this generally means that younger goats yield to older goats. This unsurprising rule holds within bachelor bands as well as within female–subadult bands, whose hierarchy can be nicely summarized by the following scene, loosely transcribed from my journal:

A fairly large group of adult nannies and immature goats lie bedded on a favorite stone turret overlooking the forest. Among them a three-year-old nanny I know as Number 100 stretches out drowsily chewing her cud, her kid beside her doing the same. Her head is only about four feet from the rump of a larger nanny who has a kid with her, but since the goats seem to measure their personal perimeter outward from their head, Number 100 is safely just beyond the big nanny's trespass zone. She is, that is, until the female gets up and turns 180 degrees to re-bed. Now the heads of the two nannies are not eight feet apart but four. What has been an association turns into a confrontation, with the big nanny staring steadily at Number 100. Number 100 and her kid are forced to rise and leave. It is typical of these crag-dwellers that they consider the bed of a lower-ranking companion more appealing than an unoccupied site. Number 100 accordingly walks straight over to a young billy, a two-year-old. He gets up and after some circling and horn threats is persuaded to leave by Number 100, who settles into his bed with a yawn after the usual preliminary pawing. Her kid does the same and curls up beside her, then lazily extends a foreleg and begins chewing its cud.

The two-year-old billy now heads directly for a slightly smaller two-year-old nanny, who jumps up from her bed and leaves after a quick horn-toss in the billy's direction. While the billy lies down in the bed he has usurped, she is taking out her aroused aggression on a dwarf fir tree, which she thoroughly slashes. A few moments later she is kicking a yearling male out of his bed. This displaced yearling tries to take over another yearling billy's bed spot but is discouraged by the other's violent pawing and the rigid present-threat he performs while still lying down. And so the smallest yearling in the band, hapless last link in the chain, bottom rung on the ladder, and low goat on the totem pole, is left standing to pick out a new bedsite.

Though predictable in certain respects, the white climber's social order is anything but static or rigid. It is a rare mountain goat that humbly accepts a subordinate position time after time without putting up some sort of resistance. This is one reason encounters so frequently escalate beyond simple low-level approaches and withdrawals, and it may stem in part from the basic similarity in appearance between the various age and sex classes of this rupicaprid. Much as a human observer finds it difficult to classify the beasts, an individual goat doesn't have enough distinguishing physical characteristics—such as the elaborate horn organs sported by male sheep or wild true goats—for other mountain goats to be able to easily ascertain its social status. Hence the constant testing on an order seldom seen among other artiodactyls.

You could also say that the white climbers just don't seem inclined to accept a "goatalitarian society;" they bend too many rules. True, kids, being the smallest members, get pushed around by every older goat when they have strayed from their mother. When its mother is close by, however, a kid assumes a good part of her status. A big nanny dominant to the mother goat could still prod the kid, but the kid can march up to, say, a two-year-old, and the two-year-old will often hasten to make room for the youngster if the mother is looking on.

Yearlings, like adolescents of many species, are not great respecters of the social order. In rambunctious moods—of which they have more than their share—yearlings go out of their way to taunt older, more sedate animals and are loathe to submit to any two-year-old without making at least a horn-feint or two before scampering away. Mountain goats even have a special threat posture they occasionally display toward individuals that usually dominate them. Bracing its front legs, the goat stretches its neck out and up, to point its head toward the higher-ranking animal chin-first. It is a stiff-legged approach and confrontation pattern, yet the position of the head and neck give the whole enterprise away as halfhearted to anyone who speaks Goat, because it is the opposite of a lowered and cocked-to-strike position.

I was able to pick out a handful of especially tough customers in different herds—the welterweights who would take on and sometimes intimidate heavyweights. I saw a handful of especially timid personalities too. Another outright exception to the rule that big goats always subdue littler ones are the animals past their prime that begin losing battles to smaller but younger and more vigorous herd members.

Finally we have the major exception and the most fascinating one: adult males. They are indisputably the most hulking and powerful of all goats, and you would expect them to reign with ease at the top of the social hierarchy. Instead they generally behave as though they were on the bottom, leaving us to figure out how the venerable process of survival of the fittest ever came up with a 250-pound billy who could be rousted out of bed and sent packing by a 45-pound yearling.

To comprehend the adult billy's peculiar status we need to add two unique behavior patterns to the mountain goat's repertoire. The first is called the low-stretch. Though its use is by no means limited to the rutting season, it is basically a courtship posture. A comparison with the present-threat, provided in Table 3, is illuminating.

TABLE 3. *Comparison of Present-Threat and Low-Stretch Behavior*

	Present-Threat	*Low-Stretch*
Presentation	Broadside display	Head-on presentation
General body position	Stiff-legged, back arched	Crouched, back lowered
Head	Tucked down and in, horns usually visible and poised for instant use	Neck extended, chin tilted up, horns kept from view and unprepared to strike
Tail	Tucked down	Held out or up
Movements	Tensed, deliberate, plodding or stomping steps	Fast, jerky, small steps, tongue flicks in and out
Vocalizations	May be accompanied by roaring, growling, or loud humming	May be accompanied by soft buzzing

Adapted from Valerius Geist, On the rutting behavior of the mountain goat, *Journal of Mammalogy 45(4):551–568, 1964.*

Valerius Geist saw the dissimilarity between the present-threat and low-stretch as an example of Darwin's Principle of Antithesis. This predicts that a species will express opposite emotions through elements of behavior that are not merely different but contrast strongly with one another. Each behavior pattern conveys a certain amount of information by itself, while the contrast between the two minimizes possible confusion of signals and adds to the overall communication potential of each.

The function of the present-threat being to intimidate, it speaks the superior's language: taut and inflated, assured, ready for action. The low-stretch, on the other hand, serves to increase a billy's chances of being allowed within the personal space of one of the most aggressive of all ungulate females during the breeding season. To avoid antagonizing her and spoiling his chances of mating he must appear as meek and mild as he can, and speak the underling's language: deflated, inhibited, and unprepared to defend himself.

I can think of more than a few parallels between the billy's low-stretch behavior and the hushed-voice, pleading, hat-in-hand, down-on-bended-knee approach of human suitors to a lady, but I'm not going to pretend that I know any more about love now than I did when I started climbing goat cliffs. I'll just say that for many creatures you will find that when

15. *A courting billy in low-stretch approaching a nanny.*

16. A billy exhibiting the conflict posture.

a courting male is not parading in front of a female to get her attention he is likely to be doing things to pacify her and get closer—things that are the antithesis of threatening, aggressive behavior.

The second unique male posture, seen when nannies or subadult males threaten a billy, looks like a mixture of the present-threat and low-stretch. It is a show of strength and a cringe all at once. The billy arches his back and presents broadside. But he is slightly crouched as he does; his neck is outstretched, and his head tilted so that the horns point away rather than toward the other goat. Geist called it the conflict posture because it appears to be the result of conflicting intentions to be dominant and submissive. The best way to learn the full meaning of the conflict posture might be to follow the career of an individual billy, such as William Goat, whom I fitted with a radio collar early in life.

From birth, billies are slightly larger and more aggressive than nannies of the same age, and usually dominant to them. As a two-year-old, William began to approach young adult nannies (three and four years of age) in size and social status. Some of the longest and most intense battles I observed were between these two closely matched classes. Then, at age two-and-a-half—just as he was on the verge of being able to best all but the biggest nannies in battle—William Goat entered the rut for the first time. He was never the same again.

William's gonads and hormone levels had been growing along with the rest of his body from birth. He gradually ceased to exhibit the juvenile sexual play, which is about equally divided between circling and butting and circling and mounting or placing the neck and chin over the other's neck and back. But as early as age one-and-a-half he began using the more formal, sex-related low-stretch and conflict postures during a few of his interactions with females. After he turned two, these postures alternated more and more with his normal aggressive poses in the presence of females.

Then came the six to eight-week rutting period, when William's testes, further enlarged, were secreting hormones in doses that controlled his social behavior almost completely. He took part in more frenzied fashion than the older billies and, unlike them, courted nonbreeding yearling females as well as breeding age nannies. I'm not sure he actually succeeded in mating, as the competition from those big males was keen. Nevertheless, he seemed to realize once and for all that there were more rewarding ways to relate to females than pushing them around. I say "realized"—what probably happened is that the jolt of hormones altered behavior-controlling neural pathways in his brain, as is believed to be the case for humans upon reaching puberty, though in our species the hormonal impact is less sudden.

The rut ended, and William, now a mature billy, continued to act sexually much of the time he was near nannies, unpredictably breaking off feeding to low-stretch toward a female. When threatened in the course of ordinary encounters, he now almost always responded with a conflict posture, unless provoked by another mature billy. Rarely did William run or jump at mature nannies and subadults or bring his horns into a dispute with them. Unwilling to use these parts of his aggressive arsenal and possibly risk driving females completely away, William ended most of his encounters with nannies and their subadult followers by stretching away, sidling away in a conflict pose, or stiffly walking away. As long as the nanny is perceived in a sexual context, threat behavior may simply be suppressed at a fundamental level. Even a kid could cause him to abandon a feeding area these days, if its nanny was nearby.

That William's responses were different from those of a truly subordinate animal was evident from the manner in which he always left at his own pace. He never fled outright, raised his tail, flattened his ears, or showed any of the usual signs of fear toward nannies after reaching three years of age. Furthermore, there were occasions both during and outside the rut when adult males like William handily dominated every other class. Notable examples occurring outside the rut can be seen around salt sources, where a male's desire for minerals seems to overpower any scruples about threatening females and young—not just at the lick site but in the general vicinity. Unaware of this, some observers, who did most of their close-up goatwatching near salt sources, wrongly concluded that the big billies are in fact the kingpins of goat society.

They aren't, at least not in any ordinary sense. Nevertheless, I doubt it was easy for William to play the pacifist his new adult role demanded he be most of the time. Once in a while I thought I could actually see the balance between opposing aggressive and sexual–subordinate drives shifting back and forth when he was using his tense conflict posture. Just before, during, or after such displays William was likely to do some violent dustbathing, scratching, shaking, slashing vegetation, or war-dancing—all hints of excess energy that show up when a goat can't satisfy a strongly aroused motivation through normal channels.

Torn between making love and making war, mature billies are unable to establish even a roughly dependable rank in mixed groups. Though a mature male might give way nine times in a row, the other classes can't be sure whether, on the tenth time, he is going to spike them, woo them, or avoid them again. Neither, it seems, can he. The result for the group is serious social instability; for the billy himself, the result is an even greater amount of stress as other classes test him and each encounter generates a conflict of potent emotions.

About half of all the mature males I recorded outside the rut were solitary. Most of the rest were in small bachelor bands. Males may have an inborn wanderlust, but the change from a role of growing supremacy to something rather like ambivalent inferiority, plus the strain it causes in social relationships, certainly contributes to their becoming independent of female–subadult groups, and generally using other ranges.

Given the feisty disposition of the white climbers, especially the zeal with which the nannies will—and indeed must—defend their kids against possible injury by older age classes, groups can prove unstable even after the mature males have been segregated. I discovered that the larger the group a particular goat was in, the more aggressive encounters it experienced over a given period of time. A group of eight, for instance, would have almost four times as many dominance conflicts per goat per hour as a group of three. There are several reasons for this, all of them related:

1. Goats in larger bands are more crowded and so press up against one another's personal space more often.
2. Larger bands contain more animals of the same or similar classes, and these goats battle over status more often and more intensely than goats of clearly disparate classes.
3. After a battle, and particularly after a heated one, the loser will some-times vent its aroused anger on a low-ranking bystander. It is the old "boss yells at man, man goes home and mistreats wife" syndrome.

Redirected aggression turns goats into scapegoats for other goats, and in larger groups one tussle can quickly become ten.

4. The mere sight of battle can excite nearby goats to begin pawing and war-dancing and then head out to pick scraps of their own. Aggression seems to be contagious in many mammal species, including our own, as those who have been in a barroom brawl or a surly mob—not to mention a war—can attest. The larger goat bands are fertile ground for the spread of conflict.

The continual turmoil in big groups disrupts efficient feeding and resting, is a drain on its members' energy (the more so because it causes stress), and makes it difficult for a nanny to keep track of and protect her offspring. When two bands meet and a large congregation does form, it is rarely very long before it fragments, sometimes into the original components, sometimes into new ones.

Groups tend to keep subdividing into calmer, better organized cliques. Calmest of all are the small male clubs whose members are of different ages and size, and small, familylike units composed of an adult female with subadults of different ages: exactly the kind of bands you come across most often in goat country.

Familylike—not necessarily family. At first I assumed, as have most observers, that the typical female–subadult bands were close kin—a nanny with her offspring of successive years. But my marked yearlings and two-year-olds often ended up following four different nannies in three days' time. Though each band they joined might resemble a family unit, all of these associations were transitory. Bands within the herd were constantly forming, exchanging members, and dissolving. I eventually realized that those goats remaining together the longest were simply those with the most compatible dominance relationships. Except for a nanny and her kid none of the group's members had to be especially close relatives.

A pregnant nanny becomes less and less attached to the kid at her side as she approaches the birth season. Before long, she begins to actively reject the juvenile, and once the new baby is born, her maternal interests shift solely to its welfare. Her main concern regarding the kid-become-yearling, which may be lingering near her, is as a potential threat to the infant. The more closely the yearling tries to approach her, the more often and more severely it is threatened away. In the end the yearling's unreciprocated attraction to her wanes, and, while it might continue to favor its mother's company to some degree, it transfers its following tendencies toward adult females in general. A subadult often shifts from one band to another immediately after a tempestuous series of conflicts with the lead nanny, or with some testy adult female or domineering fellow subadult that also happens to be following her. At other times the young goat simply begins associating and playing with subadults in a nearby band and is drawn away with them when they move off with their leader to a different part of the range.

If an adult nanny fails to produce a kid, she may retain her offspring of the preceding year. According to Hutchins, the relationship can persist should she again fail to give birth the next year. If an adult nanny gives birth but then loses the kid, she will sometimes re-adopt either her yearling or, if she has none, her two-year-old offspring. That subadult might find all the old maternal affection lavished upon it, including nursing privileges if the nanny is still lactating. Thus, I would see a subadult so big that it had to crawl on its knees to reach under for the udder happily keeping once again right by its mother's side day and night. At least for a while; it looked as though the close bond completely disintegrated after a few weeks in some cases, so that the two animals returned to their separate courses.

It is generally believed that nannies do not adopt the young of other females under any circumstances. I never found any evidence to disprove this. An adult female may temporarily tolerate an orphaned kid somewhat better than she will the usual yearling and two-year-old followers, but that seems to be about the limit of her acceptance.

The mountain goat's orneriness, which at first seemed to me so unaccountable, turns out to be part of a complex behavioral mechanism that determines the size and composition of social groups on the basis of behavioral stability. It separates a herd into a network of solitary individuals and small interchanging bands. Counting loners as a group of one, my year-round average group size for the beasts was 3.2 in the Swans and just 2.5 in Glacier. Reports from other ranges from Idaho to Alaska show standard group size to be between two and five, while some coastal populations have an average group size of less than two. This social system also separates adult males from females and subadults more than 80 percent of the time, outside the rutting season.

Now we can take our inquiry the final step and find out what effect this resulting herd structure has on the welfare of the winter-colored climbers. How does it ultimately help them live and prosper?

Looking at size first, what are the advantages accruing to an individual goat that spends most of its time in groups with from one to four other members? Offhand, it might seem that if the crag-leapers could be a little more tolerant they would have any number of reasons for keeping to larger groups. To begin with, they are born with a following tendency that is strongly reinforced throughout the first year of a kid's life, and it continues to be reinforced insofar as subadults and young adults all benefit from the leadership, experience, and general home range knowledge of older animals.

I made a little study of alertness in goat bands, clocking the amount of time individuals spent surveying their surroundings. As group size increased, each member of the band spent less time in an alert posture, and yet the cumulative alertness of the group stayed about the same or actually improved, since more goats were on the lookout at any given moment and they were looking in a greater number of different directions. So the individual is as safe or safer than ever in a large band, yet can devote more of its time to essential activities such as feeding. A solitary adult nanny, for instance, is usually occupied in surveying her surroundings 15 to 20 percent of the time during a feeding session, whereas the same nanny in a group of ten would be using perhaps only five percent of her time checking for possible danger.

An additional reward of living in large groups is better defense in the event of outright attack by a predator. Animals are also known to profit from the phenomenon of social facilitation, the general stimulation of group living that causes participants to feed, travel, play, and learn with a bit more gusto than when they are alone or in very small associations.

In his book *Ethology of Mammals* R. T. Ewer states:

> Large societies are only able to exist in situations where members can easily keep in contact . . . and only where adequate food can be found for all within the normal feeding period . . . Terrain and type of food supply are thus the two external factors which have the most influence on the evolution of social relations.

Species like bison, wildebeest, and barren-ground caribou enjoy all the advantages of aggregation listed for the goat, with very few drawbacks. The forage they require is more or less evenly distributed over the wide-open grasslands or tundra they inhabit. There is little to keep herds from becoming immense. I have watched more than 100,000 arctic caribou moving together like the streaming plasm of a single giant cell. At the other extreme of sociability are semi-solitary species, such as the small African antelopes known as duikers and dik-dik. Both are shy animals that elude their predators by slipping away into dense foliage. The habitats they use for feeding are patchy; that is, favored forage occurs in pockets separated by other plant communities and sometimes by other types of terrain.

Despite the potential pluses of gregariousness that I mentioned for the goat, the climbers' basic lifestyle keeps nudging them toward the less companionable end of the spectrum. Topographically, the "cover" on goat range—jumbled rocks, overhangs, and chutes—is just as dense in some respects as the forests and brushfields frequented by white-tailed deer, another species with a very small average group size.

Even if it were easy to keep together and coordinate their feeding activities on precipitous terrain, this might work against the goats, for it would lead to crowding on ledges and restrict maneuverability. Just as every group member gains from the knowledge of the most experienced animal, the alertness of the one with the sharpest senses, and the defensive abilities of the most fearless, so it must share the limitations of the least practiced and least skillful mountaineers among the group in a tight spot. As an extreme example we have Seton's description, in *Lives of Game Animals,* of a band of mountain goats that packed themselves onto a ledge leading to nowhere. Unable to turn back, since the hindmost couldn't make the necessary first move, they remained trapped and languished on that shelf until, one by one, they fell to their death. Most of the relatively big goat bands I located were on gentler slopes than the climbers normally use.

Another topographic factor affecting group size is the catastrophic downslope movement of rocks, ice, and snow. Because it is a significant source of death to the species, it too puts selective pressure on the animals to remain dispersed in small groups. Then no one rockfall or snowslide can wipe out more than a band or two at once. Some will always be spared to replenish the breeding unit, the herd.

While snowslides are an important agent of mortality, we have seen that animal predators have only a modest impact on this sharp-horned cliff dweller. The need for larger goat bands as antipredator devices, either in terms of alertness or defense against attack, is therefore correspondingly less. At the same time, separation into small, often isolated bands reduces opportunities for the spread of the tiny predators we call diseases and parasites. This—taken together with the harsh climate and rocky ground, both of which discourage proliferation of disease organisms and some of their intermediate hosts—may largely account for the goat's relatively clean bill of health.

Both food and shelter are irregularly distributed in goat country, particularly during the snowbound months. Four goats might find shelter from a blinding blizzard beneath overhangs and in crevices, but a fifth group member might have to wait it out on an exposed ledge. Suppose that same storm dumps two feet of heavy snow onto an already thick blanket of the stuff, confining the goats to a fraction of their already contracted feeding grounds. During this siege, which may last several days or continue for weeks, food can be found only in small pockets—a clump of fir trees here, a few sedge bunches on the outer edge of a shelf there, mosses in the fracture cracks of that wall up above. Perhaps there will be enough food to go around until the weather breaks and some of the snow melts or blows off; perhaps not. It is a sure bet that ten goats —or even six goats—would exhaust the limited local forage supply much sooner than would two or three goats. They would then be forced to plow through the cold crystals in search of buried plants or a windswept site, possibly starving in the meantime. (Figure 17 is a look at how much the goats' daily movements vary between winter and the warm months.)

Every species strikes a balance between the advantages of being a joiner and those of being a loner. For the lion pride, the success of more animals cooperating to run down prey must be weighed against the reality that meat goes furthest when divided among a few. Beavers spend a year under their parents' care, and while a damsite can always use more engineers, there are only so many trees and shrubs with edible bark growing along the edge of a pond; the yearlings are thus forced out to seek territories of their own as soon as the next litter of beaver kits comes along.

Among the white climbers, the need is to distribute a herd so that its members reap whatever benefits they can from one another's company while making the most efficient use of a sparse and widely scattered food supply on steep, avalanche-prone cliffs. As long as individuals that spend most of their time in small bands survive and reproduce at slightly higher rates than more gregarious goats do, natural selection will favor social mechanisms that put a low limit on average group size for this creature. It is no accident that bands of ten or more goats are commonly seen only in summer, right after the kidding season. Food is abundant everywhere in this season, and so for a while the rewards of group alertness and mutual protection of the infants, coupled with the value of allowing kids to play and learn together, outweigh the negative aspects of crowding.

Now we can turn to the group composition determined by mountain goat social behavior and look at its effects upon survival. I saw one billy at a lick drive off a nanny and then use his horns to pick up her kid and throw it several feet. The physical damage could have been serious, which is why this rupicaprid society can't afford to have its females and young dominated over the entire range by powerful males with lethal headgear. The billies' shift to a submissive sexual mode upon maturation effectively neutralizes that problem.

And because mature billies find life less stressful when they are off alone or in the company of a few other bachelors, they cease to compete for food and other resources on the ranges used by females and subadults.

From the standpoint of natural selection it is to a male's long-term advantage not to compete with any females he has impregnated, or with his subadult offspring. Their success is his success in maximizing the proportion of his genes in future generations. Except during the fall rut, then, the female-subadult bands have the best ranges pretty much to themselves. The adult billies inhabit comparatively marginal ranges but, because of their greater size and strength, have less trouble than other goats in coping with deep snow and are also less vulnerable to predators.

With adult males usually relegated to less desirable ranges, the aggressive adult females rank at the top of the small bands using prime habitats. Their superior status allows the most dominant adult nannies to protect their kids against all other goats as fully as possible. It also gives them and their offspring (when they stay close enough) first rights to food, shelter, and safe locations all through the year. Of course, winter is the time this advantage really pays off.

The longer a handful of goats is isolated by thick snow and furious storms, the more familiar they become with one another's status, and the better established a dominant nanny's supremacy becomes. With little effort and little resistance from the others, she can claim resources as she needs them. A long stare permits her to take over a feeding crater pawed at the expense of long effort by a smaller adult female. The stamp of her foot in one direction lets her pre-empt the warm, protected bedsite of a two-year-old. She, who may be nourishing a fetus as well as her own body, thus takes in the most food energy while using up the least. There is no better way to survive a winter and produce new mountain goats in the spring.

We have seen that to survive a winter, when the only things that grow for half a year are the glaciers, is the ultimate test of the bearded beast's claim to a place on slopes so high and slanted. And every once in a while comes that winter of winters—the bottom line, the lifeboat situation, the worst the northern mountains can throw at the goat. Think how many such crises have come and gone since this rupicaprid's colonization of the New World and its early struggles to match Ice Age environments while challenging the mountaintops. These were the extremes under which the goat's social behavior evolved as an essential adaptation.

Which goats would you choose if some dark fate hung over a herd and you could only save a fraction of the animals? Faced time and time again with winters so fierce that if all the goats shared their rations equally they would all be equals in starvation, nature selected the dominant adult nannies. Or rather, she selected a social scheme that in turn selects those females to pull through. Wouldn't they be your choice?

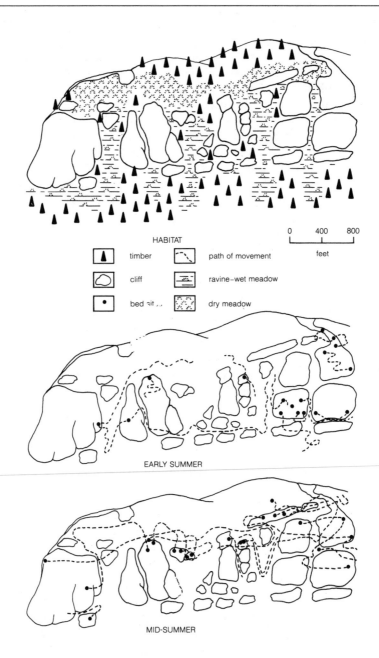

HABITAT

▲ timber		⌐¬ path of movement	
◯ cliff		ravine–wet meadow	
• bed site		dry meadow	

0   400   800

feet

EARLY SUMMER

MID-SUMMER

17.   *Typical patterns of range use in different seasons, showing widespread travel in summer months and restricted movement in winter.*

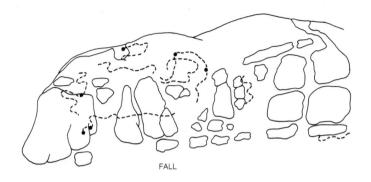

FALL

MID-WINTER

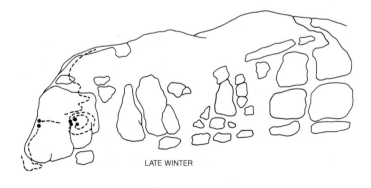

LATE WINTER

Mature females bear the young, recreating the herd. Dominance being mainly a function of size, strength, and overall health and vigor, the highest-ranking mature females tend to be the fittest to begin with, and therefore are capable of producing more and better-adapted offspring. One or two billies are enough to impregnate several nannies. As for subadults, well, the situation is grave, and the subadults have little to offer in the way of leadership or home range knowledge: mark them "expendable."

Indeed, the hierarchy stacks the odds heavily against the subordinate herd members. Any existing resource shortages become magnified for them, because they have to get past dominant animals to use what is available. In Idaho's Pahsimeroi Range, Lonn Kuck chronicled a situation in which dominant nannies claimed the part of winter-range cliff systems with the best snow-shedding qualities and most abundant food, forcing subdominant nannies and their subadult followers to less optimum cliff sections, where survival rates were lower. Bruce Smith confirmed the pattern in Montana's Bitterroot Mountains.

We already know which classes fare the worst over the snow months: kids and yearlings. As a measure of their low status in society, kids received 38 percent of all the actual horn blows I witnessed, and yearlings received an even higher 49 percent, for a total of 87 percent between them. These two bottom-ranking classes also suffered 80 percent of all the climbing accidents brought on as a consequence of aggression, kids being involved in 44 percent and yearlings 36 percent. Benjamin Dane found 18 injured goats during his studies of a herd in southwestern British Columbia. Ten of the injuries were, in his opinion, horn-puncture wounds. Three had been inflicted upon full-sized adults, four upon two- or three-year-olds, and three upon kids.

Such statistics suggest that even a dedicated nanny can't defend her offspring from older subadults at every moment, and her problems multiply if she is subordinate to many other mature nannies. A nanny may increasingly dominate her own kid if it comes to a late-season crunch. As winter snows grow too deep and crusted for the youngsters to paw through on their own, they reach the stage where they have to begin feeding almost exclusively in their mother's pawed craters. If bitter conditions wear on into March and April, and perhaps May as well, the kids discover that their mother, whose maternal drive is waning anyway with the approach of the birth season, is less and less averse to pushing them away as they try to eat right by her head instead of waiting their turn. The longer the winter, the more the kid has to settle for leftovers, though it is still a good deal better off than if it were on its own.

In view of the social hierarchy's selective effect upon goat survival, the heavy losses that often occur in the kid and yearling classes seem not only more understandable but almost inevitable. Nor do adult males survive as well as adult females. A typical mountain goat population has only about 70 to 90 mature billies for every 100 mature nannies. (Much lower male-female ratios have been reported, but these may reflect the effects of hunting, or else the greater difficulty of finding the largely solitary, wide-ranging billies during censuses.) The segregation from female-subadult ranges that leads most males to winter on suboptimal cliffs explains some of the discrepancy in the adult billy–adult nanny ratio. Competition with rival males throughout the late fall rut explains much of the rest. All the billies are worn down from their courtship efforts. Some bear debilitating wounds from their fights; a few may already be corpses.

Here I am—despite some promises I made to myself—speaking of juveniles "suffering" rotten mortality rates, and of a "dark fate" hanging over goat herds in some years. The "struggle" for existence ends up sounding gritty and overwhelming, with winter a culprit of sorts, and "harsh" social measures being required to combat it. At one level it is all true enough. Yet the language builds in our minds the implication that it's too bad the goats have to "endure" what they do.

It's not too bad. It's not too anything. It is absolutely right for the bearded climbers. By concentrating mortality in the juvenile (and, to a lesser extent, adult male) classes, the same social mechanisms that promote adult nanny survival also prevent goat numbers from falling too low—or rising too high.

Overpopulation can be a serious threat to big mammals. Mountain goats have to take extra care to guard against it for a couple of major reasons. First, their numbers are not effectively checked, or even noticeably dampened, by predators in most regions. This set them apart from most of the big herbivores on the continent until European man arrived and began purging the land of native meat-eaters, which, geologically speaking, happened yesterday. Secondly, many of the consequences of excess numbers—overgrazing, trampling, erosion—would be exaggerated in the fragile, slow-to-repair alpine and subalpine habitats that *Oreamnos* depends upon to a greater extent than its fellow North American ungulates.

As long as enough breeding-age nannies pull through, a mountain goat population can always bounce back after heavy winter losses. But if instead the goats were to become too numerous, widespread malnutrition, disease, parasitism, and psychological stress leading to abnormal behavior would sooner or later curtail their numbers in a sudden, drastic way, taking the breeding nannies along with every other class. And it would be a long, long time before the ranges grew back and there were as many goats on the mountainside again. From the standpoint of the species' welfare, then, it is better that the herds' social behavior ends up limiting their own numbers first, in their own hierarchical fashion. This isn't my conclusion: it is the conclusion of eons of natural selection.

Within its fairly exclusive niche at the top of the mountainside fauna, the white goat occupies an ecological position somewhat similar to that of the mammals at the top of the food chain: the big predators. Having few effective enemies, the large carnivores also must partially regulate their own numbers to avoid the chaotic results of overpopulation. Nearly all the powerful hunters keep themselves spaced out by establishing territories and determinedly defending them against others of their own kind. As George Schaller has shown for lions and David Mech for wolves, an invader is sometimes lucky to get away alive. Where the predators defend territories as a group, a pride, or a pack, there is also an internal hierarchy that controls access to food, mates, and other essential resources, further governing rates of population increase. Thus, apart from omnipresent man, the lion's worst enemy is the lion, Griz is the worst enemy of Griz, the wolf is the wolf's worst enemy, and so forth. And omnipresent man, at the peak of the global food chain? Same thing, perhaps: I'll leave most of that discussion to the social scientists and just suggest that, from the vantage of the goat cliffs, the parallels seem worth looking into.

It was on a high pass through the Continental Divide that I first met the billy I called Gore, and learned about mountain goat society by taking a personal part in it. F. Fraser Darling, whose study of red deer in Scotland during the 1930s was a marvelous piece of pioneering in the field of animal behavior, wrote in his introduction to *A Herd of Red Deer*, "I still go on the principle that if you are watching the higher animals, watch them as if they were human beings of a different civilization or culture, and if you are watching human beings observe them as if they were animals. Your anticipation of the next move will not be far wrong." Gore was the one who brought this message home.

I called him Old Gore at first. He was, and remains, the biggest billy I have ever seen. His hooves were getting on toward the size of a bull elk's, and his horns were long and exceptionally thick. When I got my first close look at those horns I discovered from the number of rings near the base of them that Old Gore was less than five years of age, a young giant with years of growing left.*

Along with two to three dozen other goats, Gore spent the warm months in and around this particular pass in Glacier. It is a traditional summering spot for the climbers. The cliffs are laminae of blue-grey limestone, and red, olive green, and cream-colored argillite. They are bounded by permanent snowfields and crevasse-striped glaciers, and interspersed with moist alpine meadows that are like terraced floral gardens by July.

Through the pass winds a hiking trail, and there is a stone chalet several miles to the west. Over the years the goats have not only become well accustomed to people, but have made a positive association between them and salt. In the past, salt licks were put out to attract the goats for viewing. That practice has been officially stopped, but people still give the goats salt, and by now the beasts have developed the not-so-charming habit of licking where people or their horses leave urine, a salty substance in its own right.

To the goats, the entire area for miles around the pass is a salt-lick situation, which means the billies drop their usual role of deferring to nannies. Aside from this it afforded an ideal opportunity for me to live side by side with free-roaming mountain goat bands. At times when no one else entered the pass for days I felt as if I had left my own society and adopted a new one. The problem was that although the goats accepted me as long as I moved slowly and avoided intruding on anybody's personal space, they still treated me as a very dominant animal, which is just what we humans take for granted. They were always watching to see where I would go next so they could get out of the way. When we all bedded down together there would invariably be a wider empty spot around me than around any other individual in the group.

Gore fixed that.

I had an extra interest in him all along, for in addition to being by far

---

*A ring forms at the base of a mountain goat's horn upon the commencement of renewed horn growth after each winter of the goat's life except the first. In other words, a two-year-old will have a single ring; a five-year-old, four rings; an eight-year-old, seven rings, and so on.

Gore was perhaps an extreme example of the individual variation that makes relative horn size alone a poor indicator of age. Winter conditions, as they affect nutrition, also cause variations in horn growth. For example, after several light winters in a row in coastal Alaska, Christian Smith began to notice four-year-old goats with horns as long as those of nine-year-olds that had undergone very heavy winters as juveniles.

the biggest goat, deferred to by all, he had his own extra interest in me. I was lying on my back in a meadow one afternoon when I was awakened by a sound that turned out to be Gore snipping grass a foot away from me. I lay still and looked at him, and our eyes met. I looked away first, not wanting to threaten him. With his head down grazing, his horns were too close if he wanted to respond. Then he stepped right over me and continued grazing, pausing once to look back at me. His tail was tucked down the entire time, betraying not a milligram of fear.

What was it about this huge billy? He, and he alone, trotted back and forth across the pass keeping an eye on the whereabouts of all the other goats. He also kept the closest track of hikers, meeting them as they came up one side and then watching from a promontory as they passed down the other, acting like the true master of the mountaintop. My initial thought was that he was merely making sure he wasn't missing out on any new sources of salt. Yet there was something more to the way he kept track of everybody's comings and goings, and in the way he grew uneasy when he lost sight of the nanny-led bands. Then I recognized that he was acting rather like a billy does during the rut: roaming about the rocks, usually keeping above the female–subadult bands, and checking for the approach of possible rivals. As if to confirm my theory, he began to threaten me when I was in the company of nannies.

The first threat was subtle enough. He merely stood in my path, refusing to give way. I had to go around him to proceed. The next was a mild present-threat I hardly noticed. The third was a present-threat he made sure I noticed. Gore put me a bit on edge at this point, but I was still more interested in watching his behavior than worrying about it. A day later he nailed me.

I was walking alongside a nanny, taking notes. Gore appeared beside me just within my personal space. His tail was tucked down and he was slightly tensed. He watched me intently but made no further move, so I ignored his stare-threat and turned to see what the nanny was doing. The next thing I knew, I was being lifted up with a horn in my knee and spilled onto my back. It was not a vicious thrust. By Gore's standards it was probably more like a warning prod. But it had gone right through my soft hide, and only the leg bone close to the surface at the knee had kept it from penetrating more deeply. If he had struck somewhere else. . . .

Thereafter I had a new place in goat society and new insight into its workings. I was genuinely afraid of Gore now, and both of us knew it. Like other herd members smaller than he, I was careful to give him a wide right-of-way when our paths crossed, respecting his private sphere of influence with the sincerity of a lower-ranking animal. If he drew close purposefully I crouched slightly, then stepped aside. This seemed to satisfy him. But he continued to threaten me occasionally, and I found myself becoming keenly alert to his whereabouts and moods—again as a subordinate must to a dominant goat.

Seeing me defer to Gore as I moved over the rocks and meadows, a few other big billies apparently learned that I was nothing to have to sidle away from and so began to behave more aggressively in my presence, giving me threats of their own when we came together. As my status kept slipping from dominant stranger to familiar subordinate I could do more than record the social encounters taking place around me: I could empathize in a realistic way with the goats involved in them.

I spent three or four muggy, buggy hours lying down among the goats during one long afternoon bedding period. All of us were twitching and fanning mosquitoes and blackflies away from our faces, me with my hands, they with their ears. I was using the time to count chewing rates, noting how often the goats brought up a bolus—the ball of food we call a cud—from the rumen, how many chomps per minute they made in grinding the bolus up, and how long it took the goat from the start of each bolus until it was finished and swallowed it. Pretty trivial stuff in a way, yet I had noticed in the Swans that the speed of chewing varies from one age class to the next, becoming slower with age. Kids average about two chews per second; yearlings, 1 2/3 chews per second, two-year-olds, 1 1/2; and adults about 1 1/3. Here was a possible way to estimate the age of a goat, for there are many kinds of poor light conditions under which a distant observer with a telescope can see a goat chewing but cannot be sure of its horn length against a dark rock background. Perhaps more importantly, here too was a possible way of estimating stress in the white climbers. When the beasts are disturbed, as they were in the Swans by the sounds of roadbuilding and logging, they slow down their chewing rate and often interrupt the sequences by pausing to listen intently.

So I was jotting down more chomping data to see where it might lead, and every notebook page had seven or eight squashed mosquitoes among the lines. As early evening approached we were all more than a little full of pent-up energy. An adult female was among the first to rise in our band. She started to move off feeding, but none followed, and she returned toward the group. At that point the leader of the band—a nanny with a kid—rose, stretched, shook herself, nibbled some plants, urinated, and then started out in earnest, and all the subadult followers rose to join her.

The climbers began snipping their usual midsummer fare—the most recently blossomed flowerheads from a bouquet of species. Almost at once three fights broke out. They were playful fights, though—mock battles. Michael Fox, a well-known investigator of canine behavior, has shown that wolves, like dogs, will crouch with their heads low and give a shake or shimmy before playfighting. It is both an invitation to play and an announcement that the attack behavior that follows is a sham, meant to be taken in the spirit of having a good time. Fox calls this signaling of intentions to establish the context of a behavior pattern metacommunication. The goat's way of saying, "Look, this really isn't serious," is to make quick prancing movements accompanied by a lot of head-bobbing and horn-shaking.

High-spirited and sassy, our band was soon in an uproar, with some of the members beginning to rear up, toss their horns, and go on to make whirling leaps. This is the behavior I have referred to several times before by the self-descriptive name of war-dancing. A war-dancing goat looks like a rodeo bull just let out of the chute, bucking, twisting, hooking, and slashing the air with its horns. Sometimes goats leap straight up as they war-dance. More often they spin as they jump, and I've seen goats make nearly two complete revolutions in mid-air before landing.

War-dancing shows up in play, and also during or just after status battles that are less than dead serious, and it is most common in summer when the climbers are well fed and full of pizzaz. I've seen single goats all alone on a mountain slope do it, though it is more of a group behavior. In fact it is tremendously contagious. One war-dancing band member will spark every other within sight into the dance. They do their best dancing on fellfield or meadow slopes steep enough that they can get airborne heading downhill, especially when that slope is covered with old, hard snow. Once in a while just coming upon a tilted snowbank in the midst of a feeding area is enough to send a band boogieing away downhill. Chamois have a version of war-dancing, and they are also given to glissading down snowbanks, their style being to extend their forelegs and leap into a belly slide.

One big billy now pranced my way and gave a horn-toss close to me. I wasn't as nervous about this particular fellow as I was about Gore, not at all; but then I wasn't really dominant to this billy either. In any case, I decided to give a small hop and head-toss myself. It felt kind of good. The billy sidled toward me in a present-threat and then leapt up and spun around one side of me. I didn't quite know what to do next. I wasn't in a mood for yielding, but I didn't want to tempt those horns. Just then a yearling headed down a nearby snowbank, bucking and spinning like a dervish. One by one the rest of the herd took off after him, including the

The author and Kobuk the Malemute goatwatching in an autumn storm. Beth Ferris.

This and facing page: *Various views of the winter-colored beast in winter.*

A kid follows its nanny's trail through deep snow.

Photo by Karen Reeves.

Goats pause to browse a stunted fir while crossing a late-winter meadow at timberline.

A kid stretches from a boulder perch to munch beargrass seed pods.

Members of a band in a favored summertime meadow atop the continent.

Aggressive behavior of this kind occurs frequently at mineral licks; the rocks to which these nannies cling are rich in salts.

The climbing billy at right responds in kind to the intimidating present-threat of its antagonist.

In a fairly common instance of courting behavior out of season, a billy pursues a nanny.

Though not yet sexually mature, yearlings at play sometimes mount one another in adult mating postures.

Old Gore, the big billy that asserted his dominance over the author in an incident described in Chapter 6.

billy and myself, and our troupe continued dancing its way downhill for almost 200 feet in a spray of crystals.

A spiraling kid lost its balance and landed on its chin. A nanny spun out onto her side. I kept leaping higher and higher, making one turn, then two turns while I was airborne. It was a magnificent release of tension, I found out, and just plain fun. Now when I ski down a snowfield on my bootsoles I always throw in a stretch of war-dancing, and from time to time I've been tempted to try a little war-dancing in awkward social situations down at lower altitudes.

CHAPTER SEVEN

Heat Wave

AFTER CONTENDING WITH the yearly ice age on their separate range or on the periphery of female–young wintering sites, mature billies are generally the first to move out in spring to seek new food supplies. Perhaps first trekking down to recently greened-up cliffs at low elevations, they then lead the steady upward climb through the warming days. So if you see a goat (or goats) high above the rest in May or June and it has no obviously small companions, you can be fairly confident of marking it down as a male.

I could usually confirm such a sighting by the fact that big billies start and finish shedding their fur noticeably earlier than nannies and young. By July a grown male often is completely bare of the old, slightly yellowish, long wool coat that helped get him through winter. In contrast, nannies without kids typically retain plenty of hair on their hindquarters into July. And nannies with new kids, possibly because of hormonal changes associated with pregnancy and lactation, shed most slowly of all, having lost only patches around the face, neck, and shoulders by July. I've wondered if a rough measure of early kid losses might be obtained by counting the number of nannies in July that are relatively unshed but have no kid at heel.

The adult billies appear to want to spend a lot of time alone or, at most, in pairs much of the year. In summer, quite a few of them become rather sociable, for billies. I routinely found bachelor bands of from three to as many as eight members feeding in Glacier's highest basins day after day. These were fairly constant associations of the same fellows, which goes along with my notes showing them to be less feisty and meddlesome toward one another, in terms of aggressive encounters per hour, than female–young bands. Not that nannies didn't form much larger "nursery" groups at times while their babies bumbled, butted, and explored together, but these seldom had the same make-up for long.

The style in which the goats used a range was most dependable. It was as though they had the equivalent of kitchens, bedrooms, and general living rooms, with well-worn paths along the corridors between them. A herd as a whole had predictable patterns of movement in any one area. Individuals had favorite feeding and bedding spots that they returned to whenever the band they were with approached a particular locale. And individual preferences were in turn built back into the herd's patterns, as one generation followed and learned from the previous one.

The best shortcut for learning exactly where goats winter and summer, and where their usual kitchens, bedrooms, and so on are within each of those homes, is to map out the location of pellet groups. Captive mountain goats defecate something like a dozen pellet groups a day. I don't have a precise figure for free-roaming goats but it's similar, and the pellets last for years in some spots. Winter pellets are large, roundish or shaped like a pill capsule, and full of recognizable plant fibers. Pellets indicating summer range are smaller—about pea-size, acorn-shaped, and somewhat flattened. Transitional spring and fall range will often have distinctive compact clumps of partially joined pellets, which tend to be produced when the animals change from soft, growing vegetation to dry forage or vice versa. I don't know of a sure way to tell goat pellets from sheep pellets, unfortunately. Mule deer, whose range also adjoins goat range in some regions, have similar pellets too, but mule deer drop an average of 100 or less pellets per group, whereas goats drop more like 120.

All of us are creatures of habit to some degree. Goat range is more restricted, specialized, and fixed from year to year than the home habitat of most northern ungulates. The bearded beasts therefore develop more elaborate and regular procedures for going about their daily business within it. This made my surveys in Glacier much easier every year. I was still trying to find around 300 different goats each month, but I learned where to expect them, and they rarely let me down. Same time, same ledge.

For examples, one Glacier nanny gave birth on the same protected stone shelf two years in a row. Between May and the end of June, depending upon how fast snow was retreating, the McDonald Loop herd would always move from one set of cliffs up to a certain plateau, pause, then proceed up an angled strand of outcrops to the southeast face of Haystack Butte. And for four years running I encountered three sturdy billies—probably the same three comrades each time—loafing on a particular pinnacle near Ahern Pass when I passed by on my July count.

A goat performs a predictable routine whenever it lies down. It sniffs the ground while circling a bit, like the family dog; scrapes the ground, favoring the uphill hoof on tilted spots, thus helping level the bed or remove stones; sniffs again; kneels, sometimes checking the scent again, then lies down all the way. In warm months this will be followed at once by pawing in a bedded position, unless the animal is on solid rock. Part of the extra pawing is to level things a little better. The rest depends on how much the goat feels in need of a dustbath. It may go at it so hard, alternately scratching with its rear feet and horns and sending up plumes of powdered soil, that it scoops out a wide, dusty pit in the slope. And it keeps dustbathing off and on in bed on hot days; even more on hot, buggy days.

It is mid-afternoon in August. The goats will be bedded just now and likely doing a little dustbathing. They'll be using the basin around the upper lake here in the Otokomi Valley for feeding during this part of the month. They always have. The surrounding pastures are dried out by late July, and the moist basin offers the lushest plant growth remaining. Therefore, the beasts should be bedded nearby at a comfortably cool site—definitely in the shade today. The east side of that nearby rock peninsula ought to be the place. Nothing. No dust rising. No white bodies. Some might be there, but lying down too far back from the edge to be visible. Yet the one promontory toward the top has always had a goat on it when they were around. The breezes cool it, and you can take in all the lower rocks from there, and . . . it's just goaty. No goat, though.

With these climbers a break in the expected pattern is worth looking into, since there is a good chance the cause is more than a random change of direction. In this instance a party of backpackers turned out to be the source of confusion. The hikers were traversing the cliff bottom, and I soon spotted the goats lined out along one of their trails over to the headwalls of Baring Creek, pausing to glance back at the tourists.

Big billies pass on their preferences and home-range knowledge to the younger mature males that join them each year. Nannies, of course, teach all subadults the ropes, including long and difficult routes to distant salt licks. I've followed goat trails for miles away from the rocks as they wound down through forests and across fast-moving creeks en route to a mineral source.

Older nannies continue to transmit information to the younger, mature ones. The matter of which goats in a herd actually serve as leaders of the various bands is complex in *Oreamnos* and possibly based upon quite a few hard-to-detect signs of experience and dependability. A nanny may be able to dominate every other adult female in a band through her aggressiveness, but that doesn't necessarily translate into making her the leader. On the other hand, age and the savvy that comes with it isn't the entire answer either. Yearlings and two-year-olds seem to prefer to follow a nanny with a kid at heel—whether it is their own mother or not—rather than an older nanny that has no kid.

By sometime in August the last of the old fur is gone even from the mother goats, and with their new fur growing rapidly in preparation for cold temperatures, the climbers are becoming bushy and plump-looking and iridescently white. To some extent the plumpness is genuine. Their fat has been growing along with new fur in anticipation of winter.

And none too soon. The sweltering infrared days seem only just past when, in late August or early September, the high country starts to freeze each night, gilding the slender needles of alpine larch, small cousins to the tamarack, or western larch. The leaves of the dwarf huckleberry on the ridgelines turn the burgundy of its berries. Already retired underground for the duration, the marmots and ground squirrels do not hear the bull elk begin bugling challenges to other rutting males. The elk music would reach me as I stood clad in woolen shirt and cap, blowing on fingers grown stiff in the morning air. But the frost, winter's envoy, doesn't yet linger, and afternoon often found me stripped to the waist and sweating as I hiked, listening now to the familiar hum of burly flies.

Very soon the upper slopes flare scarlet and sulphur, as if wildfire were running across them. Migrating hawks pause to hunt the cliffs and tundra meadows. If the afternoon warms, it brings out a smell of fermentation from wilted plant stalks and fallen, mottled leaves.

Once the huckleberries shrivel and drop to the ground, the grizzlies return to digging for food. By late October the fat, lustrous-coated bears will begin digging deeper than the roots and sleeping rodents to make dens of their own. John and Frank Craighead found that Griz may excavate several densites into open hillsides or beneath spreading tree roots before finally lining one with boughs, mosses, and other plant material and settling in for the winter.

The basic pattern of daily activity for goats in autumn is the same as over the rest of the year: early morning feeding, bed, less concentrated late morning to midday feeding, bed, prolonged late afternoon through evening feeding. Now, however, the nap times are shortened and the feeding intervals lengthened, and the bearded beasts are chubbier than ever. Purple aster, fleabane, and penstemon—whose flowers may persist long after other blooms have withered—are favorite early fall food items. So are beargrass seeds, which the goats strip from their tall stalks. Before long the climbers are starting in on standard winter fare.

Autumn in the tall country is a state of grace. You hold your breath, knowing that the fortune of gold surrounding you may vanish dream-quick in a single leaf-stripping snowstorm. The goats, naturally, are the last big creatures to retreat before winter, the great miser. The storms send the climbers down along much the same routes they ascended in spring. There is always the chance that the first confections of snow over the high country will melt away in the mellow warmth of an Indian summer. Such an interlude of fine weather often sends the bearded beasts right back up toward the peaks to graze and perhaps to have a last look from the mountaintops at the colors of fall around them, the western larches now beginning to glow like torches among dark phalanxes of spruce and fir on the lower slopes.

The various nanny–young bands are keeping together more than they were in late summer and more than they will in the weeks to come. The billies are almost all solitary or close to it, their little clubs having dissolved for the season.

Each day darkens sooner than the one before, and the change in day-length (photoperiod) is unconsciously registered by the mountain goat. Even the most primitive organisms seem to have some sort of internal clock by which they measure seasonal changes in their environment and prepare for critical stages in their life cycle. In most vertebrates it is the pineal gland that somehow gauges photoperiodicity. It relays its information to the body's master gland, the pituitary.

At this time of year, in swallows or swans, for example, the pituitary directs molting of summer plumage and then final preparations for southward migration. In the case of the mountain goat, the pituitary turns its attention to the gonads, which begin to enlarge and prepare fertile eggs or sperm. As they do, the gonads start secreting hormones of their own, priming the animals for specific reproductive behavior, first billies, then, three or four weeks later, the nannies.

The earliest evidence of rutting comes in late October, from two-year-old billies. Short on experience and long on enthusiasm, the two-year-old males I watched wooed yearlings and kids along with nannies of breeding age, all with an equal lack of finesse and negligible results. Many a young suitor quickly changed from bold propositioner to frantic fugitive pursued by an outraged nanny with horns far longer than his.

Arriving in female–subadult ranges one by one, shortly after the just-maturing billies make their first overtures, the older males are anything but forward. They roam the upper rocks at a fast clip, searching for bands with mature nannies. But once they have spied or smelled one, they rarely approach closely. Instead they hang back a hundred feet or more and stare at the nannies like secret admirers unable to bring themselves to step forward and declare their passion. They may even be driven off by the aroused two-year-old billies or some rambunctious yearling.

The lovestruck older males forget to eat as they gaze and gawk and gape and moon, then leave and climb over to another nanny or band of nannies and repeat their curious performance. They inch closer to the females as the days pass. Yet by the second week of November they still are not following much closer than 50 feet or so.

In addition to staring so ardently and interminably at the objects of their infatuation, these distant suitors periodically lie down and begin pawing as hard as they can, which usually results in a depression known as a rutting pit. It was less difficult now than at any other time for me to tell the sex of adult goats, because the knees and flanks of practically all the mature billies were soiled from pit-digging.

Rutting billies urinate and, I'm fairly sure, ejaculate onto their own fur. Wallowing in a pit may help them spread these rich, rank odors whereby they advertise themselves, as may rubbing the crescent-shaped gland behind the horn on grass stalks and twigs. However, I never noticed scent-marking by mature males to be as widespread as I'd expected in the rut. They and adult females and immature goats all performed some horn gland-rubbing and did so in all seasons, summer most of all, making the real significance of this behavior tough to interpret. As for pit-digging, this did not originate as a way for males to spread their sign and scent. Like the strenuous dustbathing and other comfort behavior goats may perform during aggressive interactions, it is primarily a reflection of high levels of excitement and excitement's close relative, frustration. Bison, one of the goat's North American bovid kin, use pawing and wallowing as a major part of their threat displays during the rut. Likewise, rival billies will frequently bed simultaneously and paw deep pits. But most of the pit-digging I witnessed involved a solitary suitor, and the frequency of any billy's digging declined sharply as he drew closer to the females and started to interact with them during mid-November. This implies that his pit-pawing was indeed triggered by a hormone-heightened conflict between approach and withdrawal.

In keeping with the species's mobile social hierarchy, billies don't attempt to defend rutting territories. Nor do they try to corral nannies into a harem as bull elk do with cows. I did see a few irrepressible two- and three-year-old billies pursue young nannies as mountain sheep rams do to ewes. They chased them up and down and across the rocky slopes, constantly racing ahead to cut off routes of escape and generally destabilizing the nanny band's daily activities in the process. But older males simply continue to trail at a cautious pace behind the nannies wherever they go. Occasionally one might undertake a trotting low-stretch into the nanny group. But the nannies invariably would flee from, ignore, or aggressively reject his advances, and he would soon resume his usual routine of waiting and staring. A male's favorite position on the mountainside throughout the first half of the rut is some distance above the female or females he is following, the better to keep track of them and to be able to see or scent other bands—and to spot other big males.

After coexisting in relative peace through the summer, adult billies are now potentially deadly opponents in the all-important business of passing on genes. I was recording the way one stout-chested billy attended a band with three breeding-age nannies in it when another large male came skidding down toward the females in a flurry of fresh powder snow. The defender trotted uphill at once to intercept him, causing the intruder to veer aside. The two then trotted parallel behind the nannies for about 80 feet. Next they began stamping in a circle, revolving antiparallel, displaying their size and corded strength in a full arch with lowered horns. Neither broke away as they trampled a small arena in the snow and started lashing out with roundhouse horn-thrusts that narrowly missed drawing blood. Following a particularly fiery lunge by the defender, the challenger widened the circumference of his circle. Another lunge by his rival, and he leaped away and relaxed to normal size. Unlike its equally sharp-horned rupicaprid cousin, the chamois, which will pursue a fleeing opponent relentlessly, the victorious billy turned away and stamped back toward the nannies to wait and watch. The unsuccessful intruder slowly retreated up the slope, halting every now and then to cast lingering glances at the females below.

I mentioned earlier that other observers have seen rutting billies maim and kill each other. But the battle just described is typical of the scores of male encounters I kept track of during this period. Though they could easily have turned gory, none resulted in serious injury. The communication system inherent in the billies' ritualized matches worked splendidly each time to select a winner and potential breeder while conserving the health and vigor of both contestants.

Elmer DeBock first drew attention to the fact that competition for mates, and the consequent risk of injury from fighting, becomes more intense when deep early snows confine a number of billies to a small area with few females. When travel is not so restricted—and it takes a real pile of snow to restrict rutting billies—the males keep on the move between various female bands and so are better dispersed.

A scientist once described the rutting season for moose as a period of temporary insanity. Chock full of hormone-pumped gumption and gripped by moosey jealousies, bulls have been known to charge not just any and all rival bulls but passing automobiles and, according to some stories, freight trains. Breeding is a consuming goal, and the ascendance of the sex drive is nearly as apparent in the behavior of a mountain goat billy. So given over is he to following and defending a succession of nannies as he searches for one in heat (estrus), he loses interest in food altogether; for a full month the billies I observed virtually went without a bite.

Between battling and courting and hustling from band to band and neglecting to eat, the male loses weight fast while females and young continue to put on winter fat. It isn't just billies that enter the bleak season with rut-depleted fat reserves, but rams, bull elk, buck deer, and others. Biologists believe it one reason why otherwise healthy adult males of northern ungulate species in general have markedly poorer overwinter survival rates than mature females do.

Eventually, the long, cautious, and arduous courtship shows signs of paying off for the billies; the rapier-horned, belligerent nannies grow used to their presence. Not quite within their personal space yet, but close. Finally, after a billy has made any number of low-stretch approaches, the nanny starts to tolerate him within touching distance. Each time she walks away, the reason for the male's unusually gradual and humble advances becomes clearer. Like any large goat, he is perceived by her as a threat and must take care not to scare the female off. And on occasions when she stands her ground and reveals how emphatically a nanny can and will say No, the respectful attitude of the mountain goat suitor makes even more sense. A fully grown female is, after all, not that much smaller than a fully grown male, and her horns may be even longer. I saw billies stabbed viciously in the face, neck, and shoulder by these queens of the mountain who acknowledge no king.

By mid-November, at long last, the big males are following literally right on the tails of breeding-age females, often rushing back and forth between two or three in a large band. This takes place much to the consternation of the nannies' subadult followers, who also must adjust to the continual presence of very large, very excited strangers in their midst.

The older males quickly make it obvious that they will no longer put up with the impertinence of the two-year-old billies, who earlier had the nannies to themselves (though none of the females was in heat yet). The young billies are driven to the edge of the band. There they just might have some luck with the two-year-old nannies they focus on courting now, being continually rejected by most larger nannies anyway. But not much luck. If the two-year-olds were very serious breeding competitors, I assume the big billies would take more care to force them completely away, as they do other big billies.

Just as two-year-old males end up pursuing mainly females their own age and size, so the three-year-old billies I watched appeared to concentrate on three- and four-year-old nannies. In the case of the three-year-old billies, this would have to be in a different band from one that already had a full-grown billy attending it. Fully grown males appeared to prefer fully grown (four years old and up) nannies where they had a choice.

The mating sequence itself commences when a billy abruptly crouches into the low-stretch and trots the last few feet in this submissive pose directly toward the nanny of his choice. He then sniffs her genital area thoroughly and usually licks it. Next he is likely to lift his head and curl his lip into an exaggerated sneer. This lip-curl, or *flehmen*, behavior brings scent collected during investigations of the female's genitalia to receptors that tell the billy about the type and concentration of female hormones; in other words, how close she is to fully estrous condition.

After lip-curling, the billy may break off and low-stretch over to a different nanny, if one is present. Or he may begin nuzzling the first female's back and then deliver a short, fast kick between her rear legs— a stylized prelude to mounting also seen among wild true goats and sheep. Typically, he is rebuffed here, if not at an earlier stage. Many nannies start walking or trotting away; others, notably younger, inexperienced nannies, appear frightened at times, and crouch and flatten their ears. By squatting to urinate—another form of anxiety behavior—they can succeed in distracting their pursuer, who will usually stop to taste the liquid and perform *flehmen* once again.

For his considerable efforts, the billy *still* has very little positive response from any nanny before the last ten days or so of November. (This is true in Montana; the peak of the rut may vary slightly from region to region. Based on data from other bovids, we might look for it to arrive a fraction later in ranges where kids need to be born slightly later to match late-arriving springs.) Nevertheless, in addition to making the nannies better habituated to their presence every day, all this persistent courtship by different males is having a group effect in terms of physiology: most of the females in a particular herd will probably come into heat within several days of one another, a more compressed period than would prevail without the influence of courting males.

Synchronization of estrus has been discovered among numerous herd-living ungulates. Hormones exercise a potent influence on behavior, and the pathway looks to be reversible, in that behavioral (and probably olfactory) stimuli from rutting males can in turn affect the females' output of hormones. Thus each female, which otherwise might show greater variation in her timing of estrus, tends to release eggs for fertilization at approximately the same time most other females do. (Synchronization of estrus, incidentally, has also been observed to a degree among human females. Minute quantities of airborne hormones known as pheromones, when given off with perspiration, can cause women living together, such as college roommates, to align menstrual cycles that were previously quite different.)

It has been speculated that one advantage of synchronizing reproductive timetables, at least among hooved animals, lies in minimizing predation. If females conceive in more or less identical time periods, they will gestate and give birth on a very similar schedule. Were births spread out over a greater interval, predators would have more opportunities to become attracted to an area and learn to specialize on the continuing supply of newborn babies. Having said all that, I have to add that its overall significance for goats is less than for species with larger group sizes and greater vulnerability to predators. On the other hand, it may be important for nanny goats in isolated groups to become receptive together so that a male or males will be able to impregnate them all at once. Were the next female to enter estrus too many days after the first, he might leave in search of receptive females elsewhere, and other males may or may not arrive through the snow to replace him.

Back to the action. Having nuzzled and amorously kicked his beloved, the billy makes his next step in the mating sequence a literal one—up onto her back. Or the male may jump directly from his regular stance to mount her. This becomes more common as the pace of courtship quickens and the nanny demonstrates the first small signs of reciprocal interest. The preliminaries are more and more often dispensed with altogether by the billy now. Nor is he easily discouraged. If fled from, he pursues at a relentless, steady pace. If threatened, he may respond in kind, drawing himself up to full height in an impressive present-threat. He has been exhibiting himself in full profile in front of her lately anyway, making only perfunctory attempts to return to the earliest formalities—the excuse-me-for-living shrinking and tongue-flickering of the low-stretch. If the nanny lies down to rest or discourage him, he will stand over her and lick the fur on her rump or back, concentrating on the spine like a doting mother goat, and perhaps her head and ears. Then again, he may kick and paw her until she rises and he can continue his mating attempts. More kicks between the legs. More leaps up onto the rump or at least placing of his chin over her rump. More escapes by the nanny. Then one day her coyness is gone.

Nannies accept a male for copulation by standing still with their rear legs slightly spread and their tail upraised. Once actually mounted, the male clasps the nanny's sides with his hooves, sometimes burying his chin in her back fur. He has made it this far many times. All that remains, if the nanny does not spin or gallop away, is to begin thrusting with his pelvis. She does not this time, and he does. The "act" itself is brief. I missed the consummation of goat courtship for several couples because I looked away momentarily from what I thought were endless preliminaries to write a few notes or glance at another courting pair.

For the short time they are in heat—perhaps no more than 48 hours —some nannies do a lot more than passively submit to a suitor. The last part of November is a snowy time in most Montana years, and it always seemed to storm the hardest just as the rut was getting steamy, building to its climax. An inch or two of big star-shaped crystals would gather on my shoulders as I hunched over the telescope, wiping condensation off the lens and straining to peer through the blizzard, wanting to be sure I really had seen a nanny lick the face and neck of her beau.

Imagine the worst television reception you have ever seen on a screen —ghostly images moving through speckled white veils—and you have the conditions that guard the bearded beasts from voyeurs like me at November's end. Yet I did see several nannies licking their beaux, and several more begin determinedly pursuing the suitors they had spurned for so long. A few even dug rutting pits of their own. Through the center of one fogswirl I made out a nanny running over and mounting the handsome male who had ignored her in favor of another. Still another female mounted her own kid in the presence of a courting billy. The last expression I saw on that kid's face before it collapsed into the snow beneath its mother's weight and a new snowsquall obliterated the cliffs looked to me like either profound worry or total disillusionment.

The white climber's closest approximation of our sometimes popular ideal of romance comes when a receptive nanny and courting billy form what may be called a tending bond, as cattle, bison, and certain other bovids do. Not all mating couples do this; many billies, and some nannies, are too busy hurrying from one potential mate to another. But an occasional pair will be seen together for a day or two, often well apart from the herd, accompanied only by the nanny's kid, if she has one. Side by side, they feed and rest and travel, sometimes licking and nuzzling one another, sometimes just standing with shoulders touching to gaze out over the mountainsides filling with snow, sufficient unto themselves for a while. I know this isn't the best time to intrude with scientific reasoning, but I need to point out that tending bonds are generally viewed as post-mating protection on the part of the male. By lingering with the nanny, the billy guards against the possibility that a rival might also inseminate her before her brief peak of estrus has passed.

It takes moments of violence, moments of quiet tenderness, and moments when it seems things will never work out, for mountain goats to make more mountain goats, for competition, selection, and intimate acceptance to produce a union of sperm and egg.

First to start courtship, the two-year-old billies are also first to quit, losing interest (maybe due to a drop in hormone production) during the very height of the rut among older goats. By the first week of December only a few males of any age are still following nannies, and their overtures are increasingly lackluster. As the cold days pass, these males do less courting, more feeding and, inevitably, more quarreling with the nannies, which are resuming their usual sober, belligerent attitude toward big males. And so these billies too take their leave, wading through thick snows to their own winter ranges where they will turn all their remaining energies to enduring the months ahead.

CHAPTER EIGHT

Managing Democracy

A FRIEND WHO is a hunting guide once gave me a sample of mountain goat meat. It took a lot of chewing, but I found the flavor better than I had expected after hearing others describe it. As a rule, older goats tend to be too tough and gamy to suit most palates. Nevertheless, the older and bigger a goat is, the more value it holds for the average modern hunter. This is because *Oreamnos* is widely regarded as a trophy game animal, though it has never had the status among trophy seekers of the more impressively crowned—and tastier—bull elk or sheep ram.

Even when the hunters were native Americans, the beast was probably sought as much for its horns, fashioned into ornaments and implements, and for its woolly pelt as for its meat. It seems not to have been hunted very heavily in any case, save possibly by certain groups in coastal territories, where the goats so often range to rather low elevations. One report does mention entire tribes taking part in organized goat-hunting drives near Washington's Mount Baker just before the turn of the century.

Early white settlers, loggers, and miners eliminated a few handy herds to fill out their larders. Occasionally, as in the case of the locals who used to blast away at goats on the shoreline cliffs while boating along Lake Chelau in Washington, the object was mere entertainment—like shooting buffalo from passing trains. On the whole, though, the crag dwellers clung safely to the opposite end of the scale of wildlife slaughter from that occupied by the American bison, which had the grave misfortune to roam the very habitats the invader coveted for his crops and livestock, and subsequently underwent the greatest single biocide in recorded history.

Antelope and elk also were surprisingly close to being in danger of extinction by the century's end. And mountain sheep were beginning to undergo broad declines as a result of overshooting, competition with livestock herded into high elevation grasslands for summer grazing, and diseases (often transmitted by livestock). By contrast, Victor Cahalane could write as late as 1947, in his book *Mammals of North America,* the following typical description of *Oreamnos americanus'* status:

> The mountain goat has been far less affected by man than any other North American big game. . . . With very minor exceptions, goats still inhabit the same range that their ancestors occupied when Captain Cook sailed his ship into Prince William sound more than a century and a half ago. Man has found no use for the home of the mountain goat.

Man did, inexorably, begin to find more and more uses for the goat's home in the search for more and more minerals; hydrocarbons; timber; highway, railroad, powerline, and pipeline routes; ski resort locations; and on and on. With the occasional exception of mining, particularly strip mining, and some types of steep-slope timbering, the exploitation of resources still did not directly affect the white climbers' chief habitat —the cliff ledges. But they were losing their exemption from disturbance as the racket of engines intruded from adjacent slopes and valleys. More critically, they were losing their inaccessibility—this species' best defense against the high-powered rifle and, in a sense, its only defense.

You can walk through the middle of deer range all day and never see more than the flash of an antler, if that. But once you actually enter a typical range used by goats you should have climbers in view before long. The herd isn't likely to be anywhere other than on the open faces of rock outcroppings or on equally open slopes right beside them. As soon as snow covers the upper elevations, most herds become especially concentrated on a few key cliff areas.

The goat is not a hider in any conventional sense. The last thing it will do when threatened is to try and lose itself in dense vegetation. Even the forest-wintering coastal goat ecotype heads straight for an exposed rock face when it feels threatened. Nor does the bearded beast have a critical flight, or escape, distance in any conventional sense. It senses security in terms of the steepness and difficulty of the terrain between it and the thing threatening it, not necessarily in terms of linear feet.

Clearly, the strategies that work so well to insulate the goat from other predators can be a liability when it faces a human hunter set up at a good vantage point, his weapon bearing a telescopic sight and capable of reaching with a lethal touch over several hundred yards. Moreover, because of the goat's characteristic attachment to a specific home range, a survivor is likely to return again and again to those same cliffs following a temporary hunting-related disturbance. A readily accessible herd therefore remains highly vulnerable once its whereabouts is known.

Unfortunately, these habits that render the white climber both conspicuous and quite easy to approach (within rifle range) at times also make it a tempting target for poachers.

Whatever the actual source, anything beyond occasional light shooting pressure may be more than some goat herds can sustain, and I think we finally know enough about the winter-colored beast's ecology and behavior to understand why. Why many populations increasingly under the gun from the 1950s onward have failed so dramatically. And why many have been so slow to come back even after measures intended to ease the pressure were taken.

To begin with, mountain goats grow and reproduce more slowly than most hooved game species. Female deer on average range first breed as yearlings and regularly produce twins. On range in top condition, the females of the larger cervids—elk and moose—also occasionally breed as yearlings. Mountain goat females, on the other hand, almost never have been found to breed before two-and-a-half years of age, even under optimum conditions where herds were introduced to unoccupied, food-rich areas. The sole exceptions I am aware of are several two-year-olds recently found by Victoria Stevens to have produced young in parts of Olympic National Park, where the nonnative population is still expanding in places, and two lactating two-year-olds recorded in native Alaskan coastal range by Christian Smith, plus a 1940 report of kid production by two-year-olds in South Dakota's then-expanding herd. This sort of yearling breeding could have contributed to the high rates at which some introduced herds expanded in the years immediately following transplantation.* Recall, however, that it is mainly in studies of various introduced herds (as described by Dale Hibbs, Olav Hjeljord, Chester Rideout, and Stevens and C. Driver) that we find evidence of mountain goat females routinely failing to mature until three-and-a-half years of age, once a population fills its range to carrying capacity.

Among deer, elk, and moose populations, well over three-quarters of the mature females may be expected to deliver young most years. For

---

*A few males also may become fertile as yearlings under best-of-all-possible-range conditions, though it has never been reported for native herds. Exceptions will possibly turn up in the course of more detailed investigations. Competition from dominant billies, however, would minimize the contribution any fertile yearling could make to herd productivity.

goats, the percentage is more like 50 to 65 or possibly 70 (taking into account the common practice of lumping two-year-old females with kid-producing adult females in census figures). The percentages reported vary tremendously and are often more like 30 to 50 kids per 100 mature adult females in marginal ranges or following harsh winters. Twinning is rare in most goat populations, though it does increase somewhat in association with light winter conditions.

Introduced herds in the early, or eruptive, stages of expansion into high-quality, unused range again provide exceptions, exhibiting markedly high rates of kid production, including frequent twinning. One such situation merits particular comment. In the early 1950s, Jack Lentfer conducted an important study of goats transplanted into Montana's Crazy Mountains. He not only found twinning to be quite common but reported several instances of triplets, an unheard-of occurrence in *Oreamnos* before or since. Those Crazy Mountains goats were plainly flourishing in this nonnative range. Yet since I've seen two to as many as five kids playing together and tagging along behind a single nanny for up to half an hour before returning to their own mothers nearby, and since many of Lentfer's observations were necessarily brief parts of overall population censuses, I've never been absolutely convinced about those triplets. They may be perfectly valid. The certain fact is that triplets, like abundant twins, are highly atypical, to say the least. At the time of Lentfer's investigation, however, no one knew quite how atypical they were, due to the paucity of data from indigenous herds. Thus his results reinforced the then-current assumption that *Oreamnos* could be managed like other big game. This did the white climber no good as a whole. As for the Crazy Mountains population itself, a generous hunting season, begun once the goats were believed well established among the peaks, contributed to bringing about an end to their success story, and they have not yet recovered well from the declines that ensued.

After low birth rates, the next factor we need to take note of as it affects the white climber's ability to sustain hunting pressure is the typically high rate of first-year losses goats experience. In addition, there is the unusually high average rate of second-year, or yearling, mortality, plus scattered losses in mature goats and the inevitable demise of the elderly each year. Then we have to add the unique toll of climbing accidents—both purely inadvertent and aggression-caused—along with deaths from avalanches, rockfalls, and related factors built into the mountain-edge niche. And these include every so often a let's-remember-who's-boss-here winter that fattens the glaciers and spreads famine throughout the high country—and down to the beaches along the northwest coast. Or a series of such winters.

Here, it might seem, are reasons enough to warrant strong restrictions on mountain goat hunting. But a game manager would not necessarily see it the same way at all. One of the fundamental tenets of his profession is that healthy wildlife populations produce a "harvestable surplus." And harvesting (shooting), the theory continues, actually stimulates the production of young by surviving females because they now have less competition from within the herd for available food and other resources, and therefore are more likely to stay strong, healthy, and able to carry fetuses to term. This is referred to as compensatory productivity, or just compensation. In the case of northern hooved mammals, generally hunted in autumn, it is all supposed to work out to where shooting merely removes the same percentage of animals as would ordinarily die over winter, plus an extra percentage that is made up for by high birth rates in the spring.

Emotional reactions for or against hunting aside, there is little doubt that many animals can and do compensate for shooting losses. Thereafter, however, the issue gets complicated since certain hunted species are so much better at keeping even than others. It helps if the hunted animal has evolved to exploit successional, or changing, habitats. Brushfields and young forests, for example, nurture deer, rabbits, and several types of game birds, while marshes grow moose and waterfowl. Sooner or later a brushfield will be replaced by an open forest, then by a closed forest, while the marsh will fill in to become meadow (which in turn will pass through a series of stages on its way to a climax forest). Fires, changing water channels, and other disturbances meanwhile will be creating new sites for shrubs and swampy vegetation elsewhere. The deer, moose, or other successional species must be able to colonize and rapidly expand to fill those sites as they become available if they are to compete successfully as species. Consequently, their common adaptive strategy is to produce and disperse large numbers of offspring.

It also helps if the hunted animal has evolved with consistently high levels of predation, for this too usually assures that it will have a high potential rate of population increase as a way of coping with environmental demands. And it helps a great deal—with this we come to a major assumption underlying the harvestable surplus theory—if those natural predators have been eliminated or reduced to minor levels, enabling man to partly mimic their role—fill in for them, so to speak. Again, this is the situation for most common game animals; a wolfless, cougarless, lynxless, bearless, wolverineless (etc.) deer population is an ideal candidate for "cropping," as game managers put it. Indeed, such a population confronts the Malthusian dilemma: if unharvested, it will suffer overpopulation instead, leading to overuse of its range and starvation (and probably disease and heavy parasitism), until at last it stabilizes at a level lower than before, to match its depleted resources.

I know that hunting opponents find particularly galling the hunters' argument that they are doing wildlife a favor by shooting it, but in a sense the reasoning holds true—until we start allowing big carnivores back in the ecosystems where they belong. This is not to say that the reasoning justifies always squeezing the maximum harvest we think we can get away with out of common game species. Nor should it be taken as justification for cropping carnivores like cougars, wolves, bears, otters, and so on as a necessity; they are quite prepared to handle their own population densities without our help, thank you. Nor does it apply well to prey species occupying unusual or sensitive niches—like the mountain goat.

Cliff ledges, alpine and subalpine meadows, and rocky fellfields are rather stable habitats in that the plant societies they support grow and change very slowly and are shaped as much by gravity and climatic forces as by biotic trends. They are, in other words, essentially climax communities. The tundra on a windy ridge and the grassy patches on the outcropping below it will look much the same as they ever did long after a lowland meadow has turned into a shadowy woodland. Even a high-altitude brushfield can be maintained in a more or less constant (non-successional) state by soil slippage and avalanches that scour away encroaching trees.

Just as they have no overwhelming need to scatter abundant offspring to take advantage of shifting range opportunities, ledge-living *Oreamnos* need not produce a population excess to satisfy a gamut of predators on top of other sources of mortality. We have come to appreciate that the opposite is correct; the more or less predator-immune climber lives within a dominance hierarchy that operates as a population control mechanism, vital in helping avoid overuse of slow-growing permanent home ranges. To repeat once more: social behavior in conjunction with winter conditions, not habitat transition or predators (or disease or parasites or competitors), regulate mountain goat numbers naturally—and have for millennia. The need to harvest *Oreamnos* to prevent overpopulation and overgrazing doesn't exist.

This doesn't fully explain why goats don't compensate for harvesting pressure more readily. Subordinate goats succumb for lack of food, don't they? So why wouldn't removal of at least some percentage of a herd encourage better survival and reproduction among the remainder, since more food would be available per goat? The answer is that it could, but only in some circumstances and then only with some serious limitations.

For compensation to function, the survivors have to redistribute themselves so that each does, in fact, use more of the newly vacant areas and the food these contain. As usual, goats don't fit the mold. Lonn Kuck's long-term investigation of the effect of carefully controlled harvests in Idaho's Pahsimeroi Range plainly showed why. Recall that in goat country the quality and quantity of the forage supply on a slope doesn't mean as much as usual. It's whether or not you can get at any chow at all through the ice and snow that counts. Accordingly, these rupicaprids choose their winter ranges primarily on the basis of the snow-shedding physical features discussed in Chapter 5—steepness, stratigraphy, and exposure to sunlight and prevailing winds—and then bring into play their exceptional ability to reach and eat everything there from lichens and roots to fir needles.

Dominant nannies claimed the steepest, most snow-free cliff exposures in Kuck's study area. When they were shot during the course of the hunting season (along with goats elsewhere, though hunters tend to be especially drawn to the prime cliffs, where goats are densest), other goats from surrounding, less desirable wintering sites soon moved in to fill the openings. As a result, the prime ranges offered no more food per goat than before. Survival and reproduction stayed about the same there, and didn't improve in the outlying marginal ranges. Fewer adult females were left after each hunting season, and total kid production declined accordingly. (Killing billies doesn't stimulate productivity; wintering on separate ranges, they aren't competing with females and subadults for forage in the first place.) "Consequently," Kuck concluded, "hunter mortality proved to be additive and not compensatory as expected." He simply ended up with a smaller population and a smaller overall amount of goat range as the dwindling herds contracted toward the best available cliff sites. This occurred while 12 to 13 percent of the adult population was being harvested annually—a very modest cropping rate by the standards used for managing the deer family.

Most sportsmen bent on bagging a mountain goat would prefer a billy, mainly for its thicker horns and more imposing size. Yet many of them mistakenly drop nannies instead, first because female–subadult groups tend to be larger and lower on the mountainside and therefore easier to locate and stalk, and secondly because most hunters can't distinguish the sexes at a distance. Due to the common misconception that goat bands are always family units made up of ma, pa, and their progeny of different years, an adult with a kid at heel or close by is not always recognized as a nanny. Besides, no real stigma is attached to killing nannies. Most hunters believe—as did most game managers until recently—that goat kids, being fully weaned by autumn, are prepared to go it alone should their mother disappear, which is how things are supposed to work for many common game species. Both mountain goat sexes are desirable as trophy targets. In fact, some of the longest horns on record are those of nannies. Altogether, goat hunters end up killing somewhere between half as many to as many females as males on the average, and occasionally more nannies than billies.

In addition to the obvious negative effect on herd productivity of removing breeding females, we might as well add some percentage of the orphaned kids (beyond expected losses for the kid class as a whole) to the final hunter tally. This is my guess, anyway; the actual data are still limited and mixed. I saw hunting-orphaned kids pull through an easy winter. Bryan Foster, who made a special study of the subject, recorded rather good survival of orphans through two fairly light winters. Yet I also noticed orphans that were already in bad shape by late fall. While adoption of unrelated kids is uncommon among goats, I pointed out in Chapter 6 that an adult female usually is not very aggressively aroused by a kid that tries to attach itself to her. The subadults that may also be following her are a different matter, however; I've seen orphans so harassed, particularly by yearlings, that they eventually opted to go it alone on a separate part of the cliffs. Foster also found this to be the case; orphans tend to end up solitary or with other motherless kids. I would not want to bet on their chances during an average winter, much less a severe one.

Another side effect of gunning for goats ought to go into the final harvest total, but neither I nor anyone else knows what weight to give it. This has to do with the number of animals that are wounded but never recovered by the hunters. Some will drag themselves off to die shortly thereafter in some secret cranny; others will be crippled and perhaps die later in winter; still others will pull through. Estimates from various state fish and game departments put wounding rates as high as 30 to 50 percent for other big game. If you talk to goat hunters or read their accounts in outdoor magazines, you will hear of the muscular white climber's note-worthy ability to "carry a lot of lead," which means it is pretty tough to kill cleanly. ". . . I have killed well over a hundred grizzlies without finding them any more tenacious of life than many other wild animals. They cannot stand any more punishment than the deer or the elk, and they cannot begin to stand up under the rain of bullets that an old Rocky Mountain goat will survive," wrote turn-of-the-century hunter-naturalist William Wright—after first aptly pointing out that we tend to be more impressed with the vitality of an animal that has long claws and, when wounded, takes the offensive. I'll let the subject go at that, except to recommend that we contemplate adding a few extra points—again, I have no idea how many—to the harvest percentage to account for the goats killed illegally each year.

Still another, and more subtle, result of goat hunting worth scrutinizing is excessive interference with normal rutting activities. As the preceding chapter described, the courtship process among these rupicaprids is a prolonged, elaborate series of negotiations between exceptionally aggressive females and billies hoping to be tolerated within their personal space. The billy is using every Btu of energy wooing, fighting, and traveling across snowbound ground between nanny–young bands, which may be widely separated. Harassment by gunners can seriously disrupt the negotiations and sap the billies' much-needed reserves of strength. If too many big males are shot or forced to flee from a particular area, some of the more isolated nanny groups could go unbred or else be bred mainly by low-ranking males. Unable to dominate nannies effectively through the courtship process, these subordinate billies, especially the younger ones, often cause chaotic, energy-draining social interactions, and the entire mating structure can become increasingly haphazard.

Like most vertebrates, mountain goats invest a tremendous amount of time and effort in reproductive behavior that ensures that the fittest individuals will pass on the greatest share of genetic material. This is the germ, the essence of their continuing success against environmental odds. Prime billies represent not only a concentration of desirable inherited traits but—through their strength, defensive abilities against predators, and mobility—they are the conduits that keep genes flowing from one herd to the next. Getting to the next herd may be just a short hike for the males. It can also be a critically important venture across forests, rivers, and low valleys. Mountaintop-dwelling species are more susceptible to the harmful effects of inbreeding than animals whose habitat is not so specialized or geographically scattered, and billies are the goat's form of insurance against it.

The discontinuity of suitable cliff homesites, coupled with the female goat's reluctance to leave her habitual home range and colonize new terrain, brings us to a final troublesome aspect of managing *Oreamnos* as a game animal. Once a local group is shot out it may not be replaced through emigration from surrounding areas for quite some time, especially when nearby herds are themselves subject to hunting pressure, and so contracting toward key cliffs rather than expanding away from them. Failing to re-establish a foothold on empty outcrops, the regional population becomes pared down segment by segment, the more so as hunters concentrate on the most accessible herd or herds during any one season instead of distributing shooting pressure equally throughout the rugged countryside.

Game management practices long missed the cue altogether in this respect. A standard technique for judging the welfare of a hunted population is harvest success. If enough sportsmen after a certain type of prey are able to collect it each year, this is taken as evidence that the animal is abundant and reproducing well. Paradoxical as it may sound to someone unfamiliar with the subject, the if-you-kill-a-lot-we-must-have-a-lot-left-out-there method of sampling wildlife does work—to sound the refrain again—reasonably well for typical game species but *not* for you-know-who.

Managers generally would review the annual goat kills considering vast areas as a single hunting unit. Sure, the harvest figures stayed right up there for a long time; the climber was providing a dandy crop. Having little or no actual field count information to check against, they overlooked the reality: it was the elimination of one easy-to-reach herd after another that kept the regional kill totals so high. Then came the crashes in the paperwork figures. Then came some restrictions on hunting, most of them inadequate. Then more crashes and the urgent search for culprits. Disease? Predators? Overgrazed ranges? What's going on with their food habits? Low numbers of young animals, you say? Sounds like a stagnant population. Maybe we should hunt them harder to perk up production.

I don't mean to be too glib. I've been through game management courses, and what was going on with *Oreamnos* contradicted almost everything I was taught about the population dynamics of hunted hooved animals. With a good deal of practical experience in applying these management strategies and seeing them produce acceptable results for standard hunted species, many game biologists were not prepared for a subversive like the goat. Many, too, had limited familiarity with behavioral science, but that was less important than the limited money and manpower at their disposal. It took a lot of both to clamber or fly around after snowpatches of goats, and there were more popular and economically important game critters to attend to.

Because thorough goat counts are almost as hard to come by now as ever, it is nearly impossible to pin down the true magnitude of the bearded beast's downward slide. For instance, the number of goats around at the start of the 1950s in British Columbia, the continental hub of the *Oreamnos* population, is recorded only in the ledgers of God. The province does offer a rough guesstimate of 100,000 as of 1961. Its current total is simply put at between 20,000 and 60,000. If you break the province in two, you would find that the declines were minor in the remote and relatively roadless northern half but amounted to a literal decimation throughout the southern half.

D. E. Phelps, Bob Jamieson, and Ray Demarchi and, independently, Bryan Foster analyzed the southern debacle and found it had proceeded hand in hand with rapid expansion into the backcountry of road networks for resource development. Demarchi and colleague Ken Sumanik told me of recording one group's reduction: 163 goats to three goats in five years after the high slopes were opened up by logging and coal- and oil-related operations. It was not an exceptional case. In the central eastern part of the province, a study by Bruce Pendergast and John Bindernagel revealed a drop from an estimated 740 goats in the early 1960s to an estimated 260 goats in the mid 1970s (a loss of about two-thirds) following development of the area for coal. In one newly accessible drainage, the estimated population went from 250 to one.

Decimations of an order equal to British Columbia's occurred in Alberta, which now has little more than 1,000 to 1,500 goats left outside its parks and preserves.

Alaska, which currently claims 10,000 to 25,000 goats and is therefore the continent's secondary goat population center, did not begin noticing declines in accessible areas until the 1970s—chiefly because it didn't have many accessible areas until the 1970s. A general dip in goat populations throughout Alaskan range, including seldom hunted areas, also became apparent in the 1970s and was attributed to a succession of severe winters, according to state game biologist Warren Ballard. Current concerns focus on the possible disruptive consequences of extensive logging in coastal forests containing low-elevation winter goat ranges. Quite a bit of goat habitat was protected, though, as a result of the 1980 Alaska National Interest Lands Conservation Act, with its provisions for the establishment of new parks and wildlife refuges on federal lands throughout that state.

Idaho, recognizing early on that readily reachable herds were being hammered, instituted permits and quotas for goat management in the 1950s. The one area where Idaho continued goat hunting under a general season—whereby an unlimited number of hunters are allowed to take a goat—was in the Panhandle region. Some 200 goats inhabited the Selkirk and Cabinet Mountains there in the 1950s; less than a third of that number remain, their decline paralleling that of the Selkirk caribou herd. In the rest of the state, numbers dwindled despite harvest regulations. But then it was common practice everywhere goat hunting was regulated to count, for example, 30 animals in some solitary herd and issue five permits for them every year. Only the Sawtooth Mountains herds more or less held their own, except for the accessible ones along the fringes of this range.

Approximately 2,200 to 2,500 white climbers are currently thought to remain in Idaho.

Washington was first among the states and provinces to regulate all goat hunting within its borders. One 1961 count sketched in 8,600 goats for the Cascades, where nearly all the state's herds are located, and biologists generally used to offer 10,000-plus as a rough statewide estimate. Since then, groups on the western, or coastal, slopes have been subject to local declines. Broader losses on the order of 50 percent over the last 20 years seem to have taken place east of the Cascades divide, toward Wenatchee and Lake Chelan. Excessive harvests, coupled with roadbuilding (primarily for lumbering) explain most of the drop, but biologists would like to know more about the possible contribution of longstanding fire-suppression policies. Some feel that the value of certain lower-elevation winter goat ranges, and some higher, subalpine ones as well, could have been reduced as forests encroached upon comparatively more valuable shrub forage. Whatever the actual statewide total at the moment—game biologist Rolf Johnson suggests that it is somewhere around 7,000—it includes 1,500 to 2,000 in national parks. At least 800 of these, in Olympic National Park, are the result of a transplant accomplished in the 1920s.

Numerically, the Olympic group represents the most successful introduction to date anywhere—so successful that the Olympic Peninsula has become the one place in the solar system where you will hear complaints about being overrun with *Oreamnos*. The Olympic goats are descended from a handful of Canada- and Alaska-born animals. I've met them several times and discovered them to be good-looking, friendly, and well-enough-mannered by goat standards. And no one really minds too much that they exemplify the questionable aspects of transplanting I touched on in Chapter 2—mixing up geographic gradations, or clines, of physical traits (the transplanters could at least have taken nearby goats from the Cascades) and skewing the natural evolutionary process.

What park biologist Bruce Moorhead and his colleagues are concerned about at the moment is another by-product of sticking wildlife into non-native range: upsetting the natives. The burgeoning herds have been awfully slow to disperse from the first major mountain complex they colonized. It happens to be in a unique low-precipitation belt whereas other parts of the Olympics drown in rain and snow. And in building up by leaps and bounds there, these goats finally managed to leap over most of the population-governing turnstiles I've been extolling and get in some classic crowded-ungulate-range overgrazing. Consequently, they began seriously altering plant communities and soils that, as Moorhead points out, evolved without goats—including some rare and endemic plant species. Some local fauna have also come under pressure: one mountain goat neighbor I overlooked in Chapter 4 is a little-known rodent called the mountain beaver (*Aplodontia rufa*—not a true beaver), found along the Cascades south of southernmost British Columbia. In the Olympics, it probably has a different name than "neighbors" for the goats now trampling down the slopes where its colonies burrow and monopolizing much of its food.

There used to be goats, incidentally, on the slopes of Mount St. Helens. Had they not been extirpated by overshooting early in the century, the volcano definitely would have transplanted them when it blew its top in 1981. A herd reintroduced to nearby Mount Margaret in 1972 and 1973 was apparently de-reintroduced when the St. Helens eruption buried Mount Margaret's slopes beneath ash—though a party of hikers reported seeing a band of at least temporary survivors down in the forest near the mountain's base.

Montana declines to venture past and present goat totals. I would hazard one for the present: 1,500 in Glacier Park and an equal, if not somewhat smaller, figure for all the rest of the state's native populations combined, plus several hundred more in various nonnative herds. While the state was establishing new goat ranges through an extensive transplant program, its natural nonpark populations were plummeting. Along the continental divide, the region I know, they probably fell by at least 50 percent overall and by more than 75 percent in much of it. The chief cause? The same: overharvest together with uncontrolled access. Yet in some sections overharvesting alone was responsible. Despite the fact that fewer and fewer hunters and their guides were able to find goats in the vast, roadless Bob Marshall, an unlimited number of goat permits were sold for that hunting unit until the 1970s, and it cost the resident herds far more than they could afford.

My study area, where the Swan Mountains continue northward from the western boundary of "the Bob," was a microcosm of the conditions that brought about the bearded beast's demise in so many of its former strongholds elsewhere on the continent. A fast cliff-by-cliff history of the area will help reveal just what the white climbers are looking at from their stony abode ten millennia into the so-called Holocene epoch.

A regular succession of deep stream and glacier-cut valleys notch into the Swan Range at right angles, draining its waters away to the east and west. The Swan goats always kept to the upper ends of these valleys during the green months, each herd traveling some distance north and south along the divide itself, and also across to the other side, occasionally meeting and mixing with adjoining herds. Then, as the snow clouds arrived, the different groups dropped away from one another down either side of the crest. Soon each herd had returned to its inherited winter range in a particular valley, usually toward a south-facing set of outcrops near the valley's mouth, sometimes to a gale-bared ridge.

If you visit the western slopes of the Swans today, you can drive up virtually every valley on a well-maintained two-lane dirt and gravel road. Along the way you will often pass right along the base of winter range cliffs—literally within a stone's throw of goat ledges. Farther up, having wheeled by dozens of side roads webbing away up the slopes to a quilt-work of clearcut forest tracts, you pass more cliffs—fall and spring transitional range—and soon arrive, still in your car, in the subalpine lower edge of goat summering country. Some roads will take you to within a mile of the divide itself, so you can bushwhack to reach the very highest spots an hour or two after shutting your car door. Other roads switch back so that if you were hunting, you would have the dubious distinction of being able to park and then commence firing *down* at the hooved animal that dwells highest of all in North America.

You would have one problem, of course: conjuring up a goat to sight on these days. I seldom got my scope on more than one or two—at most four—in any of the several roaded west-slope valleys I surveyed hard and often. The rocks had room for ten to maybe 25, which is what longtime local residents told me they used to see, along with temporary concentrations of over 30 or 40 per valley in the 1950s. That was the decade the first bulldozers headed uphill. They were followed by many more in the years to come.

During the years I was counting, Lion Creek still had a maximum of 15 goats and Bond Creek up to seven. They were the only two drainages in the west-slope part of my study area in which the roads stopped before they reached the lower cliffs. The Forest Service, however, has proposed pushing roads and logging leases farther up both of them.

On the eastern Swan slopes the logging roads wind upward from the main route along the South Fork of the Flathead River. In 1957, 158 miles of logging roads existed in the lower South Fork area. In 1958, the earliest year records were kept, the harvest of mountain goats—hunted on an unlimited permit basis—was 74. By 1971, the lower South Fork held 617 road miles, and hunters managed to take just eight goats, though 25 permits were issued for this unit. To put it mildly, the easy goats were gone.

Some of those South Fork road miles veered up a drainage named Sullivan Creek which lies near the Little Creek/Addition Creek valley where I spent so much time goatwatching. Prior to the road—and a logging camp set up within pistol range of a major cliff area—Sullivan Creek had 15 to 20 resident goats, according to both the woods boss of that operation and Forest Service employees. In the years I looked there the number of shaggy white inhabitants varied from zero to three, depending mostly on whether or not some billies happened through. I never found many big billies anywhere in my study area. I'm sure I missed a few, but they had also been picked over heavily by shooting in the preceding years, and now hunters here were starting to harvest mainly nannies. A few were calling on the game department to close the season.

The farthest extension of the South Fork road was from a point near Sullivan Creek on up to Bunker Creek, an intrusion of 25 miles into pristine mountain landscapes. The Forest Service decision to go ahead with constructing access and offering logging sales here was highly controversial. Hunters, fishermen, guides, and others—I know some opposed to the project made their living logging—fought it every tractor cleat of the way. They were aware that Bunker Creek held some of the best wildlife habitat and lonesome campsites left in the northern Swans, maybe *the* best. Moreover, it was a valuable buffer area for the Bob Marshall. Perhaps the right word for this place is one sometimes used as a synonym for a state of remoteness, or inaccessibility: ultramontane.

But every Forest Service region and district has an annual timber quota to meet. Officials are subject to national administrative pressure to sell the timber through bids to private logging companies. At the same time, local districts like those around the Flathead are generally under intense local pressure to open up new sawlog reserves because logging and lumber-milling are the mainstay of the local economy. A quick check of Flathead National Forest offices prior to the early 1970s would have failed to turn up a full-time wildlife biologist among several hundred employees. Over 90 percent of the personnel dealt directly with timber and engineering, clearly reflecting the prevailing emphasis. The ratio has shifted somewhat since then, but not terribly far.

The Bunker Creek sale went through, and road work began. A side road was pushed up the Little Creek/Addition Creek drainage, stopping only at the headwall, and the valley was heavily cut over. Though no one was keeping track of the effects on resident goats at the time, I suspect that the intense logging disturbance prompted most of the herd to abandon the locale in favor of the Bunker Creek portion of their range, across the ridgeline.

When Beth and I came into the country in March of 1971, the main road had proceeded around Little/Addition Creek, then past Gorge Creek, flowing out of the Bob Marshall's north edge, and on to the confluence of the North and Middle Forks of Bunker Creek. The only sign of man's presence beyond that was a rough bulldozer trail probing partway up each of the two high valleys. But the goats apparently had felt the first shock wave strongly. Both the game warden who patrolled the South Fork and a Forest Service employee who had hunted Bunker Creek told me that as many as 11 of the bearded beasts may have been poached from the North Fork cliffs during the fall of 1970. Until then I had only known of the three killed there legally that year. Three happened to be the same number that had been legally taken in the previous ten years, when Bunker Creek was still free from any road.

By July the tractors and trucks and chainsaws had proceeded up the North Fork to a point opposite our camp, opposite the trout pools and the slopes where the goats and black bears and elk and I had been studying each other. Drills bored into the rocky ground and dynamite was placed in the holes, and charges were touched off throughout the day to clear and level the wide road route. One blast spewed out a rock chunk that landed across on our fire pit, smashing a coffeepot. Two others shook me loose from the rocks I was climbing.

The goats withdrew; some to the highest ridges, others back to Little Creek. Now and then an individual or small band would return for salt at one of the two natural licks here. But they came mostly after dark now or on the weekend, when construction ceased and you could once again hear the moving water or the bleating of a kid.

Three goats—a nanny I had named Patch for the hunk of hair missing along her mane, her kid, and a collared yearling billy—lingered around the upper cliffs and ridges until September. A Forest Service ranger arrived to check out rumors of loggers baiting black bears into their camp to shoot. For a while the air smelled of huckleberries, then it smelled of smoke and the air hazed up from fires set to burn logging slash. Then there were no goats in Bunker Creek.

I returned to Little Creek to follow their activities, and on the opening weekend of hunting season (which lasts from September 15 through the last week of November), I found the logging spur road across from the cliffs suddenly cleared of fallen snags and boulders, and full of four-wheel-drive vehicles and over a dozen men in orange vests. Concentrated now in this one valley, the largest remaining herd in this entire portion of the Swans—25 to 30 goats—went unconcernedly about its business on the tile-red rocks while hunters set up tripods, sighted through telescopes, and a couple of them started lobbing one-half- to three-quarter-mile volleys of bullets across the canyon, exclaiming, walking up and down exchanging shop talk. Several agreed that what I knew to be a three-year-old nanny was a prize billy.

On the receiving end of this drive-in shooting gallery, the goats still paid little attention to the distant people or to the puffs of dust and rock splinters spanging around them, probably because these were not unlike the results of a small rockfall. There wasn't that much shooting, really. It had been more like an experiment. Now everyone was waiting to see where the goats might bed down and making plans to hike over to the cliffs, or at least a little closer.

I suppose my task as an objective recorder was simply to keep score. From the standpoint of the long-term value of my kind of research project it might indeed have been the most reasonable thing to do. What I did was go with Beth, slipping down the hillside, across Little Creek, following game trails we knew, and up to the cliffs, where we pretended to be sampling vegetation—placing ourselves so the goats would be sure to get our scent and escape upward, out of range.

Later that day a hunter passed us on the road and, failing to recognize either of us, told how he had been part of a crowd watching "two damn fool berrypickers messing around by the goat rocks" through their rifle scopes. Before dusk I was at the Spotted Bear Ranger Station telling the chief ranger that if he didn't close that spur road, I would dig it shut with a pick and shovel. It was supposed to be closed off anyway (mostly to meet Forest Service driving safety codes). I didn't think I needed to watch the goats actually collapse and stop breathing to figure out the consequences of goat hunting as a parking lot carnival. I doubted the more serious hunters liked it all that well either. He agreed, and sent up a backhoe to trench the spur road shut before the next weekend.

Yet the road over in Bunker Creek stayed open to the confluence of the forks. Heavy snows sent the elk moving early, downstream toward their winter range where Gorge Creek flows into Bunker Creek. The road intersected the wintering area. Over twice as many elk were shot along Bunker Creek as in any other South Fork drainage that fall of 1971.

Following a long, quiet, isolated winter, the whole cacophony of bulldozing and clearcutting resumed in Bunker Creek, pressing up both forks toward the subalpine basins around little melt lakes. Logging trucks rumbled up and down the road all day, and blast reports thundered through the North Fork valley, several to the hour at times. Bunker Creek ran muddy now and then as work upstream crossed it or culverts were dug in.

We spent little time in the Middle Fork of Bunker because goat sightings there were always scant compared to the North Fork. Now, however, no goats regularly used the lower cliffs of the North Fork either, their powerful attraction to salt notwithstanding. And only a few lingered at times on the ridgeline. Four grizzlies were poached: a sow with two cubs at the head of the roaded Middle Fork, and one across from Gorge Creek.

Another fall arrived. A group of ten goats including my old collared acquaintance No. 10—Pandora—left Little Creek, ironically on the first day of hunting season, and traveled to the Bunker Creek ridgetop. The next day two adult nannies were shot there and a young billy reportedly wounded. Another grizzly was killed near Gorge Creek, this one legally. As many as three others were reported by guides and hunters to have been poached elsewhere in my Swan study area. Among the goats killed in the overall study area was Billy One-Eye. He was taken on the western slope of the Swan divide. I had last seen him on the east side, at Bunker Creek. Skinning him out, the hunter—bowhunter, actually, and also a longtime Swan area resident and a good friend—learned that the billy had lost his right eye's sight long before to a bullet.

Yielding to pressure from the Montana fish and game department and other conservationists, the Forest Service had closed the road for the duration of the hunting season at a point across from Gorge Creek. It wasn't far enough. The word was out on the fantastic elk hunting here, and it was hard to find parking space among the trucks and cars. Where they could park, all the hunters had to do was step out the door to be in the major wintering site. The elk kill was as high as the year before.

Winter: again powerful winds stormed down off Thunderbolt and Bruce Ridge to topple most of the spindly trees left in, or on the edge of, logged sites. Yet snowfall was the lightest in years, and spring of 1973 found the Little Creek herd in good shape. Kids included, goat groups in the study area were about the same size they had been when I started the project in the Swans. Given the amount of depopulated winter range, especially west of the divide, I had thought they might do quite a bit better. On the other hand, they might have done quite a bit worse than keep even, had the Little Creek and Bunker Creek roads stayed open.

By late spring, I wasn't seeing the elk I was used to in the North Fork. Nor was there anything like the usual sign of Griz or black bear, once dense in the North Fork terrain I covered. Some goats started using the licks. On June 19, four days after the road opened and preparatory logging operations began, no goats remained. Nor did I see any goats in that valley during summer or fall, though I've no doubt the odd one hiked over from Little Creek while I was off searching other slopes. And still no regular Griz sign in the usual Bunker Creek spots. The scat, tracks, diggings, and sightings of the great bear I now noted were densest in the adjoining Bob Marshall section of the study area. I did see one smallish, black subadult grizzly in Bunker Creek. It was legally killed by a hunter that fall next door, in Addition Creek.

I know goats still came at times into Bunker Creek as logging wound up and the Forest Service began repairing erosion damage on steep cutover areas in the North Fork while I turned my attention toward

Glacier Park. I know because of a photograph a fish and game employee took of a man walking down the Bunker Creek road (regularly closed at Gorge Creek during the hunting season) wheeling a golf cart with a dead goat draped over it.

I always had a great time crab-crawling along the rocks close enough to heave my dye-filled balloons at mountain goats. But that's about as far as my hunting instincts lead toward these bearded beasts, and I thought I'd better make my emotional bias clear, if it isn't already fairly obvious.

I also want to make it clear, though, that while I've used part of this final chapter to build as strong a case as I could against applying traditional game harvest policies to North America's sole rupicaprid, I didn't do so in order to argue that every goat ought to be left unhunted. My personal feelings tell me it would be a splendid change if this hooved species could be one we agreed to manage exclusively as a resource for the eyes and questioning mind and imagination. The facts don't prove this to be a necessity.

Selected herds—in marginal ranges, disturbed areas, or isolated settings—should perhaps be left entirely unburdened by harvest pressure. Beyond that I can only encourage what many managers now realize as a result of their own investigations and are working toward: developing sensitive management procedures tailored to the unique physical niche and society of *Oreamnos*.

The first step, most would agree, is to set quotas on a herd-by-herd basis, or as close to that as is practical. Next? Making sure those quotas are set at conservative levels. How conservative? Some think five percent of a population could be skimmed annually. This does represent a truly conservative approach by contrast with earlier ones. Others want to shoot for ten percent, still cautious by usual game harvest standards. I would think five percent is risky enough.

However, the true percentage that could be removed without lasting harm probably varies from region to region. As Daryl Hebert has recommended, the coastal ecotype probably requires more cautious manipulation than interior populations, due to the highly variable productivity and greater isolation of many maritime herds, and because of their extreme liability to those winters that lock up even the beaches.

The proper harvest percentage will depend also upon which goats go into it. Barring the unlikely possibility that trophy-hunting sportsmen could be talked into taking mostly kids and yearlings, the next most "expendable" segment of any herd is mature males. Canadian managers have experimented with "billy only" seasons. The results were discouraging insofar as the hunters still proved unable to tell the goat sexes apart, despite education efforts by the game departments. That's no surprise. I still have to look twice to distinguish the sexes at a distance, often half-a-dozen times. And there are likely to be almost as many mature nannies without a tell-tale kid at heel as there are with one in an average herd.

I'll cheerfully throw in another headache—the need to focus mainly on subordinate billies because of the importance of prime billies to the mating structure. But then, smaller billies are even harder to pick out from nannies, and how many breeding nannies can a given herd afford to supply to human hunters? These adult females are also, in a sense, cultural repositories; they pass on very specific home range knowledge from generation to generation—information that is of particular importance to a beast living in very small bands, whose survival may turn on knowing the location of a few windblown acres.

Game management is an applied science. Its primary purpose, after all, is to encourage the sustained production of wild animals for human consumption, and its primary funding comes from the sale of hunting licenses. Understandably, then, managers are inclined to try for the maximum theoretical harvest, and revise and finagle downward from there. My proposal, since I can't say precisely what form an acceptably conservative harvest ought to take, is simply to start at levels that, if not quite right, at least err wholly in favor of the mountain goats for a change.

I do have one specific positive suggestion. Put the hunters on the job gathering more information about goat numbers and locations to fill in the blank spaces. Those I've talked to would be grateful for the challenge and chance to participate.

It seems a dismal business that from the middle of the twentieth century onward the mountain goat should have had to undergo much the same pattern of vanishing from place after place upon its first serious contact with our culture, as though we learned nothing from the earlier fate of virtually every other big wild mammal in this country. It's easy to point to past shortcomings by managers in protecting my white-clad, sure-footed heroes. It might be more appropriate to look around at the priorities of our nation and ask why game managers have never had quite the money or manpower necessary to gain crucial information about the goat in time, or even to just get them counted before the crunch came. And why are they still strapped for funds? And why do they have so little clout when it comes to influencing the way critical wildlife habitat is used by other interests?

All the funds that, say, Montana's Department of Fish, Wildlife and Parks (fish and game) receives annually from the legislature, plus sales of licenses for everything from beavers to cougars wouldn't build five miles of interstate highway or one turbine for one questionable dam. The manager can urge road closures, emphasize the value of leaving migration corridors, recommend halting work during birthing or rutting periods, and so forth. Road closures are an especially important, simple, and effective solution to many resource conflicts. Seasonal closures of roads throughout a mountain complex such as the Swans could be orchestrated to restore entire wildlife communities without precluding certain types of development. The idea of systematic road closure appears to be catching on in many regions. At the rate it is being put into actual practice, however, the glaciers might return before vigorous populations of the white climbers and some of their neighbors do.

The wildlife manager can make his suggestions. And when the political and economic atmosphere is cordial, everyone listens and a workable compromise is struck. In less enlightened episodes—and I've seen a few —the game manager, not wanting to cause too great a fuss, merely grins endearingly and hopes for the road to be closed . . . until the land manager, who, say, is a forester and anxious to get on with his job, tells the biologist to close or shorten the hunting season if he wants to protect wildlife. The fire-control officer wants the main road kept open; the four-wheel-drive club is lobbying to keep every spur road open. Meanwhile, some emotionally unbalanced goat-lover like myself is writing crank letters threatening to tear the road up and plant it with thorn trees, and then the Fish & Wildlife Service is drawn in, perhaps because the officially threatened grizzly may be jeopardized by the road and logging disturbance. But the professional antipathy that sometimes develops between state and federal biologists snarls efforts at cooperation, so there is a public hearing at which one man compares peregrine falcons to Beethoven and assures everyone that a single falcon he thinks he saw there did more for him than ten years on his analyst's couch. The local curmudgeon who attends every public hearing on everything complains once more that all Griz does is sleep all winter and eat people all summer; a woman harangues bureaucrats in general for wasting taxpayers' money on meetings; and the inevitable "We don't need more otters, we need jobs" spokesman's speech is interrupted by a shouting duel. Eight people glare their way out the door to start separate petition drives. . . .

It's called democracy, and I love it. The drawback is that the animals whose future the entire furor originally revolved around still lack a vote, and speak foreign languages we are only just beginning to translate. And so when push comes to shove in the arena of self-government, the critters

two-thirds of this nation happened only some 130 years before that, 180 years before 1983.

Marshall used the word "niche" in the older sense of a place. His statement appeals to me even more when I contemplate niche in the biological sense as a summation of the space an organism occupies and the role it plays in the web of life.

We must take care to see that the beast we call the mountain goat remains. Remains for its own sake and because it is a talisman, not far from myth, of the high, free places. Its welfare will continue to mark the extent to which we have invaded and exploited the mountain fastnesses and the extent to which Griz, Wolf, Eagle, Sheep and all the others holding on there will take part in our future. Without them, without their niches, we will be that much closer to having only ourselves and our works to look at, learn from, and touch our feelings—the self-inflicted tyranny of walking endlessly down a hall of mirrors.

Appendix I
Criteria for Distinguishing Sex and Age of
Mountain Goats During Summer

Age Class	Sex	Characteristics
KID		Small size obvious in early summer, but grow rapidly and require more careful observation from the air by late summer
		Horns barely visible early summer, and are less than approximately 0.75 times the ear length by fall
		Face very juvenile in appearance
		Nearly always following an adult female
	Male	Urination posture: stands in stretched position
	Female	Urination posture: squats
YEARLING		Larger than kid, considerably smaller than adult female in early summer; still obviously smaller in late summer
		Horns in early summer less than ear length, reach up to 1.5 times ear length by fall; horns generally with ragged rough surface texture (later becoming very smooth)
		Face still juvenile in appearance
		Subdominant behavior: frequently "picked on" by all older animals
		Occasionally solitary in late summer and winter, but most often with female juvenile groups during summer
	Male	Urination posture: scrotum visible when hair is short
		Horns usually appear heavier than females and more masculine

Age Class	Sex	Characteristics
	Female	Urination posture: black vulval patch visible when tail raised Horns usually slightly thinner than males
Two-year-old		Smaller than adult female in early summer; nearly equal by fall Horns longer than ears Face no longer juvenile in appearance but not quite as long and angular in muzzle as adults Difficult to distinguish from adults in late summer except by careful observation
	Male	Urination posture: scrotum visible in summer coat Horns obviously thicker than females' with less space between bases as seen frontally, smoother curve from base to tip as seen laterally, may look longer in proportion to head length than adult males Body slightly larger and heavier over neck and shoulders than females Usually still in company of female kid groups during summer
	Female	Urination posture: black vulval patch visible when tail is raised Horns thinner and slightly more angular (not always) than males' as viewed laterally; more space between bases as viewed frontally Neck and shoulders not as massive as males Body obviously smaller than adult females in spring; still slightly smaller in fall Difficult to distinguish from adult females without kids by late summer
Adult		Full-grown animals Faces long and angular, especially females Horns much longer than ears
	Male	Urination posture: scrotum very visible in summer coat

Age Class	Sex	Characteristics
		Rump progressively more dirt smeared in late summer and into winter
		Horns more massive than females', tapering and curving smoothly from base to tip as viewed laterally; horn bases heavy, and space between bases as viewed frontally is about one-half the width of the base and obviously narrower than females'. Horns may appear proportionally smaller than those of females or two-year-old males due to larger body and head size.
		Neck and shoulders massive with crest line forming nearly smooth, convex curve from back of head to lumbar region
		Body larger than adult female
		Usually clean shed by early July and starting to grow winter coat by early August
		Only rarely found in association with female kid groups during summer; often solitary
	Female	Urination posture: black vulval patch obvious when tail raised
		May have kid at heel.
		Horns thinner than males and more angular, often diverge in "Y" shape as viewed frontally. Space between horn bases is obviously wider than males and is about equal to three-quarters the width of horn base.
		Appear "ewe-necked" before molt is complete with thin necks and long, angular muzzles. After molt, dorsal crest line appears slightly concave or less convex than males.
		Shoulders and entire body less massive than adult males
		Rump clean in fall and winter
		Usually in groups with other females and juveniles

Adapted from Lyman Nichols, Mountain Goat Management Technique Studies. Final Report, Federal Aid in Wildlife Restoration; Projects W-17-9, W-17-10 and W-17-11, Jobs 12.2R and 12.3R. Alaska Department of Fish and Game, Juneau. July 1980.

Appendix II
Taxonomy of Rupicaprid Relatives

CLASS	ORDER	FAMILY	SUBFAMILY
MAMMALIA	ARTIODACTYLA[1]	BOVIDAE (bison, antelope, sheep, goats, cattle, etc.)	CAPRINAE
			Cephalophinae (duikers)
		Suidae (swine)	Neotraginae (dwarf antelope)
		Tayassuidae (javelinas, peccaries)	
			Tragelaphinae (spiral-horned antelopes)
		Hippopotamidae (hippos)	
			Bovinae (buffalo, cattle, bison)
		Camelidae (camels, llamas)	
			Alcelaphinae (hartebeests)
		Tragulidae (chevrotains)	
			Hippotraginae (oryx, etc.)
		Cervidae (deer, elk, moose, caribou, etc.)	
			Reduncinae (waterbuck, kob, etc.)
		Giraffidae (giraffe, opaki)	
			Antilopinae (gazelles, etc.)
		Antilocapridae (pronghorn)	
	Perissodactyla[1]	Equidae (horses, asses, zebras)	
		Tapiridae (tapirs)	
		Rhinocerotidae (rhinos)	

[1]Perissodactyla and Artiodactyla were at one time lumped in the superorder Ungulata. The common name "ungulate" is still used, but the superorder is no longer recognized.

TRIBE	GENUS	SPECIES
RUPICAPRINI	OREAMNOS	O. AMERICANUS (mountain goat)
	Rupicapra	*R. rupicapra* (chamois)
	Nemorhaedus	*N. goral* (goral)
	Capricornis	*C. sumatraensis* (serow)
		C. crispus (Japanese serow)
Caprini	*Capra* (ibex, markhor, wild true goats, domestic goats)	
	Ammotragus (Barbary sheep)	
	Hemitragus (tahr)	
	Pseudois (blue sheep)	
	Ovis (wild sheep, mouflon, urial, argali, domestic sheep, bighorn, Dall's sheep)	
Saigini[2]	*Panthalops* (Tibetan antelope)	
	Saiga (saiga antelope)	
Ovibovini	*Ovibos* (musk-oxen)	
	Budorcas (takin)	

[2]The tribe Saigini appears to be closely related to modern descendants of primitive true antelopes that gave rise to rupicaprids. These modern antelope species are the Mongolian gazelle (*Procapra gutturosa*), the Tibetan gazelle (*P. picticaudata*), and the Przewalski's gazelle (*P. przewalski*).

Bibliography

BALLARD, W. 1977. Status and management of the mountain goat in Alaska. In *Proceedings First International Mountain Goat Symposium*, ed. W. Samuel and W.G. MacGregor, 15-23. Queen's Printer, Victoria, B.C.

BANSNER, U. 1974. Mountain goat–human interactions in the Sperry–Gunsight Pass area of Glacier National Park. Progress report, University of Montana, Missoula.

———. 1976. Mountain goat–human interactions in the Sperry–Gunsight Pass area of Glacier National Park. Final report, University of Montana, Missoula.

BRANDBORG, S.M. 1955. Life history and management of the mountain goat in Idaho. Idaho Department Fish and Game Wildlife Bulletin No. 2, Boise.

———. 1970. *Alive in the Wild.* Prentice–Hall, Englewood Cliffs, N.J.

CAHALANE, V.H. 1947. *Mammals of North America.* Macmillan, New York.

CASEBEER, R.L. 1948. Food habits of mountain goats in western Montana. In M.S. thesis, University of Montana, Missoula.

CHADWICK, D.H. 1974. Mountain goat ecology–logging relationships in the Bunker Creek Drainage of western Montana. Montana Department Fish, Game, and Parks, Project Report N-120-R-3,4, Helena, Mont.

———. 1976. Ecological relationships of mountain goats, *Oreamnos americanus*, in Glacier National Park. In *Proceedings First Conference on Scientific Research in the National Parks*, ed. R.M. Linn, vol. 1:451-456. U.S. Government Printing Office, Washington, D.C.

———. 1977. The influence of mountain goat social relationships on population size and distribution. In *Proceedings First International Mountain Goat Symposium*, ed. W. Samuel and W.G. MacGregor, 74-91. Queen's Printer, Victoria, B.C.

———. 1977. Ecology of the Rocky Mountain goat in Glacier National Park and the Swan Mountains, Montana. Final report, Glacier National Park, West Glacier, Mont.

COLE, G.F. 1971. Animal ecology studies in Yellowstone National Park. Office of Natural Science Studies, Annual Report YELL-N-38, Yellowstone National Park, Wyo.

COWAN, I. McT. 1944. Report of wildlife studies in Jasper, Banff, and Yoho National Parks in 1944 and parasites, diseases, and injuries of game animals in the Rocky Mountain National Parks, 1942–1944. Wildlife Service Department, Mines and Resources, Ottawa.

COWAN, I. McT. and W. McCrory. 1970. Variation in the mountain goat *(Oreamnos americanus)* (Blainville). *Journal of Mammalogy* 51(1): 60-73.

CRAIGHEAD, F.C. JR. 1979. *Track of the Grizzly.* Sierra Club Books, San Francisco.

DANE, B. 1977. Mountain goat social behavior: social structure and "play" behavior as affected by dominance. In *Proceedings First International Mountain Goat Symposium,* ed. W. Samuel and W.G. MacGregor, 92-106. Queen's Printer, Victoria, B.C.

DARLING, F.F. 1937. *A herd of red deer.* Oxford University Press, London.

DEBOCK, E. A. 1970. On the behavior of the mountain goat *(Oreamnos americanus)* in Kootenay National Park. M.S. Diss., University of Alberta, Edmonton.

DEVOTO, B. 1953. *The Journals of Lewis and Clark.* Houghton Mifflin, New York.

ESTES, R.D. 1974. Social organization of the African Bovidae. In *The behavior of ungulates and its relation to management,* ed. V. Geist and F. Walther, vol. 1:166-205. I.U.C.N. pub. no. 24, Morges, Switzerland.

EWER, R.F. 1968. *Ethology of mammals.* Logos Press, London.

FOSTER, B.R. 1976. Exploitation and management of the mountain goat in British Columbia. Department Zoology Report, University of British Columbia, Vancouver, B.C.

———. 1980 (revised). Bibliography of North America's mountain goat *(Oreamnos americanus).* In *Proceedings Biennial Symposium, Northern Wild Sheep and Goat Council,* ed. W.D. Hickey, 624-668. Salmon, Idaho.

————. 1978. Horn growth and quality management for mountain goats. In *Proceedings 1978 Northern Sheep and Goat Conference*, ed. D. Hebert and M. Nation, 200-226. British Columbia Fish and Wildlife Branch, Victoria, B.C.

FOSTER, B.R. and E.Y. Rahs. 1983. Implications of maternal separation on overwinter survival of mountain goat kids. In *Proceedings Third Biennial Conference Northern Wild Sheep and Goat Council.* Fort Collins, Colo.

FOX, J.L., K.J. Raedeke, and C.A. Smith. 1982. Mountain goat ecology on Cleveland Peninsula, Alaska, 1980–1982. Pacific Northwest Forest and Range Experimental Station Final Report, Contract PNW-82-197, Juneau.

FOX, M.W. 1971. *Behavior of wolves, dogs and related canids.* Jonathan Cape, London.

FRASER, F. 1968. *Reproductive behavior in ungulates.* Academic Press, New York.

GEIST, V. 1964. On the rutting behavior of the mountain goat. *Journal of Mammology* 45(4):551-568.

————. 1967. On fighting injuries and dermal shields in mountain goats. *Journal of Wildlife Management* 31(1):192-194.

————. 1971. *Mountain sheep: a study in behavior and evolution.* University of Chicago Press, Chicago.

GUIGUET, C. 1951. An account of a wolverine attacking a goat. *Canadian Field Naturalist* 65(5):187.

GUTHRIE, A.B. JR. 1947. *The Big Sky.* Houghton Mifflin, New York.

HARINGTON, C.R. 1971. A Pleistocene mountain goat from British Columbia and comments on the dispersal history of Oreamnos. *Canadian Journal of Earth Science* 8(9):1081-1093.

HEBERT, D.M. 1978. A systems approach to mountain goat management. In *Proceedings 1978 Northern Wild Sheep and Goat Conference*, ed. D. Hebert and M. Nation, 227-243. British Columbia Fish and Wildlife Branch, Victoria, B.C.

HEBERT, D.M., and I. McT. Cowan. 1971. White muscle disease in the mountain goat. *Journal of Wildlife Management* 35(4):752-756.

HEBERT, D.M., and W.G. Turnbull. 1977. A description of southern interior and coastal mountain goat ecotypes in British Columbia. In *Proceedings First International Mountain Goat Symposium*, ed. W. Samuel and W.G. MacGregor, 126-146. Queen's Printer, Victoria, B.C.

HIBBS, L.D. 1966. A literature review on mountain goat ecology. Colorado Department Game, Fish, and Parks, and Colorado Cooperative Wildlife Research Unit, Special Report No. 8, Denver.

HJELJORD, O.G. 1973. Mountain goat forage and habitat preference in Alaska. *Journal of Wildlife Management* 37(3):353-362.

HOLROYD, J.C. 1967. Observations of Rocky Mountain goats on Mt. Wardle, Kootenay National Park, British Columbia. *Canadian Field Naturalist* 81(1):1-22.

HORNOCKER, M.G. and H.S. Hash. Ecology of the wolverine in northwestern Montana. *Canadian Journal of Zoology* 59(7):1286-1301.

HUTCHINS, M. 1983. The mother–offspring relationship in mountain goats *(Oreamnos americanus)*. Unpubl. diss., University of Washington, Seattle.

JOHNSON, R.L. 1977. Status and management of the mountain goat in Washington. In *Proceedings First International Mountain Goat Symposium*, ed. W. Samuel and W.G. MacGregor, 41-46. Queen's Printer, Victoria, B.C.

———. 1983. Mountain goats and mountain sheep in Washington. Washington Department of Game Biological Bulletin, Olympia, Wash.

KERR, G.R., and J.C. Holmes. 1966. Parasites of mountain goats in west–central Alberta. *Journal of Wildlife Management* 30(4):786-790.

KROG, H., and M. Monson. 1954. Notes on the metabolism of a mountain goat. *American Journal of Physiology* 17(3):515-516.

KUCK, L. 1970. Rocky Mountain goat ecology. Idaho Department Fish and Game Project Report W-144-R-02, Boise.

———. 1977. Status and management of the mountain goat in Idaho. In *Proceedings First International Mountain Goat Symposium*, ed. W. Samuel and W.G. MacGregor, 37-40. Queen's Printer, Victoria, B.C.

———. 1977. The impact of hunting on Idaho's Pahsimeroi mountain goat herd. In *Proceedings First International Mountain Goat Symposium*, ed. W. Samuel and W.G. MacGregor, 114-125. Queen's Printer, Victoria, B.C.

KURTEN, B. 1972. *The Age of Mammals*. Columbia University Press, New York.

LENTFER, J.L. 1955. A two-year study of the Rocky Mountain goat in the Crazy Mountains, Montana. *Journal of Wildlife Management* 19(4): 417-429.

MECH, D.L. 1970. *The wolf: the ecology and behavior of an endangered species*. Natural History Press, New York.

McFETRIDGE, R.J. 1977. Strategy of resource use by mountain goat nursery groups. In *Proceedings First National Mountain Goat Symposium*, ed. W. Samuel and W.G. MacGregor, 169-173. Queen's Printer, Victoria, B.C.

MURIE, A. 1944. The wolves of Mt. McKinley. Fauna of the National Parks of the U.S., Fauna Series No. 5. U.S. Government Printing Office, Washington, D.C.

MURIE, O.J. 1954. *A field guide to animal tracks*. Petersen Field Guide Series No. 9. Houghton Mifflin, New York.

MOORHEAD, B. 1981. An environmental assessment on the management of introduced mountain goats in Olympic National Park. Olympic National Park, Port Angeles, Washington.

MOORHEAD, B., and V. Stevens. 1982. Introduction and dispersal of mountain goats in Olympic National Park, Washington. In *Ecological Research in National Parks of the Pacific Northwest*, 46-50. Forest Research Laboratory, Oregon State University, Corvallis.

NICHOLS, L. 1980. Mountain goat management technique studies. Alaska Department Fish and Game, Federal Aid in Wildlife Restoration Final Report, Projects W-17-9,10,11; Jobs 12.2, 3 R, Juneau.

PENDERGAST, B., and J. Bindernagel. 1977. The impact of exploration for coal on mountain goats in northeastern British Columbia. In *Proceedings First International Mountain Goat Symposium*, ed. W. Samuel and W.G. MacGregor, 64-68. Queen's Printer, Victoria, B.C.

PETOCZ, R.G. 1973. The effect of snow cover on the social behavior of bighorn rams and mountain goats. *Canadian Journal of Zoology* 51: 987-993.

PHELPS, D.E., B. Jamieson, and R.A. Demarchi. 1975. Mountain goat management in the Kootenays. British Columbia Fish and Wildlife Branch, Cranbrook, B.C.

RALLS, K., K. Brugger, and J. Ballou. 1979. Inbreeding and juvenile mortality in small populations of ungulates. *Science* 206:1101-1103.

RICHARDSON, A.H. 1971. The Rocky Mountain goat in the Black Hills. South Dakota Department Fish, Game, and Parks Bulletin No. 2, Bismark, S.D.

RIDEOUT, C.B. 1974. A radio telemetry study of the ecology and behavior of the mountain goat. Ph.D. diss., University of Kansas, Lawrence.

RUSSELL, A. 1968. *Grizzly Country.* Alfred A. Knopf, New York.

SAMUEL, W.M., G.A. Chalmers, J.G. Stelfox, A. Loewen, and J. Thomson. 1975. Contagious ecthyma in bighorn sheep and mountain goat in western Canada. *Journal of Wildlife Diseases* 11(1):26-31.

SAMUEL, W., and W.K. Hall. 1977. Parasites of mountain goat, *Oreamnos americanus* (Blainville), of west central Alberta with a comparison of the helminths of mountain goat and Rocky Mountain bighorn sheep. In *Proceedings First International Mountain Goat Symposium*, ed. W. Samuel and W.G. MacGregor, 212-225. Queen's Printer, Victoria, B.C.

SCHALLER, G. 1972. *The Serengeti Lion.* University of Chicago Press, Chicago.

———. 1979. *Mountain Monarchs.* University of Chicago Press, Chicago.

SCHOEN, J.W., and M.D. Kirchoff. 1981. Habitat use by mountain goats in southeast Alaska. Alaska Department Fish and Game Final Report, Federal Aid in Wildlife Restoration Projects W-17-10,11, and W-21-1,2; Job 12.4 R, Juneau.

SETON, E.T. 1911. *Arctic Prairies.* Charles Scribner's Sons, New York.

———. 1927. *Lives of Game Animals.* Doubleday, New York.

SINGER, F.J. 1975. Behavior of mountain goats, elk, and other wildlife in relation to U.S. Highway 2, Glacier National Park. Federal Highway Administration, Denver.

———. 1977. Dominance, leadership, and group cohesion of mountain goats at a natural lick, Glacier National Park, Montana. In *Proceedings First International Mountain Goat Symposium*, ed. W. Samuel and W.G. MacGregor, 107-113. Queen's Printer, Victoria, B.C.

SMITH, B.L. 1976. Ecology of Rocky Mountain goat in the Bitterroot Mountains, Montana. Master's thesis, University of Montana, Missoula.

————. 1977. Influence of snow conditions on winter distribution, habitat use, and group size of mountain goats. In *Proceedings First International Mountain Goat Symposium*, ed. W. Samuel and W.G. MacGregor, 174-189. Queen's Printer, Victoria, B.C.

SMITH, C.A., K. Raedeke, J. Fox, and G. Contreras. 1982. Habitat use by mountain goats in southeastern Alaska. Alaska Department Fish and Game Progress Report, Federal Aid in Wildlife Restoration Project W-21-2, Job 12.4 R, Juneau.

STELFOX, J.G. 1971. Bighorn sheep in the Canadian Rockies: a history 1800 to 1970. *Canadian Field Naturalist* 85(2):101-122.

STEVENS, V. 1983. The dynamics of dispersal in an introduced mountain goat population. Ph.D. thesis, University of Washington, Seattle.

STEVENS, V., and C. Driver. 1978. Initial observations on a tagged mountain goat population in the Olympic Mountains. In *Proceedings 1978 Northern Wild Sheep and Goat Conference*, ed. D. Hebert and M. Nation, 165-174. British Columbia Game Branch, Victoria, B.C.

VAUGHAN, M.R. 1975. Aspects of mountain goat ecology, Wallowa Mountains, Oregon. Master's thesis, Oregon State University, Corvallis.

WRIGHT, W.H. 1909. *The grizzly bear*. Scribners, New York.

YOUDS, J.A., D.M. Hebert, W.K. Hall, and R.A. Demarchi. 1980. Preliminary data on mountain goat population growth. In *Proceedings Northern Wild Sheep and Goat Council*, ed. W.O. Hickey, 482-519. British Columbia Fish and Game Branch, Victoria, B.C.

Index